The
Entrepreneur's
Fieldbook

D1465992

The
Entrepreneur's
Fieldbook

John B. Vinturella

Entrepreneur-in-Residence, Loyola University New Orleans
President, Tammany Supply, Inc.

Prentice Hall
Upper Saddle River, New Jersey 07458

Senior Editor: Stephanie Johnson
Assistant Editor: Shane Gemza
Editorial Assistant: Hersch Doby
Editor-in-Chief: Natalie Anderson
Marketing Manager: Tami Wederbrand
Production Editor: Evyan Jengo
Associate Managing Editor: Judy Leale
Managing Editor: Dee Josephson
Manufacturing Buyer: Diane Peirano
Manufacturing Supervisor: Arnold Vila
Manufacturing Manager: Vincent Scelta
Cover Design: Bruce Kenselaar
Composition: Publication Services

Copyright © 1999 by Prentice-Hall, Inc.
A Simon & Schuster Company
Upper Saddle River, New Jersey 07458

All rights reserved. No part of this book may be reproduced, in any form or
by any means, without written permission from the Publisher.

Library of Congress Cataloging-in-Publication Data

Vinturella, John B.
    The entrepreneur's fieldbook / John B. Vinturella.
      p. cm.
    Includes index.
    ISBN 0-13-081219-6
    1. Success in business.   2. Entrepreneurship.   3. New business
enterprises.   I. Title.
HF5386.V56   1998
650.1—dc21   98-2844
                                                   CIP

Prentice-Hall International (UK) Limited, London
Prentice-Hall of Australia Pty. Limited, Sydney
Prentice-Hall Canada, Inc., Toronto
Prentice-Hall Hispanoamericana, S.A., Mexico
Prentice-Hall of India Private Limited, New Delhi
Prentice-Hall of Japan, Inc., Tokyo
Simon & Schuster Asia Pte. Ltd., Singapore
Editoria Prentice-Hall do Brasil, Ltda., Rio de Janeiro

Printed in the United States of America

10 9 8 7 6 5 4 3 2 1

This book is dedicated to my parents.

The person who got me started on an entrepreneurial career was my father, John "Johnny" J. Vinturella. He was never comfortable working for other people, with the possible exception of an overseas stint for Uncle Sam in the "big one," WWII. He combined a keen eye for opportunity with a competitive spirit in a way that made success inevitable. We miss him.

My mother, Josie Anselmo Vinturella, came from entrepreneurial stock herself, and understood and accepted risk. She never held my dad to the limitations of secure employment and was a source of constant encouragement for his ventures, and later for mine and those of my younger brothers.

Contents

Preface

Can entrepreneurship be taught? In the broadest sense of the term, the answer is probably no. But many of the skills of successful entrepreneurs can be taught, and sensitivity to business opportunity can be sharpened. A thorough and orderly approach to business planning allows us to assess whether an opportunity exists and to determine how to take maximum advantage of that opportunity. From there, a hardy individual can decide, with a little less uncertainty, whether to pursue that opportunity.

After teaching a course in entrepreneurship several times to college seniors and MBA students, at two different universities, using several different textbooks, I detected a need for a new kind of text. The concepts of entrepreneurship cannot be absorbed passively; they are based on powers of observation and critical thinking, development of skills in estimating and projecting economic results, and the integration and application of knowledge from course work, life experience, and attempts at understanding human nature. This, therefore, is a highly interactive text that departs somewhat, in content and technique, from traditional approaches.

FEATURES

First of all, this text contains a lot more questions than answers, because for most of the issues we consider there is no one right answer. Some of the questions asked have an apparent response, many have several responses that are equally appropriate, and a few are purely rhetorical. What is most important is that the questions be provocative, causing the reader to think, to search for applicable experience, and to find that answer that is "right" for the reader.

To further this interactivity, we have allowed space to jot notes in response to many of these questions and to the study and review questions following exercises, and cases, and at the end of each chapter. This enhances the reader's involvement in the subject matter and becomes a progress report on the refinement of the venture idea.

Case studies are integral to achieving our objective. One case study threads its way through this entire text, describing the consequences of decisions made at various stages of a business on its later fortunes over a period of 20 years; not coincidentally, I was intimately involved in those decisions. I hope these cases help your entrepreneurial development as much as they have mine.

Other highlights of the text include the following:

- Text is written from the point-of-view of a person with hands-on experience running a successful small business for 20 years.
- Enrichment materials such as entrepreneurial profiles, descriptions of valuable resources, minicases, and in-depth case studies drive home the concepts of entrepreneurship.

- Many examples, resources, and market research are drawn from the Internet, giving the reader the latest information and an appreciation of the usefulness of the medium.
- Two complete business plans, and a very detailed business plan template, are included in the text. The first plan is distributed across the two chapters on business planning, illustrating each plan section as it is discussed. The second is an adaptation of a student business plan that is within the scope of a final project in an undergraduate course.
- Special features such as progress checkpoints, views of experts on specific issues, brainstorming opportunities, and so on are included in each chapter.

ORGANIZATION OF THE TEXT

Chapter 1 begins with some introductory remarks and definitions, then quickly gets into the process of developing opportunity awareness and the search for venture ideas. Many instructors will want to get the students to choose a prospective venture quickly, to serve as a basis for more personalized assignments and workshop sessions. As backup, and for those who have not chosen a venture, we discuss a coffee shop idea in its various stages as we progress.

While on the subject of sources of venture ideas, we discuss entrepreneurship on the Internet in depth in chapter 2. As students search for business opportunities, the Internet and World Wide Web will be mentioned so often that some discussion is necessary at this stage. In addition, many of the example businesses in the chapter show particularly innovative thinking, and illustrate concepts that can lead to lively in-class brainstorming sessions.

Some instructors may feel that the Web site implementation material is outside the scope of their course, or should be postponed until student ventures are chosen. Either can be done without loss of continuity.

Once we have narrowed our choices of prospective ventures, we begin in chapters 3 and 4 to evaluate them. This consists of gathering market data, then conducting a screening process to find the best idea to pursue.

We begin with extensive treatment of the market research process in chapter 3. This includes planning for effective market research, selecting from the wide range of resources available to us, understanding the limitations of the process, and sharpening our understanding of what the results tell us.

In chapter 4 we test the "fit" and feasibility of the ventures under consideration. Fit refers to personal factors related to pursuing an idea, such as whether we would enjoy the work, are comfortable with the risk involved, and so on. If we pass this "screen," we look to market factors, that is, whether a sufficient market exists for our product or service. The critical test then becomes the feasibility of the venture, that is, whether it will make money and whether we can muster the resources to get the business to that point.

Some instructors may wish to use this text for a two-semester course, ending the new ventures portion (chapters 1–4) here or possibly after chapter 5, and requiring a detailed feasibility analysis. The second semester, supported by the remainder of the text, would then focus on business planning.

With one or two feasibility-tested ventures in mind, chapter 5 leads us through consideration of various start-up options in preparation for a detailed planning process. Does the venture lend itself to a gradual start-up process, using a homebase, starting while maintaining a full-time job, and so on? Is a franchise our best chance for success? Should we consider, and how do we evaluate, purchasing an existing business?

Chapters 6 and 7 build a business plan for a start-up venture step-by-step, and numerous illustrations guide the process while reinforcing the lessons learned. These illustrations include two detailed business plans and a very comprehensive business plan template.

In chapter 6 we review, refine, and finalize the considerations and decisions that we have made previously, in the context of the appropriate section of the business plan. It has been my experience that this approach gives a structure to the planning process that makes it less intimidating and more effective.

Given the detailed concept developed in chapter 6, we explore in chapter 7 our options for financing the venture. We consider a wide array of financing sources and approaches, examine our financial proposal from the point-of-view of potential funding sources, and discuss presenting and "selling" the plan.

After the business plan is developed, we discuss in chapter 8 some advanced topics of considerable interest to most entrepreneurs. First, we look at the immediate post-start-up challenges, such as addressing cash flow strains, adapting to the lessons the market teaches us, sharpening our focus, and measuring performance; we then consider planning for growth.

ACKNOWLEDGMENTS

The reviewers provided extremely helpful feedback, and I thank them for their input. They are: Joseph Anderson, Northern Arizona University; David Deeds, Temple University; Jack Kaplan, Columbia University; Justin Tan, California State University at San Marcos; Charles N. Toftoy, George Washington University; James Walker, Moorhead State University; Warren C. Weber, California State Polytechnic University at Pomona; and William B. Gartner, University of Southern California.

In refining the work that became this book, I owe particular thanks to my wife, Susan Howell. Susan spent countless hours editing for clarity and pointing out areas where further explanation was required. The book is considerably more useful and readable for her efforts. Our son, Matthew Oiler, was very helpful in my Internet work, editing the graphics used and with general computing support.

About the Author

John B. Vinturella is president of Tammany Supply, Inc., a wholesale plumbing and building supply house he started in 1978 in Covington, Louisiana, and which was recently named a "Blue Chip Enterprise" by the U.S. Chamber of Commerce. He is also a management consultant specializing in strategic planning and continuous improvement programs.

Dr. Vinturella is also currently Entrepreneur-in-Residence at Loyola University New Orleans and Visiting Lecturer in Management at Dillard University in New Orleans. He was previously Entrepreneur-in-Residence at Tulane University's A. B. Freeman School of Business. He has authored a computing textbook and numerous articles on entrepreneurship and family business. Dr. Vinturella can be reached via e-mail at jbv@jbv.com or on his home page at www.jbv.com.

Entrepreneurship

Derived from the French entreprendre, *which means "to undertake, to pursue opportunities, to fulfill needs and wants through innovation."*

"Tell me and I'll forget; show me and I may remember; involve me and I'll understand."
Chinese Proverb

CHAPTER

Entrepreneurship: Concepts and Issues

1

Chapter Objectives

After completing this chapter, you should be able to

- Define *entrepreneurship,* and discuss the characteristics of an entrepreneur.

- Compare your personal characteristics and preferences to a profile of widely recognized characteristics of successful entrepreneurs.

- Examine your attitude toward risk within the context of the requirements of a start-up venture.

- Evaluate business ideas as opportunities.

- Generate business ideas from your knowledge and interests.

- Cultivate your creative thinking process.

- Understand how people are motivated to "take the plunge."

WHAT IS ENTREPRENEURSHIP?

Introduction

The following sections introduce rather abstract concepts for a person just beginning to consider whether he or she ought to start a business rather than take a job, or leave a secure job for a chance at greater self-fulfillment. Let us try to refine our understanding of entrepreneurship by asking some specific questions.

Is everyone who runs a business an entrepreneur? Many would not consider the newspaper carrier, shoeshine person, and grass cutter to be entrepreneurs, though these are often the youthful pursuits of those with an entrepreneurial bent. Does it matter whether the business is only part-time? Whereas some part-time activities are basically hobbies, or undertaken to supplement income, some entrepreneurial ventures can be tested in the marketplace on a part-time basis.

Entrepreneurship is the process of creating or seizing an opportunity, and pursuing it regardless of the resources currently controlled. The *American Heritage Dictionary* defines an *entrepreneur* to be "a person who organizes, operates, and assumes the risk for business ventures."

At what scope does self-employment become a "venture"? The primary objective of many self-employed people is merely to employ themselves (and others if necessary) at a moderate to good salary; some are even willing to eke out a living to do what they enjoy. This approach is often referred to as a "lifestyle" business and is generally accompanied by little, if any, plan for growth.

These questions are not intended to develop a precise definition of entrepreneurship, but to help us understand our attitude toward its many forms of expression. We may each answer these questions differently, yet all answers are appropriate within our own frame of reference. Entrepreneurship is more an attitude than a skill or a profession. Some of us may prefer a corporate or public service career path, but many would choose an entrepreneurial opportunity that "feels right."

Would you consider a person who inherits a business to be an entrepreneur? From the point of inheritance on, it is their own money and financial security at risk. They could possibly sell the business, invest the proceeds in blue-chip stocks, and live off dividends. Some might consider managing a personal stock portfolio for a living as an entrepreneurial venture.

Would a person who inherited a small or marginal business and then took it to new dimensions be considered an entrepreneur? The inheritor could have tried merely to keep it going, or even to pace the decline of the business to just carry them to retirement. In a family-held business, long-term success is often a central goal.

✓ *Checkpoint: What is your entrepreneurial background?*
What experiences have formed your attitudes toward entrepreneurship? What influences have contributed to these attitudes, positively and negatively? Family business? Experience of parents, other relatives, friends?

_____

_____

_____

_____ ✓ ✓

ENTREPRENEURIAL PROFILE — Ted Turner

R. E. "Ted" Turner, founder of Turner Broadcasting System, is an example of an entrepreneur who used an inherited business as a springboard to a massive financial empire. After taking over a billboard business begun by his father, Turner began to expand, buying up billboard companies and radio stations. Soon he made the leap to television and staked out a leadership position in the emerging cable industry.

Although later extensions of his media holdings included some overreach, and required very complex partnerships and alliances, Turner remains a classic example of the second-generation entrepreneur who is not satisfied with merely maintaining his inheritance. The following is excerpted from Turner's biography on the company's Web site:[1]

Turner was born in Cincinnati, Ohio, on November 19, 1938. At age 9, he and his family moved to Savannah, Georgia. He graduated from Brown University, where he was vice president of the Debating Union and Commodore of the Yacht Club.

Turner began his business career as an account executive for Turner Advertising Company and became president and chief operating officer in 1963. Turner entered the television business in 1970 with the purchase of Channel 17, an Atlanta independent UHF television station.

Six years later, on December 17, 1976, he originated the "superstation" concept, transmitting the station's signal to cable systems nationwide via satellite. Turner diversified the company in January 1976 by purchasing Major League Baseball's Atlanta Braves. In January 1977, TBS acquired a limited partnership in the National Basketball Association's Atlanta Hawks.

On June 1, 1980, Turner inaugurated CNN, the world's first live, in-depth, round-the-clock, all-news television network. A second all-news service, Headline News, began operation on January 1, 1982, offering updated newscasts every half-hour. CNN International launched in September 1985 as the company's global news service; CNNI is distributed in more than 210 countries and territories worldwide.

Several years, acquisitions, and startups later, Turner's Atlanta-based company is a leading supplier of entertainment, news and sports programming worldwide. Its ownership includes the TBS Superstation, Cable News Network (CNN), Headline News, CNN International (CNNI), Turner Network Television (TNT), SportSouth, TNT Latin America, Cartoon Network, Cartoon Network Latin America, TNT in Europe, Cartoon Network in Europe, Turner Classic Movies (TCM), TNT and Cartoon Network in Asia Pacific, CNN Airport Network, CNNfn, the financial network, Castle Rock Entertainment, New Line Cinema and Turner Pictures. Its operations also include theatrical distribution, U.S. and international program syndication and licensing, professional sports and real estate.

Currently, Turner is chairman and a member of the board of directors of the National Cable Television Association and a member of the board of directors of the Martin Luther King Center for Nonviolent Change, the Greater Yellowstone Coalition and the International Founders Council of the Smithsonian Museum of the American Indian. He is also president of the Turner Foundation, the Turner family's private grant-making organization, focusing on population and the environment.

Turner is an active environmentalist and has received numerous civic and industry awards and honors, including being named Time Magazine's 1991 Man of the Year. He is also known as a superior yachtsman, having won national and world sailing titles, including a successful defense of the 1977 America's Cup, the 1979 Fastnet Trophy and four Yachtsman of the Year awards. In October 1995, Turner accepted, on behalf of the team, the Atlanta Braves' first world championship trophy. He is married to actress and businesswoman Jane Fonda.

Are franchise owners entrepreneurs? Many feel that for those who have access to a large up-front investment, franchises are sure things. Is operating a franchise, with its well-defined formula for success, much different from income from "passive" investments? What is the appeal of franchise ownership?

Are there entrepreneurs in large companies? How can a company promote an entrepreneurial attitude, or "intrapreneurship," within its operation? Are different qualities required of a successful division manager than of a president of a successful independent company of similar size? Is an entrepreneur necessarily a manager?

Entrepreneurship is generally characterized by some type of innovation, a significant investment, and a strategy that values expansion. The manager is generally charged with using existing resources to make a business run well. Are these incompatible roles? Are most managers entrepreneurial?

These questions have no one correct answer but are meant to stimulate your assessment of how you view entrepreneurship. This is often a useful first step in deciding whether some entrepreneurial pursuit might become a part of your career path.

Self-Analysis

Peter F. Drucker, author of *Innovation and Entrepreneurship,* says that anybody from any organization can learn how to be an entrepreneur, that it is "systematic work." There is a difference, however, between learning how to be an entrepreneur and succeeding as one. "When a person earns a degree in physics, he becomes a physicist," says Morton Kamien, a professor of entrepreneurship at Northwestern University. "But if you were to earn a degree in entrepreneurship, that wouldn't make you an entrepreneur."

What makes a person a likely candidate to be a successful entrepreneur? Several yardsticks have been proposed, but the real challenge is in accurately applying them to ourselves. The Small Business Administration's *Checklist for Going into Business*[2] suggests that we begin by examining our motivation.

The SBA checklist leads the prospective entrepreneur through a skills inventory that includes the hiring process, supervisory/managerial experience, business education, knowledge about the specific business of interest, and willingness to acquire the missing necessary skills. A commitment to filling any knowledge or experience gap is a very positive indicator of success.

✓ **Checkpoint:** *How well do you fit the entrepreneurial profile?*
How important to you are the reasons commonly given for people going into business for themselves: freedom from work routine, being your own boss, doing what you want when you want, boredom with the current job, financial desires, and a perceived opportunity?

Which of these might be sufficient to get you to take the risk?

_____

_____

_____

_____

Personal characteristics required, according to the SBA, include leadership, decisiveness, and competitiveness. Important factors in personal style include willpower, self-discipline, comfort with the planning process, and working well with others. Rate yourself, as objectively as you can, in these dimensions.

_____

_____

_____

_____ ✓ ✓

✓ **Checkpoint:** *Do you have what it takes to own/manage a small business?*
You will be your own most important employee, so an objective appraisal of your strengths and weaknesses is essential. Some questions to ask yourself are:

- Am I a self starter?
- How well do I get along with a variety of personalities?
- How good am I at making decisions?
- Do I have the physical and emotional stamina to run a business?
- How well do I plan and organize?
- Are my attitudes and drive strong enough to maintain motivation?
- How will the business affect my family? ✓ ✓

Does entrepreneurship still sound like fun? How does the sense of intensity and personal responsibility implied by this checklist sit with you? Does this direction still seem a few years away?

Opportunity Mindset

The process of creating or seizing an opportunity is less the result of a deliberate search than it is a mindset of maintaining a form of vigilance that is sensitized to business opportunity. This frequently relates to the prospective entrepreneur's current profession or interests, where he or she perceives a process that can be more efficiently performed, an attractive new service or improvement of an existing service, or some business or geographic niche that is being underserved.

‼ Successful entrepreneurs recognize an opportunity while it is still taking shape. Business opportunities are often based on broad trends, which may be demographic, such as the "graying" of America (creating opportunities in health services, for example); sociological, like the "green" movement, with its emphasis on recycling and environmental sensitivity; and cultural, caused by changing economic conditions and technological developments.

Opportunities can also frequently be found in current and developing business trends such as the globalization of business, the need for outsourcing created by downsizing, and the burgeoning service economy. There are often localized opportunities, based on geography, natural resources, or the abundance of human resources.

Can you think of any opportunities for your area?

ENTREPRENEURIAL PROFILE   Scott Cook[3]

Scott Cook got the idea of forming the Intuit software company in 1982 from his wife's reaction to the complexity of a bill-paying program she was using. With a little market research, Cook realized that there was a real opportunity for a consumer-friendly financial planning program.

He enlisted a Stanford University senior named Tom Proulx to develop the prototype of a program called Quicken, and began to seek venture capital in late 1983. The simplicity that Cook felt was the program's greatest strength, however, was perceived as a weakness by most prospective investors.

With two small investors, all of his savings, and loans from his parents, Cook created $400,000 of initial capital and began to promote the product. By the spring of 1985, the money was gone, and Cook was forced to lay off his six employees. He was near bankruptcy, and the strains brought his marriage, in Cook's words, "within inches of blowing up."

The turnaround came in late 1985. One promotional strategy began to pay off, and several banks bought the program for resale to their customers. Direct mail sales followed, leading to retail distribution and, several years later, a public offering. According to Cook, "At the time of its release in 1984, Quicken was the forty-third personal finance software package on the market. Now, Quicken is the number one best-selling personal finance software product on the market, holding more than 75 percent of the market share."

The Risk Factor

Why isn't everyone an entrepreneur? Obviously, no opportunity is a sure thing, even though the path to riches has been described as simply "you make some stuff, sell it for more than it cost you . . . that's all there is except for a few million details." The devil is in those details, and if you are not prepared to accept the possibility of failure, you should not attempt a business start-up.

It is not indicative of a negative perspective to say that an analysis of the possible reasons for failure enhances our chances of success. Can you separate failure of an idea from personal failure? As scary as it is to consider, many of the great entrepreneurial success stories started with a failure or two.

Some types of failure can indicate that we may not be entrepreneurial material. Foremost is reaching one's level of incompetence; if I am a great programmer, will I be a great software company president? Attitudinal problems can also be fatal, such as excessive focus on financial rewards, without the willingness to put in the work and attention required. Addressing these possibilities requires an objectivity about ourselves that not everyone can manage.

Other types of failure can be recovered from if you "learned your lesson." A common explanation for these failures is that "it seemed like a good idea at the time." Or, we may have sought too big a "kill"; we could have looked past the flaws in a business concept because it was a business we wanted to be in. The venture could have been the victim of a muddled business concept, a weak business plan, or (more often) the absence of a plan. Sometimes factors outside our control can play a part, such as a natural disaster or recession, and may offer little information as to our entrepreneurial mettle.

Are there any safeguards against failure? No! Even the best conceived and implemented business ventures can become market experiments that simply did not work.

Our goal here is to follow a planning process that can minimize risk. That is the best we can do, and the degree to which we can enhance our confidence about a venture must enter into any decision about its pursuit.

1.1 *Expert Opinion*

When small businesses fail, the reason is generally one, or a combination, of the following: *inadequate financing,* often due to overly optimistic sales projections; *management shortcomings,* including inadequate financial controls, lax customer credit, inexperience, and neglect; and *misreading the market,* often indicated by failure to reach the "critical mass" required in sales volume and profitability due to competitive disadvantages or market weakness.

The best approaches require patience and a commitment to preparation well in advance of start-up. This could be a long-range process to a better understanding of our strengths, weaknesses, and limitations, and of filling knowledge and experience gaps.

We are all self-employed; even as employees of a firm, we are still primarily personal career managers. Trends toward downsizing and outsourcing will almost certainly lead to smaller companies using networks of specialists. *Fortune* magazine suggests that "almost everyone, up through the highest ranks of professionals, will feel increased pressure to specialize, or at least to package himself or herself as a marketable portfolio of skills."

✔ ***Checkpoint:*** *How are you doing at personal career management?*
How marketable is your portfolio of skills? Do you have several years of experience, or one year of experience several times? Are you continuing to learn and keeping up with developments in your field? Is there some aspect of your field in which you could be considered expert?

_____

_____

_____

_____ ✔ ✔

The path to an entrepreneurial venture might begin by earning a salary in the business you expect to enter, while learning more about it, and waiting for the opportune time to go out on your own. This time can be used to develop support networks, both professional and personal, and generating ideas to bounce off people whose opinions you respect.

Once an idea is thought to represent a real opportunity, we must be able to research the market, know what data is important and how to gather it meaningfully, and know what actions this information indicates. This information can then be worked into a detailed plan, and then refined into a blueprint for success.

1.2 ***Expert Opinion***

Douglas Gray, LL.B., is a Vancouver-based speaker, lawyer, columnist and author of 15 business books. In the November 1996 issue of TCP Online (www.tcp.ca), Mr. Gray suggests some specific reasons that some businesses fail:

Money mismanagement. Problems include insufficient funds to meet startup and operating expense needs, cash flow problems, too much debt, not enough money to grow, charging insufficient prices for products or services to make a profit, inadequate financial planning, poor credit and collection practices, and inadequate bookkeeping. Many entrepreneurs "bleed" the business by taking more money from the business than it can afford. It is important to save some of the earnings as a buffer for unexpected business expenses or to reinvest in the business.

Poor marketing. Many entrepreneurs simply don't know who their prospective customers are. They have not done their marketing research, have not identified their market, segmented it, or actively promoted to it on an ongoing basis. You may have a great product or service, but if the message does not get out, the business will suffer accordingly. Preparing and following a written marketing plan is necessary.

Mistaking a business for a hobby. Many people enjoy what they are doing, but never consider it more than a hobby. The object of operating a business, of course, is to earn a salary, recover all your expenses and make a profit.

Failure to evaluate themselves realistically. The failure to make a frank assessment of personal strengths and weaknesses, needs and desires is a common mistake. You may find that your business requires skills that you do not possess, such as goal setting, decision making, and selling. Objective feedback from your family, friends, relatives, and business associates is necessary.

Failure to set and revise goals. Many people do not determine their goals or objectives, or, if these targets are set, they are ineffective because they are not measurable, specific, or realistic. Failure to reassess goals can create serious problems. Various direct and indirect factors can affect your goals and require them to be modified in order to remain viable and effective. For example, unexpected problems could occur, such as illness of the owner, new competition, overly ambitious timetables, supplier delays, an increase in lending rates, or loss of a major client.

Lack of commitment. Personal motivation and desire to stick with the objective, regardless of the normal ups and downs, is essential. Some people give up their commitment too easily if the goal is not attained quickly and without difficulty.

There are many ways to achieve business success. Learn about philosophies and techniques for personal success, motivation, goal setting, and time management through books, videos, magazines, seminars, and conferences. Read about people who have been successful. Network with other business owners and cultivate relationships with successful entrepreneurs. Identify role models and try to learn from them.

SMALL BUSINESS OPPORTUNITIES

Opportunity Defined

An **opportunity** is attractive, durable, and timely and is anchored in a product or service that creates or adds value for its buyer or end user. Opportunities are created because there are changing circumstances, inconsistencies, chaos, lags, or leads, information gaps, and a variety of other vacuums, and because there are entrepreneurs who can recognize and seize them."[4]

What businesses are currently in rapid change and uncertainty? Where is today's chaos? Where are our area's lags, leads, and gaps? Do we see a service vacuum we could help fill?

Ideas may be easy enough to generate, but an idea is not necessarily an opportunity. Building a better mousetrap, for example, does not ensure success; other factors include fit, timing, and resources. Let us look at an analysis of the factors determining the opportunity potential of an idea in the context of our interest in opening a business in a particular area.

MINICASE 1 **Neighborhood Coffee Shop**

In the eastern section of town, which is growing rapidly, food and business services are not quite keeping up. The "East" is fairly isolated from the rest of the city by water, an interstate highway, and an industrial park, forming a separate and distinct market. People are saying that the East desperately needs a good coffee shop and an office supply store. (Who are these people? Are they just in our immediate circle? Are they representative enough of the area to extrapolate from?)

COFFEE SHOP EXAMPLE

Let us analyze some factors that indicate the opportunity potential of an idea.

- The "window of opportunity" is opening, and will remain open long enough.

  We cannot be the only entrepreneurs that perceive these opportunities.
  How long before the need becomes compelling enough for others to jump in?

- Entry is feasible, and achievable, with the committed principals.

  Two friends want to be partners with me in a venture; one is managing a coffee shop across town, and willing to manage a start-up. We could muster the capital for a coffee shop, but an office supply store seems outside our reach.

- The proposed venture has some competitive advantage.

  We were among the first to locate in the new area, and are very active in the local business community. We know of an ideal site, and the building manager is a friend. She is willing to subcontract the beverage and light-meal/dessert services the building provides to tenants.

- The economics of the venture are rewarding and forgiving.

  Materials costs are a small percentage of revenues; site preparation and equipment costs are minimal.

- We can break even at what seems to be an easily achievable volume.

The conditions for starting a neighborhood coffee shop seem favorable, but there must be more that we can do to critically evaluate the venture while improving our chances of success. Would published market data be of any help? Can we survey the market ourselves?

We will test this business idea periodically as we further develop our opportunity-evaluation skills. The first critical test: Could we withstand Starbucks' entry into the market?

(Note: Seattle-based Starbucks Coffee Co. is a leading retailer, roaster, and brand of specialty coffee in North America. According to Starbucks management, the company has experienced more than 60 percent sales growth for eight consecutive years including retail store growth from 11 stores in 1987 to more than 850 locations in 1997, with plans for 2,000 stores by the year 2000.)

Sources of Venture Ideas

Where do business ideas come from? The best source is what you know. Often, ideas come from work experience or from personal interests, such as hobbies; other ideas can come from friends and relatives, and your educational background (see Figure 1.1).

Ideas can also be generated by market research. For example, a recent survey by AT&T Capital and the American Institute of Certified Public Accountants

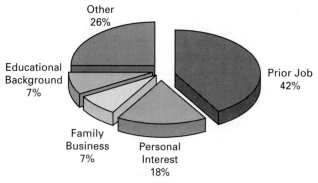

Source: National Federation of Independent Businesses.

Figure 1.1 Sources of Business Ideas

dramatizes the shift of the United States to a service economy; service companies made up 46 percent of business start-ups in 1994, up from only 19 percent two years earlier. Over the same period, manufacturing start-ups declined from 54 percent to 15 percent. Certainly, service industry growth is good news for prospective entrepreneurs. Service businesses are relatively easy to start, and economies of scale are not generally sufficient to give larger companies a significant competitive edge.

Why do service businesses seem to dominate job growth? Is it because people today value their time and enjoy the convenience that services produce over more tangible products? Is automation providing productivity gains that are allowing increasing demand to be satisfied with relatively few additional workers? Or, is it because services must be produced locally, whereas goods for local consumption can be produced anywhere in the world?

COFFEE SHOP EXAMPLE

Many services are highly localized. Are national data useful for consideration of a neighborhood coffee shop?

Can we acquire meaningful data on just our market area, the northeast corner of a metropolitan area, serving 18 percent of its population?

How do we relate current data to future projections?

For an indication of the products and services that people will need in the near future, we can look at projections of those industries that are expected to produce the most new jobs by the year 2000 (see Figure 1.2).

Do these projections indicate merely that the large companies in these fields will become even larger, or are these areas in which an entrepreneur can compete? Do you see opportunities for yourself in any of these areas?

Our coffee shop idea fits within the fastest growing industry, eating and drinking places, though in competition with national franchises.

Is it in competition only with other coffee shops, or with other casual dining or snack-food places too?

What personnel or supply services might we be able to provide? In what areas do you think most businesses need help?

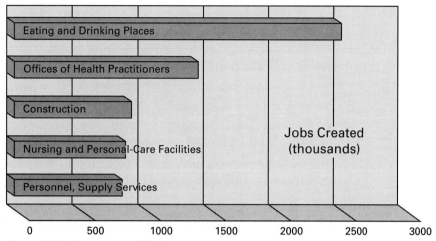

Eating and Drinking Places

Offices of Health Practitioners

Construction

Nursing and Personal-Care Facilities

Personnel, Supply Services

Jobs Created
(thousands)

0　　500　　1000　　1500　　2000　　2500　　3000

Source: U. S. Department of Labor

Figure 1.2 Where the New Jobs Will Be

For what types of help do businesses look to consultants? Can "brain power" be a service? Can it be exported? What forms might this take?

✓　*Checkpoint*

Is there some consulting function you can perform that people need? What skills do you have that separate you from "the masses"? Can these be turned into a business?

_____

_____

_____

_____

Which service businesses do you enjoy dealing with? What distinguishes these service businesses from other similar businesses? What lessons can you draw for any business you might start?

_____

_____

_____

_____ ✓ ✓

‼ It is not enough anymore to just say that "the customer always comes first"; there must be meaningful, tangible evidence. You might begin to keep a notebook or file with approaches toward service that particularly impress you.

Trend Tracking

Futurist Faith Popcorn, in *The Popcorn Report*, suggests some broad areas of cultural and psychographic change that are creating new areas of opportunity:[5]

- For the first time, wilderness is safer than civilization.

    This is creating a "paranoia" industry (security systems), fostering "cocooning" (home entertainment), and "cashing out" (moving to the country and the simpler life).

- For the first time, nature is our enemy rather than our ally.

  This is generating interest in "safe thrills," "down-aging" (ways to feel younger than we are), and ecology-mindedness.

- Say no to drugs, yes to "foodaceuticals."

  Our food must feel indulgent, yet promote health.

- We all need a little "adrenaline-adjusting."

  We need help in feeling better about ourselves ("egonomics") and in dealing with our frantic lifestyles; we are becoming vigilant, if not vigilante, consumers.

Popcorn suggests that a venture that taps into two or more of these needs in a competitive way will be a winner. Have you considered a business that addresses any of these ideas?

Specific ideas are often suggested in the business and entrepreneurship literature. From various sources we have compiled a list of suggestions:

Food and Recreation

Family entertainment centers (number of children under age 12 will increase by 2 million by the year 2000).

Ice cream/yogurt shops ($2.7 billion market in 1994).

Tea salons (less-caffeinated, predicted to cut into gourmet coffee shop growth).

Brewpubs ($900 million market with 300 brewer-restaurants and 155 microbreweries).

Pretzels (passed $1 billion in sales in 1993, soft pretzel stores coming to a mall near you).

Personal and Business Services

Children's learning centers (tutoring, and contract services to schools).

Specialty travel (themed vacations, custom tours, participatory opportunities).

Environmental services (products from recycled materials, compliance assistance to corporations).

Specialized staffing services ($28 billion North American market for temporary help services).

High Tech

Computer training centers ($4 billion market with room for creative niche players).

Multimedia services (a $30 billion market for presentations, training, reference publishing).

Home Office Computing magazine suggests several businesses, formerly perceived as promising, that are now saturated: electronics repair, real-estate sales, word processing, wholesaling, and laser-cartridge recharging. Other useful sources of inspiration include *Business Week, Inc.,* and *Success* magazines, the business section of the local newspaper, and the local business weekly. Broad trends can be tracked merely by being a reasonably well-informed observer of the popular culture.

Are these types of opportunity listings useful? Is it already too late by the time a particular type of business is publicly acknowledged to be an opportunity? Is it better to wait for the "first movers" to clarify exactly what services consumers want, and then enter with a more focused product?

Do we need to move into a hot new business, or are approaches to well-established industries just as promising? Do you think more people have gotten rich with new computer software products, or with McDonald's franchises? Is there a family business that you can take to a new location, or to otherwise higher levels?

Exercise 1.1 Opportunity Scan

Scan the current literature for opportunities that fit your strengths and interests.

Describe a specific business that would take advantage of one of these opportunities.

_____

_____

_____

What are your strengths and weaknesses for developing such a venture?

_____

_____

_____

What are the critical factors for success of the venture?

_____

_____

_____

_____

Creativity and Innovation

Do you consider yourself to be creative? Can creativity be developed?

For some people, being creative involves trying not to be embarrassed by their own ideas; for others, it is a matter of being aware that things can be done in

---

1.3   *Expert Opinion*

Here are some suggestions from the Web site CreativityWeb, edited by Linda Schiffer, for things you can do to improve your creativity:

- Study books on creative thinking techniques and put them into practice.
- Attend courses on creative thinking and put the ideas into practice.
- Keep a daily journal and record your thoughts, ideas, sketches, etc., as soon as you get them. Review your journal regularly and see what ideas can be developed.
- Indulge in relaxation activities and sports to give the mind a rest and time for the subconscious to digest information.
- Develop an interest in a variety of different things, preferably well away from your normal sphere of work. For example, read comic books or magazines you would not normally get. This keeps the brain busy with new things. It is a common trait of creative people that they are interested in a wide variety of subjects.
- Do not work too hard; you need time away from a problem to be creative after periods of intense focus.

Source: www.creativityweb.com

many different ways. Some are self-aware or confident enough to have fewer inhibitions and can let their creative natures work.

Innovation, in a business context, is generally thought of as the product or application of creativity. Peter F. Drucker suggests that innovation "is the specific instrument of entrepreneurship."

In *Innovation and Entrepreneurship* Drucker suggests that there are seven sources of innovative opportunity. Four relate to a specific industry or service sector: the *unexpected,* the *incongruous, process needs,* and *structural change.* The other three relate to the human and economic environment: *demographics; changes in perception, mood, and meaning;* and *new knowledge.*[6]

COFFEE SHOP EXAMPLE

The *unexpected* factor in the recent success of gourmet coffee shops is the willingness of the consumer to spend two or three times the cost of a generic cup of coffee for exotic, flavored, or brand-name coffee. An *incongruity* is the popularity of fat-free desserts ("healthy" indulgence) to go with that coffee.

The *structural change* in the industry is the emergence of franchises. Environmental changes have also contributed to this phenomenon. As the baby-boomer generation has aged, the preferred place to meet has moved from the bar to the health club to the coffee shop.

Let us consider information about some current trends to see if we can relate them to potential opportunities in the context of Drucker's categories. For each of the following, see if you can find a niche on which to build a business:

- The unexpected

  The Atlanta-based International Association for Financial Planning recently observed a 60 percent increase over the previous year in calls requesting referrals for a local financial planner. A spokesperson for the IAFP says, "People are realizing that financial planning is not just for retirement or saving for a child's college education; it's for all stages of a person's life." Individuals and businesses have increasingly been turning to financial planners, either for personal planning or for tightening a company's operating costs; the unexpected factor was the dramatic year increase. Something about economic conditions or family milestones turned the acknowledged advantages of professional financial planning to an immediate need, creating a shortage of qualified practitioners and an entrepreneurial opportunity.

- The incongruous

  Many Americans, in particular single parents and dual-income families, are feeling increasingly and intensely pressed for time. The incongruity is that many wish to lead simpler, easier lives without giving up those activities that take the most time and effort. The opportunity created is in offering personal time-saving products and services that relieve people of tasks that they find less than fulfilling, not worth the time, or particularly unpleasant.

- Process needs

  Individuals and businesses are spending unprecedented sums of money to acquire the education, training, and skills necessary to remain competitive in a rapidly evolving marketplace. Success is often a factor of how much knowledge is built into our product or service, that is, how well it is adapted to the task or to customer preferences. The process need to create smarter products requires smarter workers and better tools, creating opportunities in consulting and training.

- Structural change

    "Health care will be a hot field for the rest of your life and mine," says Ann Howard, executive director of the American Federation of Home Health Agencies. "Approximately 15 percent of the country's gross national product is spent on health care." Howard believes the health-care industry will flourish because of an aging population, myriad technological advances, and people's expectations of readily available medical care. One of the health-care industry's fastest growing segments is home-based health care, which is well suited for entrepreneurs because of its ease of entry. "These days, anything short of surgery can be done in the home," Howard says.

- Demographics

    Today, senior citizens are the fastest-growing segment of the nation's population, and they possess more wealth than any other age segment and are living longer than previous generations. Ten years ago, 30 percent of Americans over age 50 had a living parent. Today, that number has reached 80 percent. By the year 2020, the nation's population of senior citizens will top 53 million, according to the U.S. Bureau of the Census. The combination of leisure time and discretionary funds make seniors a great market for new ventures in services relating to their comfort and recreational needs.

- Changes in perception, mood, and meaning

    According to the Hallcrest Report II, an industry report by Hallcrest Systems, Inc., a security and management research firm in McLean, Virginia, the amount of money that citizens and businesses spend on security products and services will double from $52 billion in 1990 to $103 billion by the year 2000.

    The New York–based Direct Marketing Association expects annual consumer catalog sales to grow by 5.5 percent, with total sales reaching $51.9 billion by the year 2000.

- New knowledge

    In 1996, for the first time, computer sales outnumbered television sales in the United States, and one in four homes now has Internet access, says Carol Baroudi, coauthor of *Internet for Dummies* (1997) and a recognized expert on the Information Age.

Let us now consider an example of an entrepreneur who works in the area of "new knowledge," at the leading edge of technological development.

ENTREPRENEURIAL PROFILE Gregg Garnick

After earning a degree in marketing and finance, Gregg Garnick worked in distribution for Kierulff Electronics, a small semiconductor company near Philadelphia. There he learned the industry and the language of technology, and made valuable contacts that have, through the years, helped guide his business decisions. As a field sales engineer, Garnick visited various companies and tried to convince them to integrate his company's chips into their products. As a result, he says, "I became very comfortable with technology—selling technology, talking technology."

One of the companies Garnick called on was Commodore Computers, whose premier model was the Amiga. Garnick felt that the Amiga was technologically ahead of its competitors and found himself enthusiastically imagining ways to exploit its full potential. This led to his leaving the safety of his job at Kierulff to start Great Valley Products, a company formed to produce peripheral hardware for the Amiga, such as hard-drive controllers, video cards, and sound cards. His partners in the Great Valley endeavor were people he met on his previous sales calls.

At first, the company was successful, but then Garnick noticed a disturbing trend on the horizon. Despite the Amiga's sophistication, Commodore was in trouble. "Commodore was unable to market their technology effectively," he explains. "And many times, the best product doesn't always win." Realizing that Great Valley's fate was tied to Commodore's and seeing the handwriting on the wall, Garnick decided to cut his losses and ended his association with Great Valley. Shortly afterward, Commodore went out of business, and Great Valley Products soon followed.

By keeping his finger on the pulse of the industry, Garnick was able to avoid a disaster and learned a valuable lesson about the workings of the marketplace. His next venture, he resolved, would not focus on technology to the exclusion of marketing. Garnick started another high-tech venture, Quadrant International, to address what he saw as a gap in the market. "I looked at the PC market, and they were doing very little in the way of digital video," he explains. "And I said, 'It's gonna come! It's absolutely gonna come!'"

In its short life, Quadrant International has achieved impressive initial success. In 1995, the company's first full year of operation, Quadrant International realized net revenues of $1.2 million. This was an increase of more than 1,000 percent from the company's 1994 revenues.

The numbers for the first half of 1996 are even more encouraging, with net revenues reaching $3 million. Garnick estimates that revenues for the entire year will top the $6 million mark.[7]

Is innovation a sure path to business success? "Here's an alternative view," says John Case in "Innovate! Quick!" in the August 1988 issue of *Inc.* magazine:[8]

> How many companies—excited about new items that no customer really wanted—have innovated themselves into bankruptcy? Chuck E. Cheese's Pizza Time Theatres seemed like a surefire new restaurant format. It wasn't, and the company nearly collapsed. Koss Corp., a diversified audio manufacturer, invested heavily in a new portable radio with headphones dubbed the Music Box. It flopped, and Koss wound up in Chapter 11.
>
> No one—not Pizza Time, not Koss, not even giants like Du Pont or Procter & Gamble—has yet learned to distinguish innovations that will sell from those that won't. (Du Pont lost about $100 million before discontinuing production of Corfam, a much-touted leather substitute.) But even hot-selling innovations don't guarantee success. People Express rode its popular no-frills flights all the way to never-never land. Osborne Computer sold plenty of its cleverly designed portables, but went broke anyway.
>
> Innovation, in short, is unpredictable, expensive, hard to manage, and therefore capable of destroying a company as easily as saving it. Does that mean that companies shouldn't innovate? No. It does mean that introducing a new product or service is only the starting point of a long, demanding process. You have to put your innovation into the hands of consumers, teaching them not only how to use it but why they might want to.
>
> This nostrum, too, should be obvious. If it were, Ampex would be the leader in VCR manufacture, RCA in TVs, and a company called Bowmar in pocket calculators. People Express's Donald Burr and Osborne Computer's Adam Osborne seemed to know exactly what their respective markets wanted at the moment they built their businesses. But they weren't able to create operational systems that could meet the demand smoothly, effectively, and efficiently, and so fell prey to competitors.

Reinforcing the central message of the previous comments, an innovation may be the basis of a business, but that is only the beginning. A well-conceived business plan, with a solid marketing approach, good strategic thinking, and realistic financial projections, is the blueprint for a successful business.

Once we are aware of where the opportunities are, and which of them we might be equipped to take advantage of, we can advance to a set of actions that we will call the entrepreneurial process.

THE ENTREPRENEURIAL PROCESS

Although the conditions under which people start or acquire businesses vary greatly, certain steps may be considered common to all.

Commitment

Do I really want to start or own a business? Is there a product or service that fits my talents or desires? Am I ready?

Am I willing to take on the personal demands of entrepreneurship? For example, can I work a full day as an employee of another firm, then work at my coffee shop evenings and weekends until it can support me full-time?

Can I muster the resources to make the venture a success? Can I live without a regular paycheck, a predictable work schedule, and for a while without vacations or other benefits? Am I prepared for the possibility that I might lose my money and property, and damage my health and self-respect?

For women and minorities, there are additional considerations relevant to their chances of success. Why is it more difficult for them? How much is due to discrimination and skepticism by their supervisors, and how much is due to their own "confidence gap"? Do they have to be "better" to make it, or is entrepreneurship the only true meritocracy? Do disadvantages occur only at start-up?

Catalyst, a study group committed to advancing women in business, addressed the gender gap through a recent survey. Although women make up 46 percent of the work force, they make up only about 10 percent of corporate officers at the 500 largest U.S. companies, and only 2 percent of their 2,500 top earners. Sherrye Henry, of the U.S. Office of Women's Business Ownership, notes the rapid increase in women-owned businesses, suggesting that corporate discrimination "is partly fueling this energetic economic development."

ENTREPRENEURIAL PROFILE   Lillian (Katz) Vernon

As a recently married Mount Vernon, New York, housewife in the 1950s, Lillian Katz set out initially to supplement her husband's income. Using money the couple had received as wedding gifts, she bought a small classified in *Seventeen* magazine that advertised a monogrammed purse and belt. First year revenues were about $32,000.

In 1960 the mail-order firm published its first catalog, and the company grew rapidly as more women entered the workplace and turned to the convenience of catalog shopping.

Today, Vernon is chairman and CEO of a corporation with over 3,000 employees. Revenues in 1995 were about $238 million from about 4.9 million orders.

The U.S. Census Bureau reports that 18.5 percent of businesses with employees that were started between 1991 and 1994 were owned by women, up from 12 percent of companies in existence by 1980. Businesses owned by women generally tend to be smaller, with 78.5 percent having fewer than 10 employees, compared to 68.2 percent overall.

Selection and Evaluation of the Venture Idea

The basic rule is simple: Find a market need and fill it! The process of finding the need and the method used to fill that need are where the difficulties arise.

Based on my opportunity scan, does the market need a product or service that is not currently being provided? Is there a needed product or service currently being provided in a less than satisfactory way?

Is some particular market being underserved due to capacity shortages or location gaps? Can I serve any of these needs with some competitive advantage?

What type of business could best seize some opportunity that I have chosen to pursue? Do I need partners? Where will I locate? Whom would I serve, and how? Would my chances be improved by buying a franchise or an existing business, as opposed to starting a venture from scratch?

1.4 *Expert Opinion*

Remember that a business idea is not a business opportunity until it is evaluated objectively and judged to be feasible. You may wish to choose two to five of the ideas that seem most promising for more detailed study. Trying to consider too many would spread your time, energy, and focus too thin. At the same time, if you focus too early on only one business idea, you are more likely to become attached to it, and could lose your objectivity.

Testing the feasibility of your top business ideas involves time and effort to collect key information. At this stage, most of your research efforts should focus on whether there is a market for your product or service. A first pass might consist of consulting recent journal articles that evaluate the market of interest; most libraries have computer-based indexes of periodical articles, such as InfoTrac. Other useful library resources include industry trade books, directories, and other sources of industry statistics.

Exercise 1.2 Preliminary Market Research

At your library, search for relevant information on your business idea. (If you are not actively considering a venture, investigate the coffee shop industry.)

What sources of information are most likely to contain data useful in determining the market prospects for your venture (popular literature, business literature, annual reports, trade sources)?

_____

_____

_____

How directly applicable are these data? How can we make these data more applicable to our specific venture? What additional information would you like to have?

_____

_____

_____

_____

Data collected from industry sources and journal articles are often referred to as *secondary* data, in that the data were collected by others for purposes not directly related to our specific venture. Sometimes this can be sufficient, though we may find the need to fill the gaps with *primary* data.

Collection of primary data can be very expensive. It generally consists of conducting market surveys, in person or by telephone, of a statistically significant random sample of our prospective clientele. We will discuss market research in considerable detail later.

MINICASE 1.2   Eavesdropping on Some Coffee Shop Advice

From an e-mail message to *Inc. Online:*

> I know it has been overdone, but my neighborhood is in dire need of a coffee shop. My husband and I LOVE coffee and interacting with people and would like to open a coffee shop/house in our area in order to bring everyone together. There is no other gathering spot where friends and/or neighbors can gather. We live in a "walking" part of the city.
>
> The big problem is this: We have no coffee shop experience. I am a freelance graphic designer and my husband is an attorney. We have the design and legal questions answered, but nothing else, really.
>
> We know what we would want in this coffee house. How do we find quality suppliers? How do we go about financing (is one way better than another)? Where should we start? Who should we talk to about this? We are currently brainstorming a business plan. Any help is appreciated. Post here or e-mail us.

Response:

> Use Internet search engines to find a coffee supplier. When you do, check them out with Dun & Bradstreet.
>
> You should do a survey test prior to committing yourself. Ask your City Traffic Department to conduct a count as to what automobile traffic is like at the site you prefer. If they do not want to do this, then ask if they have done any counts close to your location.
>
> Traffic flow is very important. Try to locate on the side of the street where you have the most traffic in the morning. That is when people might be in the mood for a cup of coffee or muffin or whatever. If you are located on the wrong side, your sales will suffer.
>
> As to financing—If you need less than $100,000, try the SBA Low Doc program. Under this program, paperwork and red tape are greatly reduced.
>
> My credentials—I am a retired SBA officer in practice for myself. Good Luck, Bob.

Study Questions

1. Did the inquirer ask the right questions? What else might you have asked?

_____

_____

_____

2. Were the respondent's answers helpful? Do you agree with all of them?

_____

_____

_____

3. If you are the inquirer, are you ready to go to the next step?

_____

_____

_____

ENTREPRENEURIAL PROFILE   Josh Reynolds

What do the hula hoop, pet rock, and mood ring have in common? For better or worse, all three are considered fads—products that hit the market with the force of a comet, only to disappear in the blink of an eye. If you're like most entrepreneurs, you probably envision a longer life span for your product or service, but Josh Reynolds can attest to the rewards of harnessing comets.

A former stockbroker, Reynolds introduced the mood ring in 1975—and watched as his biofeedback device took off beyond anyone's expectations. "I had five million dollars worth of orders in the first two weeks!" says Reynolds. A year later, Reynolds introduced a biofeedback bracelet that pulsed with the beat of the wearer's heart, followed soon after by a negative-ion-charged air purifier, and the Thigh Master.

"You get quick penetration in the market, but the problem with many fads is that [inventors] don't expect them to take off so fast and they can't meet the demand," says Reynolds, who now has his own product development and marketing company, New Wave Partners. "That happened to me with the mood ring; that's why so many people were able to copy it."

Planning

Once a business idea is selected, the concept must be sharpened by a detailed planning process. The result of this step is a comprehensive business plan, with its major components being the marketing mix, the strategic plan, operational and logistical structures, and the financial proposal.

Strategic issues relate broadly to the company's mission and goals. Every venture must continually assess its strengths and weaknesses, the opportunities to be seized, and any threats to the success and plans of the business. Operational issues relate to company structure and the scope of the business. The operational plan addresses tangible items such as location, equipment, and methods of distribution. Decisions on these issues largely determine start-up costs.

Marketing mix issues focus on how the product or service is differentiated from the competition. A business can differentiate itself on any of what are often referred to as the *four P's of marketing:* product characteristics, price structure, place or method of distribution, and/or promotional strategy. How did our neighborhood coffee shop differentiate itself?

The financial proposal includes an estimate of the amount of money needed to start the venture, to absorb losses during the start-up period, and to provide sufficient working capital to avoid cash shortages. It projects sales and profitability over some period into the future, generally three to five years. Where outside funding is sought, it also describes distribution of ownership of the venture and methods of debt repayment and/or buyback of partial ownership.

Implementation

The business plan is the blueprint for the implementation process. It focuses on the four major subplans: marketing, strategy, operational/logistic, and financial.

While the business plan often goes through some revision, it generally represents a rather advanced stage in the planning process. The primary product or service to be offered, based on the results of the market research, should be determined. Whether the business will be a start-up, purchase of an existing business, or a franchise should certainly be firm at this point. Often, a specific business location is indicated, or at least a specific area.

Time estimates in a business plan should allow for meeting all the necessary regulatory requirements and acquisition of permits to get to a "customer-ready" condition. The amount of funding required and a general approach to raising these funds should be determined.

The remainder of this text will assume that the reader is past the commitment step, and will concentrate on the selection, planning, and implementation steps in the entrepreneurial process. Before doing that, however, we will build some added perspective on the nature of small business.

THE NATURE OF SMALL BUSINESS

What does small business have to do with entrepreneurship? A small business is the usual product of entrepreneurship.

Over half of business start-ups consist of one or two employees (see Figure 1.3). What kinds of businesses can you enter with only one or two employees? Do you consider a professional office (medical, law, accounting) to be a business?

Can a person start a large business? Only 4 percent of businesses employ over 20 people at start-up. What kinds of businesses are larger start-ups likely to be?

The number of small businesses in the United States is about 20 million, and is increasing at the rate of nearly a million a year. Ray Boggs, of the IDC/Link market analysis firm, reports that while *Fortune* 1,000 companies trimmed 4.2 million

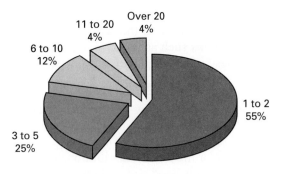

Figure 1.3
Business Starts, by Number
of Employees

jobs between 1986 and 1996, small businesses were adding 9.2 million jobs. To what do you attribute this trend? Is corporate downsizing contributing to the growth in small business formation and expansion?

Small businesses are characterized by independent management, closely held ownership, a primarily local area of operations, and a scale that is small in comparison with competitors. Many are small by design, or are lifestyle businesses, where the primary objective is employment for the principals. Many are intended to be larger entrepreneurial ventures, with the intention of generating substantial growth in scale of operations and profitability.

Why do people start small businesses? The reasons are varied, but they cluster around five basic objectives (see Figure 1.4). The most frequently cited motivation for business start-ups is to allow the entrepreneur to achieve independence; money is secondary. Is this surprising?

The other reasons named most often are that an opportunity presented itself, a person took over the family business, or the person simply wanted to be an entrepreneur. What is your motivation?

For context, what reasons might people offer for joining a large corporation? For choosing a government career? A union job?

What kind of people start businesses? Are their skills any different from those of people working in a large business? Do they need to be their own boss because they are incapable of working for other people? The opposite is more often the case.

Personal characteristics shared by most entrepreneurs include the desire to control their own destiny. This confidence leads to their valuing control, freedom, flexibility, and self-reliance. They generally value achievement over money; they de-

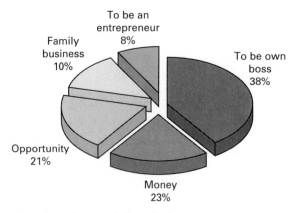

Figure 1.4 Why People Start Businesses

sire responsibility and personal fulfillment. Most entrepreneurs are not gamblers; they have a preference for moderate risk. (How moderate do you think?) They are always searching for opportunities, and are willing to pursue some.

Most successful entrepreneurs tend to be proactive, assertive, and highly observant. They are efficient, quality-conscious, and good at planning and procedures. As business operators, they are committed to partnership with employees, customers, suppliers, and their community.

Would these skills or personality traits lead to success at any venture? Which are vital for success as corporate employees? Are start-ups for overachievers only? What are the chances for success for any person willing to work hard, set goals, and be accountable for the results?

IMPLEMENTATION ISSUES

A primary inhibitor of business start-up is that few people have the financial cushion to give up a job for the uncertain income of a start-up venture. In an AT&T/AICPA survey, survey respondents whose companies were founded in 1994 identified inadequate funding as their biggest hurdle (named by 31 percent). Overall, 28 percent said lenders were too conservative, 16 percent reported being unable to find investors, and 12 percent claimed a lack of collateral.

The loan request should include a credit application, financial information such as tax returns and personal financial statements, and a brief business plan emphasizing projected financial performance of the new venture. The plan should demonstrate how the business will generate sufficient cash flow to repay the loan, as well as specify collateral and show the borrower's personal investment.

In addition to servicing the loan, cash flow should also cover operating expenses, and provide for some reinvestment for the increasing financial demands of a start-up venture. Against collateral, banks will often lend up to 80 percent of the market value of real estate, and up to 50 percent on business assets such as equipment, inventory, and current accounts receivable. Lenders and investors often require that the bulk of start-up monies be provided by the business owner. This assures these stakeholders that the owner is committed, and has confidence in the financial projections.

The prospective new business owner approaching a lending institution should keep in mind the **five c's of credit:** character, cash flow, capital, collateral, and (economic) conditions. Character consists of the borrower's integrity, experience, and ability; particularly close attention is paid to a borrower's credit history, which is a matter of record. The other criteria are addressed in the loan request.

When the entrepreneur cannot meet the requirements of commercial lenders and does not have a favorable arrangement with partners or other investors, the remaining options are difficult and expensive. These options include public-sector guarantees, finance companies, and the venture capital market. We will discuss the issue of venture financing in greater detail in a later chapter.

Even where the start-up investment consists largely of other people's money, the amount of financial risk for the entrepreneur is beyond what most can responsibly handle. For many with the financial means, the stress of bearing complete responsibility for the company's direction and performance is the discouraging factor.

1.5   *Expert Opinion*

The most challenging tasks to entrepreneurs surveyed by *Home Office Computing,* named by more than half of respondents, were: "getting new business/clients," "managing my time," and "promoting my business." Another interesting question was what they missed about the corporate world. The top three responses were "company-paid health insurance," "a regular paycheck," and "retirement plans."

A survey by *Home Office Computing* magazine, reported in their April 1997 issue, offers additional insight into the entrepreneurial mindset. Note that a sample of their subscribers who choose to respond is not scientific, but it should be fairly representative. Respondents were a bit more specific about their reasons for going into business than in the *USA Today* survey cited in Figure 1.4. The top three reasons named were "got fed up with corporate life," "laid off or downsized," and "to make more money."

Most (81 percent) would take a pay cut if that is what it took to keep the business going. Few (37 percent) would sell the business, even if a good price were offered. Three-quarters of respondents were in service businesses, and about a third worked with a family member.

Some of the more tangible characteristics of new businesses and their owners were measured in a 1989 survey of almost 3,000 businesses commissioned by the National Federation of Small Businesses and American Express. Among the more interesting findings were that about 64 percent were start-ups, and 30 percent were purchased, with the remainder inherited, promoted, or otherwise brought into ownership. About 11 percent of the businesses operate under a franchise name.

The age profile of owners or principal managers is shown in Figure 1.5. Why do you think so many new business owners and managers are in their thirties? Are entrepreneurs born (demanding parents, ethnic tradition) or made? Is it for you? At what age? What else do you need to do to be ready?

Various estimates have been made for the failure rate of business start-ups, based on various concepts of failure and of appropriate survey methods. The consensus seems to be that fewer than half of new businesses survive the start-up trauma. Perhaps, a major reason for what seems to be a high failure rate is that it is so easy to start a business. There is no institutionalized check of qualifications in the United

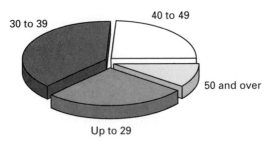

Source: Various industry sources.

Figure 1.5 Age Profile of New Business Owners

1.6   *Expert Opinion*

A proven way to sell a product or service is knowing how and why it stands out in the marketplace. Jeff Blackman is a Glenview, Illinois, business growth specialist and author of *Peak Your Profits* (Career Press). He tells how to create your USP:

Make a propostition that each customer who buys your product or service will receive a specific benefit or benefits. Your USP can be how your business is operated; how your product is developed, manufactured or marketed; or elements that go into your product or service that are of significantly higher quality than that of your competitors.

Make sure your competition doesn't offer the same proposition; yours must be unique. Your USP can be something that your competitors have but have failed to capitalize on. The first company to define that benefit and educate their customers has a unique and profitable pre-emptive advantage.

The propostition must be strong enough to continually attract new customers.

Source: Reprinted with permission from *Entrepreneur Magazine*'s Guide to Sales & Marketing, online version.

States; on the contrary, our tax dollars fund the Small Business Administration and other agencies and programs that encourage business formation.

Successful business owners tend to be those who can find some competitive edge, even when their product or service is similar to those around them. Marketing professionals often call this edge the *unique selling proposition,* or USP. Pinpointing and refining one's USP, however, is not a simple matter. An approach is unique only in the context of our competitors' marketing messages.

Some marketing messages go beyond product and service characteristics. For example, Charles Revson, founder of Revlon, insisted that he sold hope, not makeup. Similarly, United Airlines sells "friendly skies," and Wal-Mart sells "always" the low price. Do these slogans convey how each company views their customers? Does their selling proposition appeal to your preferences?

Surveys consistently show the American regard for entrepreneurs; approval of a son or daughter starting a business exceeds 80 percent. Business owners scored first in a Princeton University survey of positive influence of selected groups on "the way things are going," ahead of technology, the church, and environmentalists.

Entrepreneurship is part of our culture, recognized as far back as 1840, when Alexis de Tocqueville, in *Democracy in America,* said, "What most astonished me in the United States is not so much the marvelous grandeur of some undertakings as the innumerable multitude of small ones."

Exercise 1.3   Company Prospectus
Recast your business idea in terms of its competitive advantage.

What are the characteristics of the industry in which you will be competing (size, types of customers, trends, current distribution of market share, and so on)?

_____

_____

_____

Identify your specific market. How might your market perceive your offering as superior to what is currently available? How can you promote and convey this advantage? What market share can you capture?

_____

_____

_____

_____

Summary

While most of us have a fairly clear image of entrepreneurship, development of a useful working definition of an entrepreneur is a challenge. This is more than an exercise in semantics; our concept of the entrepreneur profile can be the basis for evaluating our fitness for the role, deciding whether to pursue an entrepreneurial venture, and the timing and scope of that pursuit.

Unlike most other career paths, there is little consensus on how to prepare a person for a career as an entrepreneur. Many feel that entrepreneurs are born, and that there is no appropriate formal preparation. We contend that, given certain personal characteristics, a person with entrepreneurial interest can be taught an approach to recognizing and evaluating opportunities that will minimize the risk that forms the downside of the business venture.

The necessary personal characteristics are fairly easy to identify. The problem is in evaluating ourselves objectively against subjective measures such as leadership, decisiveness, and competitiveness.

Planning and teamworking skills can be developed, but the same cannot necessarily be said for willpower and self-discipline. Sensitivity to the existence of an opportunity can be sharpened, but our tolerance for risk can be hard to raise. We can begin our fearless self-assessment by seriously considering the following questions:

What are my real reasons for considering going into business?
These need to be strong enough to sustain you when the excitement of the start-up has passed and the everyday grind begins.

Do I have an adequate support structure?
If you have a spouse, or are relying on some other form of family support, make sure that they understand the sacrifices involved and the pressures these will put on relationships.

Do I respond well to continuous pressure?
Start-up pressures will suspend vacations and holidays and take up much of your weekends. Even after start-up, business concerns seldom end when you lock the door at closing time.

Can I place developing this business over other interests and goals for the foreseeable future?
There is more to life than work, and maintaining a balanced and healthy lifestyle can be a challenge for the self-employed.

Fortunately, we do not have to decide right away. There is an entrepreneurial process, which we will discuss in detail later, that takes us through a series of steps that makes clear the final decision of whether to undertake a venture. Along the way, we will develop a better understanding of the fit and feel of the actions required due to our unique temperament.

The steps in the process may be broadly defined as:

1. Commitment: Am I ready to deal with the uncertainty of not getting a regular pay-check, and the lack of any structure other than that which I provide?

2. Selection: Is there a market need that I can fill competitively? Do I have the necessary information and experience?

3. Planning: What is my strategy, and how will I differentiate myself from competitors? What is the sales potential of my idea? How quickly can it be achieved?

4. Implementation: Where do I locate? What size and scope of business is called for? How much capital is required? Do I need partners?

This chapter has dealt rather broadly with the issue of commitment. Following chapters will address the selection process in detail.

Review Questions

1. How does the dictionary define *entrepreneur?*

   _____

   _____

   _____

2. How do expectations of an entrepreneur differ from those of a manager?

   _____

   _____

   _____

3. Why isn't everyone self-employed?

   _____

   _____

   _____

4. What are the primary reasons for the failure of entrepreneurial ventures?

   _____

   _____

   _____

5. When is a business idea an opportunity?

   _____

   _____

   _____

6. Where do most business ideas come from? How can we generate new business ideas?

   _____

   _____

   _____

7. Why are service businesses the fastest growing type?

_____

_____

_____

8. How well do I fit the entrepreneur's profile?

_____

_____

_____

9. Is there some product or service I could competitively offer the market now? If not, what type of business might some future offering come from? When?

_____

_____

_____

CASE STUDY 1
Used-Book Store

INTRODUCTION

"We've got the merchandise and the store; all we need now is an identity."

Dwight Payne summed up the status of a new venture he just initiated with friend Gary Heap. Payne and Heap reside in Santa Barbara, California, where they attend college and pursue their mutual hobby of science-fiction book collecting.

"Dwight and I are really into science fiction," Heap explains. "We have pooled our book collection and have over four thousand volumes— Heinlein, Van Vogt, Asimov, Bester, Moorcock, Pohl. You name the book; it's somewhere in our collection."

"Not only that," Payne adds, "we've got SF magazines going back over 25 years. All neatly cataloged and indexed. I'll bet it would cost us $20,000 to assemble this collection today."

Payne and Heap decided that, at the end of this school year, they will dedicate the summer to getting a used-book store started in Santa Barbara as a means of supplementing their income year-round. They elaborate:

Payne: Gary and I figured that we might as well try to capitalize on our love of books and reading. Both of us are familiar with used-book store operations because we have haunted them so regularly in building our collection. We've been to just about every used-paperback operation in southern California. A lot of them seem to be profiting.

Heap: My uncle owns a storefront near the university, and we made a deal for him to rebuild it as a used-book store; it's just about finished. He also cosigned an inventory loan for $4,000 for some start-up working capital. In exchange he gets 25 percent of our sales for two years. Not a bad deal, actually, since it is such a good location to serve the hordes of avid readers in the university area.

Payne: Just three weeks after lining up the building, Gary and I lucked into a deal in Ventura. The owner of a pretty good-sized used-paperback outlet put his merchandise up for sale to raise some quick cash.

Heap: We swung a good deal with him—over 10,000 paperbacks, magazines, and comics for $3,500, and $1,500 for all the shelving we will need. We borrowed the money from some fraternity brothers, rented a U-Haul truck, and carted the stuff home.

Payne: It filled the building about halfway. We're currently cataloging the stuff. We got a great deal. Most of the books are in good shape and recent. It's a good mixture of fiction and non-fiction, including westerns, mysteries, gothics, biographies, and a few technical books.

Heap: We're virtually ready to open the doors, but we still haven't decided on what competitive strategy to use. We don't want to be just another used-book store. There are a half-dozen of those around town. We want to be something different in our image and in the way we operate.

Payne: We want to be able to attract customers based on our differentiated image and unique style of operating. We're looking to be something a little different. And profitable!

STUDY QUESTIONS

This case is a do-it-yourselfer. Rather than passively accepting decisions, policies, and estimates, let us generate them ourselves to get a feel for what is involved in roughing out a preliminary plan.

1. The Marketing Concept
    Suggest a marketing concept for the store, including a name.

    _____

    _____

    Who are the customers? What are they looking for?

    _____

    _____

    _____

How will Dwight and Gary meet their customers' needs (company image, policies)?

_____

_____

_____

How will they become known (advertising, promotions, competitive edge)?

_____

_____

_____

2. Reality Check
    Decide on days of the week and hours the store will be open.

    _____

    _____

    Estimate staffing required and hourly salary costs. Do Dwight and Gary really work for free?

    _____

    _____

    _____

    What is a reasonable expectation of customers per day?

    _____

    _____

    Average purchase per customer?

    _____

    _____

    What are pessimistic and optimistic values of these estimates?

    _____

    _____

How much will they have to spend on advertising and promotion to meet these estimates?

_____

_____

_____

What are the most effective advertising media for this venture?

_____

_____

_____

What will they pay, on average, for each book?

_____

_____

_____

How much can they get, on average, for each book?

_____

_____

_____

3. Feasibility Worksheet

To facilitate our evaluation of the feasibility of this venture, we will put together a projected (often referred to as *pro forma*) income statement. In the previous section we developed estimates for much of the data required, which we can relate to monthly sales (pessimistic, ex-

pected, and optimistic), cost of goods, and expense amounts for wages and promotion.

We should add 25 percent to wages paid for the payroll estimate, to account for taxes, sick days, and so on. Debt service payments may be assumed to total $400 per month. Estimate rent and utilities and any other expenses that you feel might be incurred.

Fill out the Pro-Forma Income Statement that follows, or use a spreadsheet in this format for the calculations.

Find a break-even sales estimate, that is, the value for sales that produces the same result for gross margin and total expense. When gross margin generated by the venture equals the venture's expenses, profit/loss is equal to zero; this sales level is called the break-even point.

4. Conclusions

Where does the break-even point fall in the pessimistic-expected-optimistic spectrum? What does this imply?

_____

_____

_____

Would you do it if you were they? Why or why not?

_____

_____

_____

Dwight and Gary's Bookstore: Pro-Forma Income Statement					
Monthly Estimates		*Pessimistic*	*Expected*	*Optimistic*	*Break-even*
Sales	−				
Cost of Goods	=				
Gross Margin					
Payroll	+				
Rent	+				
Utilities	+				
Promotion	+				
Debt Service	+				
Other	=				
Total Expense					
Profit/Loss					

Notes

1. Various sources, including www.turner.com.

2. www.sba.gov

3. www.intuit.com

4. Jeff Timmons. *New Venture Creation.* New York: Irwin, (1990), p. 71

5. Faith Popcorn. *The Popcorn Report.* New York: Harper Business (1992), pp. 4, 5.

6. Peter Drucker. *Innovation and Entrepreneurship.* New York: Harper Business (1993), p. 35.

7. Saul Ravitch. "Wired for Succes," *Entrepreneurial Edge* 1 (Winter 1997): pp. 74–77.

8. John Case. "Innovate! Quick!" *Inc.* vol. 10, no. 8, (August 1988): p. 19(2).

CHAPTER

Sources of Venture Ideas: Entrepreneurship on the Internet

2

Chapter Objectives

After completing this chapter, you should be able to

■ Understand the Internet's value to the entrepreneurial process, its limitations, and indications of where on-line commerce is headed.

■ Relate to the experiences of those who have seized Internet opportunities.

■ Conceptualize a Web site to help you achieve personal and business objectives.

■ Assist your company, or corporate clients, in designing effective Web sites.

■ Investigate venture funding resources on the Web.

■ Track the future development of the Web with an eye toward opportunities it may create that form a fit with your capabilities and interests.

WHAT'S ALL THIS FUSS ABOUT THE INTERNET?

In its November 14, 1994 issue, *Business Week* observed that "this very public and amorphous collection of computer networks [the Internet] exploded as the techno-fad of the decade." Do not be put off by the word "fad"; the article is titled "The Internet: How It Will Change the Way You Do Business."

The January 1997 Internet Domain Survey showed that domain names, those familiar Internet addresses with endings such as ".com," grew from 240,000 in 1995 to 828,000 in 1996. During that period, the number of "hosts," or connected computers, went from about 9.5 million to over 16 million.

There are tens of thousands of "storefronts" on the Net, including electronic "malls" and corporate magazines (e.g., IBM's *Think*). Median annual income of Internet users is said to be $54,000. The IntelliQuest Information Group estimates the population of the Internet to be about 47 million, and it is increasing by hundreds of thousands a month worldwide. They further estimate the 25- to 34-year-old age group to form 30 percent of the on-line population, and females to comprise 45 percent.

The user-friendliest service on the network is the World Wide Web. Here various entities introduce themselves through a "home page," which can serve as the entry point to electronic catalogs and marketing materials complete with photographs. For example, one can sample the wares of Rolls-Royce of Beverly Hills or browse through the Interactive Citizen's Handbook to the White House.

The Web can be a powerful research assistant; there are nearly 3,000 Web sites based in academia. Virtually every major business puts product and service information on the Web, including business directory services and magazines. Programs that search the Web on keywords provided by the user help in finding the specific information needed.

From my home, I can use a search program to find a bibliography on a subject of interest to me without even knowing whose computer site it is coming from. I can click on one of the titles, and have the article retrieved from whichever site it resides in. I can also maintain a personal home page, with my qualifications and samples of my work (www.jbv.com).

The potential of the Internet is still so far from being realized that it is creating a lot of opportunities directly. New and improved ways of connecting to the system—such as support in Windows95 and Mac OS, and software products to help navigate it—are constantly being developed. Check your local bookstore for published guides on navigation, and for the Internet Yellow Pages to help you explore the many features of the Net.

Service companies have been formed to help businesses set up Web home pages with menus of product information, order forms, updates, and related discussion groups, among many other features. They will also get your site listed in Web catalogs, track issues that interest you, and strategically publicize your electronic showroom.

Exercise 2.1 Opportunity Scan via the Web

Test the resources available for searching the Web on a topic of interest to you, such as our coffee shop example. Visit sites of major companies in the industry. Search the archives of business magazines for articles that give background and statistics.

Rate the Web as a source of information concerning your opportunity. Consider accessibility, speed of response, ease of finding relevant information, and quality and depth of information available.

_____

_____

_____

_____

The seers are predicting great things for the Net. David C. Churbuck, in *Forbes,* says that "the day is fast coming when Internet servers and the telephone system will replace the U.S. mail for the delivery of everything from mail-order catalogs to obscure scholarly documents." In *Fortune,* Peter Huber predicts that "before long the Net will incorporate television and telephone, and all their demographics. The Internet way of delivering information will then swallow up all the others—broadcast, cable, movies, disks."

! ! Prospective entrepreneurs can join discussion groups related to starting a business. Eric Gagnon, author of *What's on the Internet,* says that in these groups "you'll find experienced, streetwise entrepreneurs . . . on hand to provide useful advice." The "subscriber" posts an inquiry, and then checks the e-mail inbox for some thoughtful, and sometimes not-so-thoughtful, responses.

Will these promises be realized? Fortunes will be made and lost on attempts to find out. Do you see any possibilities for yourself or your business idea?

The "Frictionless" Economy

In his book *The Road Ahead,* Bill Gates of Microsoft writes of "friction-free capitalism" made possible by developments in communications, chief among them the Internet and its World Wide Web. In this context, "friction" is everything that keeps markets from functioning as the "perfect competition" of economics textbooks. This friction can be a function of distance between buyer and seller, costs of overcoming this distance, and incomplete or incorrect information.

Friction manifests itself by causing barriers to entry for new competitors, limiting the number of outlets from which the consumer has to choose. Large companies, with multiple sales outlets and economies of scale, have greater power to direct the marketplace.

The degree of friction in the developed world has been decreasing for some years now. Affordable air travel, overnight delivery, and improved telephone and fax communications have shortened these distances between buyer and seller. Credit cards and toll-free numbers have spawned at-home shopping from sources across the country.

The Web has taken the friction in our economy down another notch. In principle, we can sell products and services to a worldwide audience as easily and effectively as our largest multinational competitor. Let us consider an example.

MINICASE 2.1   CDnow, a Web retailer of music CDs based in Penllyn, Pennsylvania

In his article "Nowhere Men" (*Inc.,* June 1996), John Grossmann asks about CDnow: "No store. No catalog. No sales staff. Is this the future of retailing?"

CDnow sells music CDs, cassettes, videos, and related products, but doesn't have a traditional retail store. CDnow was conceived from day one as a low-overhead virtual business.

Company founders are Jason and Matthew Olim, fraternal twins in their mid-twenties. CDnow's start-up costs, as envisioned by Jason, proved minimal. He spent $1,500, which he'd saved for a bass guitar, on a new computer, and another $500 for a software license. His savings provided an additional $12,000. But except for that and a $70,000 loan from an outside investor that he has begun to pay back, he has financed the growth out of revenues.

In August 1994, six months after Jason conceived the idea, CDnow sold its first album. First-month sales totaled $392. During the same month a year later, sales of CDs, cassettes, and T-shirts brought in $189,000. In 1995 sales for the company's first full year reached $2 million, more than double Jason's projections. Sales for 1996 approached $10 million, and in 1997 exceeded $17 million.

Music sales are well suited to electronic commerce, a logical extension of mail-order sales. Now there are several competitors to CDnow, including Music Boulevard, which recently merged with N2K, a multimedia-development company, and 1-800 MUSIC NOW, MCI's phone-order CD business, which recently added a Web site.

Study Questions

Visit the Web site at www.cdnow.com before answering these questions. Browse and get the feel for doing business this way.

1. Do you buy any of the products offered by CDnow? From what type of store? How would you compare the shopping experiences?

_____

_____

_____

2. How would you rate the company's long-term chances? On what do you base this rating? What changes would you make to the site? Any related products that you would like to see added?

_____

_____

_____

3. Can you think of any other products that lend themselves to this approach? Can you apply any of the CDnow experience to a venture idea of your own?

_____

_____

_____

Where is electronic commerce, popularly referred to as "e-commerce," headed? In an article in Business Week's Enterprise Online web site (www.businessweek.com/enterprise/news/en71226.htm; December 26, 1997) entitled INCREASINGLY, THE WEB IS FOR HIGH ROLLERS, Dennis Berman[1] suggests that:

> Becoming a hot Web property has never been easy, but during the Net's early days of late 1994 and 1995, anything seemed possible. And for some companies, it was. While established media and retail companies waited on the sidelines or launched modest Web efforts, a handful of precocious startups—such as music-retailer CDNow, computer hardware merchant Cyberian Outpost, and the online magazine Women's Wire—quickly cemented their reputations amongst Netizens. And with so few competitors, the small fry could do it on the cheap.

Those days are probably over. Startup costs for high-profile Web sites have begun to skyrocket, mainly because a saturated market for all types of media is forcing unproven Net players—and even established ones—to pump in lots of marketing dollars or face oblivion.

This costly race for what many call "mindshare" is likely to change one of the most deeply held perceptions of the Web: that the medium's barriers to entry are minimal. That will become less and less true as large corporate players, from TV networks such as CBS to catalog retailers such as L.L. Bean, move into cyberspace, toting their deep pockets behind them.

Berman quotes Peter Gardner, vice-president at Technology Funding, a Silicon Valley venture capital firm: "If you didn't move in before the heavy-hitters arrived, it's going to be awfully hard to do now." Gardner says there are still limitless commercial possibilities for the Net, but they will "tend to be in more narrow niches" such as sites for medical specialties or various types of engineers.

While there is little doubt that Web success stories will continue, Berman expects that "unlike in years past, more of these new hotshot companies will likely be launched from cash-rich boardrooms and fewer from kitchen tables."

"Is anybody really making money with e-commerce?" asks technology writer Jiri Weiss.[2] That depends on how you crunch the numbers. According to ActivMedia, less than a third of online merchants are actually making a profit from their sites. On the other hand, studies show that most Internet users read up on a product online and then buy it elsewhere. So, even if a Web site isn't generating many online sales, it could still be contributing to sales via other channels.

As for companies focusing on business-to-business e-commerce, they're not out to turn a profit so much as they're trying to cut expenses and improve customer service.

The consumer side of the market is still immature: "sex sites" make up about a tenth of all retail business done online, according to Forrester Research. But those sites are not alone. Computer companies such as Dell and Gateway 2000 claim that as much as 10 percent of their sales are made over the Internet.

SEIZING THE OPPORTUNITY

Some entrepreneurs have figured out ways to generate revenue on the Web. In a survey of 1,100 Web-based businesses, 31 percent claimed to be profitable, according to ActivMedia (www.activmedia.com), a Peterborough, New Hampshire, research firm.

In a 1996 *Wall Street Journal* article, William M. Bulkeley suggests that there are lessons to be learned from the "winners":[3]

Get Businesses to Pay, Not the Consumer

Some Web ventures have thrived by using the Internet's communications advantages to reverse the traditional buyer-seller relationship. HappyPuppy.com, a Seattle-based site for computer-game fans, works on this principle. The site, owned by Attitude Network Ltd., Naples, Florida, offers free demonstrations and reviews of new games. Computer and game companies pay HappyPuppy $30 per thousand surfers who view their ads. As of November 1996, HappyPuppy had 50 advertisers and 1.5 million visits a month. Industry observers estimate that the site became profitable in early-1997, and by mid-1998 was receiving over 3.5 million visits a month.

Web Surfers Are Bargain Hunters

When users see that the Web can save them money over real-world transactions, they flock in—as a host of electronic brokerage firms have discovered. Buying stocks on-line costs as little as $12.95 a trade, well below the fees that full-service or even discount brokers charge for telephone transactions. The market analysis firm Forrester (www.forrester.com) estimates there are now 1.5 million brokerage accounts on-line and projects that that number will grow to 20 million accounts in 10 million households by the year 2001.

Offer a Huge Selection

Companies can profit on-line by exploiting the Net's ability to reference vast amounts of information. Amazon.com, Inc., a Seattle-based on-line bookstore, is cited as a model by many Internet consultants. The company's Web site lets buyers browse among nearly a million titles, most of which are stored in distributors' warehouses rather than its own.

For any entrepreneur considering going on-line to sell a product, customer service is the key to winning market share, says Jeff Bezos, the 33-year-old force behind the company. Since it opened in July 1995, Amazon.com, which offers its titles at discounts between 10 and 30 percent off the cover prices, has beaten the brick-and-mortar competition on two counts: selection and price.

In a sense, Amazon.com practices a back-to-the-future form of Internet retailing by providing personal attention reminiscent of mom-and-pop stores. By sending e-mail notices to regular customers to alert them to new titles in areas of their interest, and planning customized storefronts showcasing titles based on previous buying patterns, Amazon.com tries to cement customer loyalty. "I advise everyone to focus on customer service because word-of-mouth is incredibly strong on-line. It fueled our growth," says Bezos, who now has 280 employees.

Don't Quit Your Day Job; Web-link It

Some specialty retailers have found that the Internet does not provide enough business to live on, but that it can enhance an existing line.

Perry and Monica Lopez thought there was a pretty small market for the 400 or so kinds of hot sauce stocking the shelves of Hot Hot Hot, their Pasadena, California, store. Back in 1994, however, one of their customers—a computer-science major fresh out of the California Institute of Technology—offered to design a Web site to hawk their sauces to a larger market. The couple selected 180 sauces and dreamed up clever, entertaining descriptions for them. The Web designer built the site and set up their server to handle transactions and payments.

In 1995, their first year on-line, 20 percent of Hot Hot Hot's revenues came from Web purchases, and today, on-line revenues are about 40 percent of total sales. "We get about 1,000 hits a day and have a response rate of between 1 and 2 percent," says Monica. "We never could reach that audience without printing and mailing catalogs, which we could never afford to do."

    2.1   *Expert Opinion*

Author's Note: One of the great frustrations of Web "surfing" is the relatively small percentage of sites that are genuinely useful. Some of the search engines and several Web-oriented magazines offer site ratings, which can be very helpful. In the text that follows, I have indicated sites that I find myself using frequently or that I feel are among the best of their type.

With both a traditional and an on-line storefront, the Lopezes have learned that what sells on the Web is not necessarily what sells over the counter. Inner Beauty, Pure Hell, Capital Punishment, and the Blow Your Head Off four-pack are top on-line sellers, Lopez says, but are snatched up more slowly in the store. "Packaging doesn't matter on-line, but a good name and funny description do," she says.

To Bulkeley's list, we can add the following:

Sell to an Affinity Group

Mary Pietrowski skipped Main Street altogether and went straight to the Internet to open her first business. Her Web venture, A Woman's Spirit, is an on-line book-store exclusively marketed toward women. A former marketing executive with a high-tech company, Pietrowski believed in the Web's potential and, as an avid reader, hit on the idea of a narrowly targeted on-line bookstore. "I really wanted to do something more personal, and this was a way to form a business I had a passion for," she says. Working from a home office in Framingham, Massachusetts, she wrote up a "very detailed" business plan that was approved for $55,000 in Small Business Administration loans within a week.

"I started this because I know no one has time to read through all the book reviews and find what is good. But I needed to be more than a shopping center. The value for the on-line consumer comes in the community you give them," she says. To that end, Pietrowski's site features book reviews, on-line interviews with popular authors, chat rooms, and bulletin boards. Each week, she draws up a list of "hot books," which she reviews and sells at a 10 to 20 percent discount. Best-sellers are also discounted 20 percent. "Price does matter to people, but I think the real draws are convenience and the sense of being in a place that is created for you," she says.

Pietrowski rents CD-ROM book directories, at a cost of about $350 a month, and as orders come in, she buys the books from distributors, and wraps and sends them to customers.

Sell the Tools of the Web

Product sales on the Web brings with it business opportunities to serve these operations. Dave Einzig, founder of Einzig Interactive Photographers in New York City, uses his background in photography to design virtual reality technology to build interactive Web sites and catalogs. "Our technology allows you to walk into a store and look around with the mouse. You can actually walk to the Web site's counter and purchase products. My technology uses photography instead of graphically created images so you are seeing an actual picture of the product." He spent $2,000 on equipment to start his business, and now has about 100 clients including Hewlett-Packard and IBM.

Match Buyers with Sellers

Pierre Omidyar, who cofounded an early on-line shopping venture now owned by Microsoft, has since launched eBay, an on-line auction house unlike most others in that it features a wide variety of items put up for sale by individuals, not businesses. When Omidyar realized the profit potential of his weekend hobby of connecting on-line acquaintances with something to sell to those looking to buy, he and Jeffrey Skoll, a friend with an MBA from Stanford University and a few computer ventures under his belt, started eBay in September 1995.

Sellers on the site list an item in one of sixty categories for three, seven, or fourteen days, much like a classified ad, and pay a small listing fee. Surfers can bid on listed items by sending an e-mail to the site. At the end of the specified auction time, eBay's software automatically selects the highest bidder, connects the two parties, and instructs them to handle payment and shipping themselves. eBay's revenues come from the listing fees and commissions on each sale—5 percent for items selling for up to $25 and 2.5 percent for those over.

In 1996, eBay held 200,000 auctions generating $4 million in sales. Astoundingly, in the first seven weeks of 1997, Skoll says, the company completed $6 million in transactions. "Once word gets out that something is good and useful on the Web, that news spreads rapidly, far more quickly than with any other medium," says Skoll.

Provide Information in a More Usable Form

For Chris Cooper, a search for on-line stock updates in 1993 proved fruitless. Surprised by the lack of easily accessible financial data, he began offering stock quotes and related financial information to any investor using a home PC. "I saw an opportunity to address the needs of millions of people by providing financial information in an easy-to-use format," says Cooper.

With $250,000 from savings and private investors, he started Quote.com in Santa Clara, California. He banged out software that could present data in bright, understandable layouts using charts and graphs. Cooper mixed the stock quotes he licensed from Standard & Poor's and Dow Jones & Co. with financial data and news headlines compiled from the Web and traditional venues.

Quote.com went on-line in late 1993, broke even two years later, and is now turning a profit. Some information is free to all surfers, but subscribers access more in-depth information by paying fees of up to $100 a month. Cooper counts 180,000 current subscribers, and says revenues come in roughly equal percentages from subscriptions, banner advertising, and selling his data to other businesses, including, appropriately enough, Internet trading houses like e.Schwab and eBroker.

Entrepreneurs providing editorial content, such as magazines, advice, commentary, weather reports, or, as Cooper does, financial data, can start small by creating the content themselves or licensing content from other sources. Such ventures typically thrive on subscriptions and advertising revenue, but the jury is still out on the best way to make content sites lucrative.

"The business model for these sites has not been perfected," says eBay's Jeffrey Skoll. "Advertisers have not jumped on board enthusiastically. There is plenty of room for sites with an innovative paradigm here."

Provide Specialized Databases

Like Quote.com's Cooper, Jamey Bennett was frustrated by the lack of a central source of information on a particular industry—book publishing. Bennett had gained contacts and knowledge during his seven years as a consultant to publishing clients and as the co-publisher of a line of art books. He and his brother, John, saw their on-line opportunity and, undaunted by their lack of computer skills, began work in the basement of Jamey's New Jersey home.

With off-the-shelf software as a guide, they learned HTML, the programming language of the Internet, and created a site they hoped would soon become established as a definitive source of book and book-related information on the Internet. Accordingly, they dubbed the venture BookWire—The First Place to Look for Book Information.

"From day one we worked out of the basement, and got going for far less than $100,000," says John, who serves as BookWire's technology manager. Investing in a computer, Internet access, and a server to house the database, they built a site that includes an annotated index of about 3,000 book-related Web sites, as well as book reviews, lists of publishers, literary agents and bookstores, schedules of conventions and author book-signings, and other information free to the surfer. Revenues come from advertising sales and subscriptions to an e-mail news bulletin covering the industry.

In November 1996 the company was bought by Cahners Publishing, a New York City publisher that owns several properties, including the journal *Publishers Weekly.* The Bennetts remain at the helm of the division, and John says plans are under way for adding more subscription-only content to the site.

THE SEARCH FOR THE "KILLER APP"

In the December 9, 1996, edition of the *Wall Street Journal Interactive Edition* Michael Bragitikos asks: "Just What Will Take the Net from a Novelty to a Necessity?"[4]

Many observers feel that the Internet is still missing the elusive "killer app." The term refers to the sort of must-have program or function so compelling that it gives legions of people a reason to adopt the underlying technology in the first place.

For the personal computer, the first killer app was a program called VisiCalc. It was the first electronic spreadsheet, and suddenly legions of business-school graduates, accountants, and others who pushed numbers around for a living had a reason to own a PC.

But what will be the Internet's killer app—the thing that convinces the globe's unwired millions to log on for the first time?

Industry observers have plenty of candidates. But several have lost some of their initial luster or remain far in the future. The technology to support secure methods of paying for on-line purchases, once thought of as a lure that will bring people on-line, is now seen as necessary for Internet commerce to thrive. A truly rich graphical environment ("virtual reality"), meanwhile, awaits higher-speed connections (greater "bandwidth") or other solutions to the rapid information flow required.

Here's a quick sampling of some of the current contenders for the killer-app mantle. Don't be surprised, however, if, a year from now, an entirely new crop of candidates has emerged.

Zzzap!

So far, the games best suited to playing on-line have been slow and strategy-oriented, such as chess. But some analysts believe that multiplayer, arcade-style games could hold the key to turning the Net into a mass medium.

One precursor to the trend may be the new computer games featuring a variety of on-line play options. For example, Microsoft's NBA Full Court Press basketball game includes options both for playing over modems and for multiplayer network play. In the latter, up to four people can play at once, and they can even open a chat window on screen to engage in real-time, remote trash-talking. It isn't a great leap from local-area network play to imagining play over a wide area via the Net.

Another and perhaps a more immediate indicator of the future of on-line gaming came in November 1996 when Sega began marketing the $199 Saturn Netlink, a custom 28.8 kilobits-per-second modem that plugs into existing Sega Saturn game players. In Netlink, Sega believes it will have a big advantage over PC-to-PC gaming because every Sega Saturn owner will have the same hardware.

"When you turn on the Saturn you'll be given the options of playing [by yourself] or playing on the network," says Kerry Bradford, general manager of Sega Online.

Netlink allows users to browse the Web, and send and receive e-mail, over a standard television set. But those aren't its main selling points, says Bradford. Netlink will, for example, enable a person in Japan to dial into the network and trade kicks, punches, and judo flips with someone in the United States on Virtual Fighter, Sega's popular bare-knuckled pit-fighting game.

The games that Sega will offer initially that have multiplayer capability are ones like the auto-racing Rally Championship, in which the players don't need to see results immediately after they have thumbed their commands into the control pad, Bradford says.

At least until bandwidth increases, however, the popular "twitch" games, where it's vital that a contestant wait only a few milliseconds between the time he throws a punch and the time his opponent's head whips back, will be offered only on a point-to-point, or two-player, basis.

Reach Out and Touch

Imagine calling a friend in Australia, talking for an hour and a half and paying nothing. That's the vision of those touting telephony, or telephone calls that use the Internet rather than telephone lines, as the key to unlocking widespread acceptance of the Net.

As with so much on the Net, the technology is still at an early stage—but it's evolving rapidly. Make an Internet call at busy times and your voice will sound choppy and have a metallic ring to it, as if you were talking into a steel drum. But call during off-peak hours, and the quality approaches that of the major long-distance carriers.

Mike Pearce, senior vice president of VocalTec, the Israeli company responsible for the hugely popular Internet Phone software, predicts that Internet telephony could approach the standards offered by established telecommunications companies' service within a year, as bandwidth increases and more efficient ways of moving packets of information across the Net are devised.

Impediments do, however, remain; computer-industry giants such as Microsoft and Intel have entered the fray, and some agreement about setting standards for Internet telephony is beginning to emerge. The attitude of telephone companies is a huge problem. Long-distance carriers, for example, can be expected to fight any attempts to use the Net to erode their core businesses, whereas local carriers are unhappy at the prospect of having to maintain an infrastructure with local lines constantly tied up by computer users making data calls.

Other problems are more concrete. For one, there's no on-line way to let an Internet user who's off-line know that you want to talk on the phone.

But some phone companies see Internet telephony as a boon—or perhaps simply as an inevitability. Telecom Finland Ltd. announced recently that it plans to unveil a limited Internet-phone service, marking what is apparently the first time a traditional phone company is offering Internet telephony that could cannibalize its core business. Will other phone companies follow suit, perhaps spurring the advance of Internet telephony more quickly than even its advocates believe? Time will tell.

Rolling the Dice

"Internet gaming is coming, and there's no way to stop it," says Peter Demos, president of Nevada-based World Wide Web Casinos, operators of the Net Pirates progressive Internet slot machine. Demos expects that in five years the prospect of cost reductions will cause 20 percent of gambling to become Internet-based. "Casinos normally have 20 percent profit and 80 percent cost," he says. "We figure it (on the Internet) will be just the opposite—80 percent profit and 20 percent cost."

Another interesting operator is Virtual Vegas. They are developing technology for casinos to bring their activities on-line, and are seen as a potential model for gambling sites of the future.

But there are still problems plaguing on-line gambling, including the uncertainty surrounding its legal and regulatory status and the difficulty in handling financial transactions on-line. Before people can gamble in most on-line casinos, they must first set up an offshore bank account in a country that permits this method of funds transfer. This process usually takes about two weeks, says Anthony Cabot, a gaming-law partner with the Las Vegas firm of Lionel, Sawyer & Collins. Even then, Cabot says, "I wouldn't feel comfortable sending my money to a bank in Belize."

Methods of payment aside, Cabot believes that the big problem with on-line gambling is that "people have a decided lack of trust" in the operators of Net casinos. "They don't know who these people are—they could be criminals, they could be legitimate businessmen."

This is also one of the reasons Cabot believes that on-line sports betting has more potential than on-line casino gaming. A game like blackjack, for example, "is very easy to rig because the operator has control over the event. There's no way to assure that the game is honest." (World Wide Web Casinos' Peter Demos says his company plans to address such concerns by having its odds audited by the accounting firm Coopers & Lybrand.)

People may start to develop trust in these Net casinos if one of the larger established casinos—one that is licensed in New Jersey or Nevada—steps in and sets up a Web site. However, Cabot says that won't happen until the legality of Net gambling is resolved.

What Else?

There's always the possibility that something else, completely unexpected, will emerge to take the globe by storm. Perhaps it will be some exotic new technology that today is barely a gleam in a developer's eye. Perhaps it will be something prosaic, like the ever-increasing use of electronic mail.

But there's also the possibility—some would call it the likelihood—that no single killer application will emerge at all. "A 'killer app' is applying a 70s word to a 90s world," says W. Russell Neuman, a visiting professor specializing in new media at Harvard's Kennedy School of Government. Instead, he raises the tantalizing possibility that the killer app is the network itself.

The term "application," he observes, "sort of assumes a stand-alone machine." The whole point of the Internet, however, is to create a flexible, interconnected platform; developments such as Java technology, allowing a vast array of functions to be created and run from the Net itself, may suggest a future environment of yet unseen possibilities.

Microsoft recently acquired a company with an interconnected platform with the potential for wide acceptance. WebTV is a set-top box and an Internet service that allows viewers to tune to cable and broadcast channels, and brings picture-in-picture capability (WebPIP) to standard televisions so that audiences can now view TV and Web programming at the same time. The system also provides Web content directly linked to TV shows for seamless integration of TV and Web programming.

With WebPIP, viewers can instantly switch among full-screen TV, full-screen Web, and the combined picture-in-picture TV and Web displays. The WebTV Network service features TV Crossover Links, which complement and enhance TV programs by providing access to integrated Web sites that are directly related to popular TV programs. The WebTV Receiver detects Web links and data embedded in video broadcasts and notifies viewers with a small icon that appears on their television screens.

Stay tuned for future developments.

IMPLEMENTATION ISSUES

Selling to an affinity group, matching buyers with sellers, and providing information in a more usable form are all strategies that have been around since well before the Web came onto the scene. We do not mean to imply that all current opportunities rely on the Web, or even require a Web presence. The previous examples are intended to show, however, what fertile ground the Web provides for creative thinking, and how the Web can leverage our efforts by presenting our ideas, services, and products to a global market.

! ! Becoming "Web-savvy" has considerable benefit to the prospective entrepreneur. We discussed earlier its value as a communications medium and as a research tool. Online versions of popular magazines such as *Income Opportunities, Inc., Entrepreneur, Home Office Computing,* and *Internet World,* and sites such as Entrepreneurial Edge, and the U.S. Small Business Administration can be tremendous sources of business ideas and can point the way to a wide array of useful resources.

Building a Web site can also be a very useful exercise to the prospective entrepreneur, since the process is a microcosm of building a business. The steps include the following:

- Concept development: Objectives, parties involved, scope.
- Specifications and planning: Technical details, timeline, budget.
- Design issues: Decisions on the general look and feel of the site.
- Content production: The product to be offered the customer.
- Testing and quality control: Refinement based on early experience.
- Launch and marketing: Ready for "prime-time," active promotion.
- Continuous improvement: Monitoring of "traffic," keeping content fresh.

Let us go through the planning process for a personal Web site, and for a business Web site, bearing in mind that the steps are analogous to a business start-up. The following discussion will leave much of the mechanics of site development to other sources, while focusing on process.

Development of a Personal Web Site

You should begin the design of a Web site by asking yourself "What are my objectives?"

Exercise 2.2   Personal Web Site

Develop an electronic résumé to which you can refer prospective clients or employers, or just to establish a Web presence. The electronic form allows you to include much more information than hard copy, allowing the reader to browse as little or as much detail as desired. You may also, or alternatively, wish to build a recreational site, to open a dialogue with like-minded Web surfers by basing the page on some hobby or interest. For example, a very popular home-page theme is the call to fellow *Star Trek* devotees.

The culture of the Web is such that good Web "citizens" provide information content in areas where they have something to say or contribute, in exchange for the information they receive from other sites. A personal, or "vanity," site should offer more than simply biographical data, and this additional content may be thought of as the product you are offering to your Web clients.

Suggest topics within your interests or expertise where you might have something to offer the Web community. What form might your offering take?

_____

_____

_____

_____

As in business, we must constantly evaluate our product, adding to and updating it to keep it fresh enough to generate repeat business. As in any quality control program, customer feedback is invaluable, and should be encouraged with an e-mail link on key pages.

Development of a Business Web Site

In designing a business Web site, the importance of clear objectives is even greater. It is not enough to justify having a business Web site simply "because the competition does." Whether we are contributing to a company Web site, developing a site for our own business, or basing a business on the Web, there are general design principles that can be applied. Bill Sweetman of Hip Hype, Inc., in his article "Web Site Strategies" offers a series of questions to help focus Web site design.[5]

What are your objectives?

Do you want to generate business leads? A Web site makes it easy for potential customers to find you, and find out about you. Your online storefront or office can be open 24 hours a day, 365 days a year.

Do you want to reduce distribution costs of promotional material?

For example, consider a typical corporate brochure. How much does it cost to print the brochure, stuff it in an envelope, address it, and put a stamp on it? Although your site shouldn't be simply an on-line brochure, what if you could deliver similar information, immediately and internationally, via the Web? (If you are sensitive to environmental issues, keep in mind that you'd also be saving trees.)

Do you want to provide the latest new product information to customers or build a database for communicating directly with them?

Changing the information on a Web site makes more fiscal sense than phoning, faxing, or snail-mailing your customers every time you want to let them know about new products or services. If you give visitors to your site an incentive to give you their e-mail address, you can also send them inexpensive e-mail updates on your company (assuming you get their permission first).

Do you want to survey customers and create new business opportunities?
Your corporate Web site could be a cost-effective way to qualify potential customers and get valuable feedback from existing ones. You can also use your site to experiment with ideas by showcasing a product prototype online and sampling surfers' opinions.

Do you want to increase international distribution and market penetration?
Rather than set up a physical office in another country, consider breaking into that market using the international reach of the Internet. A Web site is no substitute for the real thing, but it could be a cost-effective way to establish a beachhead in a new territory.

Do you want to conduct electronic commerce?
Now that secure on-line payment is a reality, you can complete sales transactions without having to go through (and lose a percentage to) a distributor. Is your current method of order fulfillment expensive or inefficient? A Web site could help cut costs.

Do you want to reduce your customer-service costs?
Toll-free 800 phone lines are expensive for a company and often frustrating for its customers. You could save a fortune by moving customer service to the Web.

Do you want to support your existing advertising and marketing efforts?
TV commercials are great, but what if they work (heaven forbid!) and the viewer wants more information about your products or services? The Web could be the perfect way to satisfy this potential customer's thirst for info.

Do you want to provide product directions to your customers?
Put your instruction manuals on-line and update them based on customer feedback so that the manuals are always up-to-date.

Once our objectives are clarified, our emphasis shifts to building a successful Web site, one that meets our business objectives and encourages people to return time and time again. Sweetman reminds us to remember that "content is king," and offers the following suggestions:[6]

- Keep the content on your Web site fresh; you cannot allow your site to remain static.

  Plan to update the site a minimum of once a week or do not launch it in the first place.

- Be sure to integrate the Web initiative with that of the company's.

  It's still not uncommon for the folks from marketing to discover, usually to their horror, that the folks from the computer department have already put their company on the Web. It's time for some of these departments to bury the hatchet.

- Think about the experience you're offering.

  Your company's annual reports and press releases might be of interest to a portion of your visitors, but your content should go beyond this minimum effort.

  For many companies, it is better to think customer service, rather than selling. Heavy-handed on-line sales pitches do not work. Helping your customers find what they need does—even if this means linking to the competition!

  Do not ignore the power of e-mail. All this talk of the Web obscures the fact that plain old e-mail is a powerful tool. Use it to correspond with customers, create a customer-support mailing list, set up auto responders that will send prewritten information to anyone who writes in, or create a monthly e-newsletter that goes out to preferred customers.

  Make it easy for people to get to your content. Web surfers are not going to wait more than 10 seconds for your home page to load. If they have to wade through endless screens to get to what they want, they will quickly give up. Remember, there is no such thing as a Web site that's too straightforward.

  Take advantage of the unique characteristics of the medium. The Web is an interactive, real-time, two-way medium. Lose sight of this and you will soon have a "ghost site" on your hands.

Publicizing a Web Site

Carol S. Holzberg is an anthropologist and computer journalist based in Shutesbury, Massachusetts. In her article "Publicity Ploys" Holzberg offers a series of options for improving sales and attracting business even before you develop a Web site.[7]

If all you have so far is an e-mail address, list your company's products and services with the on-line business directories and classified-ad sites. The more ubiquitous your Internet presence, the easier it will be for potential clients and customers to find you.

Register with Four11 (www.four11.com), an online directory that enables people to reach you by phone or e-mail as long as they know your name. They have a database of over seven million e-mail listings and will include your e-mail address free of charge.

You might also want to join the WhoWhere? on-line community. You can add your e-mail address, company name, snail-mail address, and home page to its directory at no charge.

Post an attention-grabbing classified advertisement. Several places on the Internet will list your advertisement free of charge. Links to dozens of them are available from www.webcrawler.com if you enter "classified ads" in the search field.

One of the best advertising resources available is a site called "Classified Ad Sites That Are FREE to Post" (www.magpage.com/~rispoli/free.html). For some helpful hints on writing attractive classified ads, follow the tips listed at "How to Write Profitable Classified Ads" (uran.net/pq/profit.html).

If you already have a Web page, consider listing it with a variety of different directories, catalog services, and search engines. In keeping with the maxim that "the best things in life are free," the Internet provides ample opportunities to promote your company's Web page at no charge. Most of the popular search engines offer free Web site listing services.

Be sure to follow the Submit It link available on AltaVista's "Add URL" page (URL, or uniform resource locator, is the formal name for the Web addresses we have been referring to). Submit It (www.submit-it.com) offers a free Web promotion service for companies and individuals. You fill out an electronic form, and Submit It automatically registers this information with 15 sites, including Yahoo!, Infoseek, Yellow Pages Online, BizWiz, MallPark, and WebDirect.

Several places on the Internet will list your company's Web site at no charge, but you must find them and complete an on-line submission form for each one. Enterprising advertising companies have sprouted up to handle these time-consuming tasks for you. While they charge a fee for their services, they complete all the necessary forms and submit your company information to high-traffic sites.

The Yahoo! directory has a list of companies that promote Web sites, including locations that will promote your Web site or list your URL for free. Yahoo! also offers links to Web promotion indices (i.e., megalists of Web site publicity services). Multimedia Marketing Group's WebStep Top 100 (www.mmgco.com/top100.html) features links to the best 100 places that will list your site for free.

Banners are colorful (and sometimes animated) Web page graphics that incorporate a marketing message to attract people to your site. They appear on almost every commercial Web page because they have proven to be a successful marketing ploy. Ad rates for banner advertising depend not only on the amount of traffic a site receives, but on audience demographics.

Internet advertising isn't cheap, but if done correctly, it's an effective way to promote your product and make your presence felt on the Web. Shop around and try out some of the promotion companies to see which ones generate the most site visits and hence the most income for you or your company. Remember, with a few keystrokes you can send a message to thousands of people.

Exercise 2.3   Establishing a Web Identity

Develop a promotional strategy for your Web site using some of the techniques outlined in the previous section.

Begin by writing a one-paragraph site description and identifying keywords that are likely to be used in searches by the surfers you hope to attract.

_____

_____

_____

_____

Contributing to a Corporate Web Site

Joel Maloff, president of an Internet consulting firm in Dexter, Michigan, asks "Do Execs Get the Net?"[8] (*Internet World,* November 1996). Has the Internet really begun to change business? Has it reached the boardroom, and, if so, what do captains of industry think of all this hyperstuff and cyberspeak? The answers probably are not surprising, but some of the implications are.

- Some key executives still believe the Internet is a fad and that it will go away.

- Few senior executives have seen a well-considered business case, including cost justification, for deploying Internet-related services. The "gut feel" approach still predominates.

- Failure to fully consider and justify Internet efforts has led to the mistaken view that deploying Internet services can be done in an incremental manner. Many executives believe it is at best a part-time function for technical people.

- Many large multidivisional enterprises continue to pursue separate Internet strategies among their various business units, causing wastefulness and unnecessary redundancy, with no enterprise-wide coordination.

If these are issues that your company faces today, you should assist company leadership in acquiring the necessary information to effectively guide your business into the electronic-commerce arena of the next decade. If these are issues present within organizations that you are attempting to market to, they will likely represent barriers to acceptance of your proposals.

The Internet offers businesses functionality that has been missing or too expensive in the past. Unfortunately, many executives have been led to focus on the technology rather than on the critical impact that the Internet will have on how they interact with their customers. Businesses need to recognize this, and to craft an effective approach to optimizing their use of the medium.

Questions that need to be asked include: "Web sites are visually exciting, but what will they do for us? Can they make us manufacture more effectively? Can they really bring in more customers? And how many of our customers actually use this Internet thing?"

Those organizations that view the Internet as part of their core business strategies will prosper. Those that merely allow themselves to be carried along by the wave may gain some benefits, but not as many as are possible through clear thinking. Those companies that resist the Internet will experience erosion of their businesses as the tidal forces of the Net continue to swell.

The issue of **disintermediation**—removing the middleman from the sales cycle—is causing serious concern among many in service industries. Any industry that uses sales agents, such as insurance, banking, real estate, and so on, has the potential to use the Net for direct sales to consumers. On the other hand, by "neutralizing" the existing sales networks of larger and more established firms, this method of distribution could encourage entrepreneurial activity.

Is it likely that the Internet or other electronic-communications methods will render totally obsolete these intermediary roles in the near future? No, but the Net will have an impact on them, by intensifying the competitive climate, with likely benefits to consumers.

WEB SITE PROFILE Travelocity[9]

Created by a pair of billion-dollar companies, Travelocity is a huge Web site founded and owned by SABRE Interactive and Worldview Systems Corp. But despite the depth of the pockets behind the project, there are lessons here for smaller businesses.

Even with more limited resources, entrepreneurs should consider some of the approaches they took—designing a site through a joint venture, for instance, or developing clear projections to use in measuring a site's success. Travelocity also demonstrates some nuances of on-line psychology, such as not asking people to register until they have had a chance to spend some time looking around.

The site was launched in March 1996; by mid-1998, the site reached a major milestone:

> "Reaching $5 million in weekly sales is a great complement to positive commentary on the services and products Travelocity provides to our customers," said Terry Jones, chief information officer of The SABRE Group. "By developing features designed to meet individual travel needs, we will continue to set new records."
>
> According to an April report by Media Metrix, a leader in the field of usage measurement services for interactive media and digital technologies, Travelocity was the only travel booking site ranked among the Top 25 Web sites at work with an overall audience reach of 6.5 percent. These percentages are based on Web-active individuals that visit a site once in a given month.
>
> "Our ranking among Top 25 Web sites in the workplace illustrates the growth and popularity of the online travel industry," said Jones. "When adding the easySABRE member base to the existing Travelocity audience, The SABRE Group's online travel products have more than 3.5 million members, generating more revenue per member than other online travel products."
>
> Travelocity provides reservation capabilities for more travel providers than any other Internet site with more than 420 airlines, more than 39,000 hotels and more than 50 car rental companies. This reservation capability in Travelocity is paired with access to a vast database of destination and interest information.

RAISING VENTURE CAPITAL ON THE WEB

In addition to providing opportunities, the Web can often assist in acquiring start-up financing. A Web site for pairing ventures with investors (referred to here as *company*) could explain its purpose as follows:

> Historically, the single greatest problem entrepreneurs face in getting people to invest in their ventures is exposure to those people and organizations with investment capital. Some of the best ideas fall by the wayside because they were not seen by the right person(s) at the right time. That's why *company* was developed.
>
> *Company* helps entrepreneurs showcase their executive summaries to every potential investor on the Internet. Of the latest survey figures, 87% of all new start-up ventures are financed, not by venture capital firms, but most often by private investors . . . "angels."
>
> These people are difficult to locate, but they are out there! Angels typically invest anywhere from a few thousand dollars to millions. For deals under $500,000 they are the major source of funding, far outweighing venture capital firms. *Company* is the best method for investors to see your venture.

Although we will deal with venture financing in detail later, we have included two listings from "matchmaking" sites here. Most such sites list ventures of all types, though both these sites involve Internet ventures. The listings are followed by a minicase on another venture seeking financing.

The listings are merely introductory descriptions intended to open a dialogue between mutually interested parties. The first response from a prospective investor would probably be a request for a detailed business plan. It is useful to evaluate these proposals as being competitors with your ideas in pursuit of investors. Listings have been edited slightly:

Web Site Listing 1: Internet Order Processing System

Concept

Enable business-to-business electronic commerce by allowing companies to

- Take electronic orders via the Internet and World Wide Web (Orders R Us).
- Have orders totally electronically administered, including complicated contract compliance, without human intervention.

Electronic commerce helps companies become more competitive and helps engender lasting customer relationships. Electronic order processing helps to increase revenues, reduce errors, speed the flow of orders, and cut overhead thereby increasing margins.

Advantages

The system allows customers to place electronic orders using their own part numbering and nomenclature systems, purchase under multiple buying agreements, check status of orders and their accounts, and peruse on-line catalogs with appropriate promotional, up and cross selling links. The system can also remind users to purchase, using template orders based on past buying patterns.

As recently mentioned in *Business Week,* the company has unique proprietary technologies that support total electronic order processing. In addition, these technologies instantly support any kind of change, exception, and/or customization required to the underlying business system to meet the specific needs of the business.

Market

The Internet Order Processing Market has two segments: Business-to-Business and Consumer. The Business-to-Business segment comprises distribution, manufacturing, and retailing companies, over 650,000 in the United States alone. Many of these companies are considering replacement of their legacy systems, or front-ending their existing systems with new technology. Our product, with built-in electronic commerce, will exploit both the NT and the Internet Business-to-Business waves to success.

Capital Needed

The company is using software development contracts to bootstrap the company. Need equity financing of $750K–$1M to smooth out cash flow needs and provide working capital. Looking for investors with relevant experience and networks which can help the company's growth. Plan to take company public in 2 years, to facilitate acquisition strategy.

Web Site Listing 2: Internet Health Care Venture

Venture

A health-care management services organization utilizing state-of-the-art file-server technology to distribute its services to member health-care practices and home health-care agencies through a combination of Internet and wireless media.

Advantages

Our leading-edge technology coupled with our proprietary application software and innovative member services will allow the creation of a fully automated and completely portable health-care business office allowing for the administration of point of service care at a fraction of the current cost for managing these services.

Market

Of the almost 1 million licensed health-care practitioners and home care agencies, less than half are utilizing any form of office automation, with less than a third able to bill electronically for their services. In 1995 these providers received over $370 billion for their services.

Management

We have assembled a senior management team with extensive experience in physician practice management, health-care information systems, health-care marketing, managed care, and electronic claims processing. Our founders have an exceptional track record of having created and positioned companies in this sector for Initial Public Offering (IPO) or acquisition by publicly traded companies.

Capital Required

We are seeking $1 million in seed capital from a maximum of two investors, which will be utilized for organizational costs, initial products and services development, and to allow management to concentrate on securing the $15–20 million required to launch the venture with full-feature function. Our exit strategy calls for an IPO or sale at the end of the third year.

MINICASE 2.2   **Collectibles Internet Marketplace**

For many years, collectors had to search various sources to pursue their passion for collecting, including auctions, print publications, independent dealers, shops, shows, and flea markets. The collector's marketplace is an extremely large "virtual community" defined by a common desire to acquire antiques, collectibles, and memorabilia, and by the disposable incomes available to satisfy that desire. Collectors' searches through magazines, auctions, and flea markets can sometimes be fruitful and fulfilling, but always tiring and unsure.

The company intends to provide the opportunity for collectors to follow their passion by being informed, and make purchases, in the comfort of their own home. The company will accomplish this by offering the means for the consumer to be entertained and educated about a myriad of diverse topics via television while offering a multiuse platform of services, resources, entertainment, and interactivity via the Internet and PC-TV.

It is estimated that more than 50 percent of all Americans are involved in some way in collecting. Industry reports and trade journals' research project a worldwide market of collectibles-related products/services to be over $25 billion annually.

Conservative estimates project *the company's* market share, with our intensified marketing plan, product/service development, television/Internet services and customer orientation, to be at least 0.5% to 1%—generating $125,000,000–$250,000,000 annually by the end of the year 2000.

Study Questions

1. Is this medium likely to be attractive to collectors? To those offering collectibles for sale? What do you feel are the keys to success for the venture?

_____

_____

_____

2. Does the projected market share seem achievable? With no revenue until late 1997, can it grow that large in three years?

_____

_____

_____

3. While this is only an excerpt from their listing, what is your impression of the business? What additional questions would you like to ask?

_____

_____

_____

Summary

The following, excerpted from the *Wall Street Journal Interactive Edition,*[10] aptly summarizes the topics we have been discussing:

Slowly but surely, real commerce is going on-line. Ask its proponents, and they'll tell you that the allure is overwhelming. No store ever closes on the Internet, and no location is isolated from the rest of the planet. Merchants that hang out an electronic shingle in cyberspace don't have to worry about shelf space and can target their marketing to interested customers at a fraction of the cost. And the sheer size of some on-line stores is far beyond anything that can be done with brick and mortar.

Consider the Amazon.Com Inc. on-line bookstore, which offers more than one million titles. "You can't do that with a physical store, and you can't do that with a paper catalog, which would be the size of seven Manhattan phone books," says Jeffrey Bezos, chief executive of Amazon.Com, based in Seattle.

Mr. Bezos figures his own overhead costs are half those of a large superstore, allowing him to discount 300,000 titles—nearly "twice as many titles as the largest superstore in the world carries," he says. Moreover, the operation can run with 39 employees, compared with the 60 employees it would require to run a store with 100,000 titles, Mr. Bezos estimates.

In addition, letting buyers e-mail Amazon offers "a tremendous amount of feedback from your customers and the semi-anonymity that allows people to say what they really think," he says. After sifting through e-mailed gripes, Amazon added additional shipping options, made sending gifts easier, listed titles that won literary awards and simplified searching options.

Of course, traditional bookstores such as Barnes & Noble have gone on-line and can do much the same, drawing from a wealth of distributors and catalogs to offer customers a vast selection. The larger chains have not yet adapted to the medium to the extent that Amazon.Com has, though Mr. Bezos expects them to.

CROWD-FREE SHOPPING

Shopping on-line also offers the convenience of being able to shop 24 hours a day, seven days a week. CDnow started in 1994 and took in more than $2 million in compact-disk sales in its first full year, showing early growth of about 20% a month. It now has 75,000 customers who can peruse—at any time of the day or night—a listing of 165,000 titles, with detailed information on each. Users happily spread the word electronically.

"My growth is all word-of-mouth," says Jason Olim, president of CDnow Inc., adding that his company has spent only $50,000 on advertising. Olim differs with many who say that the Web is less of a selling tool than another element of our marketing program. "There are a lot of people out there who are developing on-line presences because they feel they have to, and not because they have justification," he says. "Selling is a reason to bother with the Web. Marketing isn't."

In fact, some retailers say, some consumers are so enamored of Internet shopping that they sometimes pay more on-line than they would off-line. Jerry Kaplan, founder of Onsale Inc., a Mountain View, Calif., company that auctions computer goods and electronics on-line, says he recently sold a television set that would normally cost $245 at stores for $340, an $800 notebook computer for $909 and a $530 laser printer for $570.

Opening bids for such items can be as low as 15 cents. The trick, says Mr. Kaplan, is to make the experience fun by appealing to people's competitive instincts. "At our site, it has to do with competition, winning, beating other people," Mr. Kaplan says. "At most places, people buy. Here, they win," creating an experience "that's part Las Vegas, part P. T. Barnum and part Price Club."

Now for a dose of reality: Electronic commerce has a ways to go. Yes, some pioneers are blazing the trail, but the mass market isn't quite ready to follow. It will be soon though, as more people have reliable and user-friendly access, adapt to this new method of shopping, and feel as comfortable with on-line payment methods as they do giving a credit card number over the telephone.

In fact, so far the Internet is mostly a game of bait-and-switch: See our Web page, now contact us by phone or fax to get the real goodies. On-line retailing "is just barely in the shopping-center phase," says Allen Wiener, an analyst at Dataquest Inc. in San Jose, Calif. On-line vendors, he says, are still "figuring out what color they should paint their stores and what music should be playing."

By most estimates, only $350 million was rung up on on-line registers in 1995—pocket change compared with the $1.7 trillion tallied in the retail industry and $60 billion in catalog sales. Still, many analysts say the on-line market's annual sales could reach $5 billion by the end of the decade.

JUMPING THE HURDLES

Even hitting that modest mark, however, will take some doing. The technical hurdles are high. The World Wide Web, the Internet's business district, can be slow enough to make Moscow bread lines look like a drive-thru. Security fears, dull sites and unreliable technology also are putting a damper on electronic commerce.

In addition to the technical hurdles, psychological factors can dampen people's enthusiasm. If one wishes to shop at home, catalog shopping is at least as convenient (easier to browse while watching TV, for example), and often safer (colors are truer and pictures generally clearer). For many people, all the negatives add up—making the on-line experience not worth the trouble.

"Today there's not enough compelling stuff out there to convince people to close a book, shut off their TV and walk inside to turn on the computer," says Richard Fernandes, executive vice president of interactive services at CUC International Inc. Some people, particularly older consumers, may never be suited to on-line shopping. But those who do are choice customers; Mr. Fernandes says that online shoppers are "three to five times more profitable [than off-line customers] because of lower member acquisition costs, lower operating costs and higher renewal rates."

FLEXIBLE INVENTORY

Adds Bill Rollinson, co-founder of the Home Shopping Network Inc.'s Internet Shopping Network, based in Palo Alto, Calif.: "This medium and doing business this way is very scalable, so as you increase the volume of customers, your costs don't increase." And the medium's real-time capabilities allow him to change the inventory in the on-line mall at any time and in a matter of hours.

Sometimes even the strangest merchandise finds a mate on-line. Michael Shevenell, president of Cove Systems Software Inc., provides computer support for Web sites. His clients range from the Dusseldorf tourism office to an elephant gift shop. The latter sells "ceramic elephants, stuffed elephants, elephants hanging from the ceiling. Just anything that has to do with elephants," he says, noting that the company sold $5,000 worth of pachyderm knickknacks in one recent month to customers as far off as Australia and Japan.

Another client, Zeigler's Distributors Co. in Oakhill, Fla., has brought in $20,000 in orders for its Bare Soles "topless sandals," which are strapless and use an adhesive to stick to your feet. Pete Zeigler, the company's owner, says he has received orders from South Africa, Malaysia and Japan.

But Mr. Shevenell cautions: "Everyone thinks they're going to make a tremendous amount of money on-line, and it's just not the case. Not every product sells." He says the Psychic Vortex Center of the World, a psychic hot line, went on-line months back with a Web page posting a costly telephone number for users to dial and see into the future. The seers at the Sedona, Arizona, outfit, however, didn't get many takers. You would think they would have known.

Review Questions

1. What are the components of marketplace "friction"?

_____

_____

_____

2. How does the Internet help overcome this friction?

_____

_____

_____

3. What are some common characteristics of successful Web businesses?

_____

_____

_____

4. What are the components of Web site development?

_____

_____

_____

5. What are the principles of effective Web site design?

_____

_____

_____

6. How can we publicize our Web site?

_____

_____

_____

7. How can the Web assist in funding a venture idea?

_____

_____

_____

CASE STUDY 2
DistribNet, Inc.

INTRODUCTION

After 20 years of heading a Minneapolis engineering firm, Beavy and Associates, Jay Beavy was ready to try something a little different. He had tried to get out of the everyday responsibilities of the business once before, but felt drawn back when the company hit a rough spell.

This time, his separation was a more gradual and better-planned process. Four years earlier, he had begun teaching on an adjunct basis at the University of Minnesota. Jay enjoyed his relationship with UMinn, comfortable that his practical experience was of benefit to the university, while forcing him in a pleasant way to stay current in his field.

The lead engineer at B&A had begun to assume more and more of the administrative load, and Jay was functioning more as a board member than an employee, participating primarily in networking with clients and in policy-setting meetings with key employees. The only real exception to his disengagement was the corporate computing function. His interest in computing had begun in graduate school, 30 years earlier; Jay had even taught computer science at the college level soon after receiving his doctorate.

Since entering business, Jay had prided himself on keeping his firm at the state-of-the-art in its thorough and imaginative use of computing. More of an applications specialist than a true hacker, Jay had contracted much of the company's computer implementation work to MSI, a local firm headed by a former college classmate named Jerry Greer.

As part of his disengagement program from B&A, Jay was taking on more personal consulting work in management and computing. His civic activism and university relationship had developed networks that were providing prospects. At Minnesota, his enthusiasm about the Internet, and early application of it as a teaching tool, had earned him some local attention as an expert.

In mid-1996, Jay decided that his next business venture would be to provide Web site design services to area businesses, and that the time to start was now.

FORMING THE PARTNERSHIP

In his computer consulting activity, Jay had worked on several projects with Randy Mueller, a student at UMinn with expertise in computing networks. He set up a meeting with Randy and Jerry Greer to brainstorm about the possibilities.

Jay's reasoning was that this could be an effective partnership. Many clients of Jerry's company were considering Web sites, and were asking Jerry if his firm could help them or recommend someone who could. Randy filled in some required expertise, and had the time and flexibility to sell and demonstrate the offerings of the new venture to prospects.

Jay proposed that initial investments total $12,000, and that he would be managing partner and hold 40 percent of the ownership, offering Jerry 30 percent. Jay offered the remaining 30 percent to Randy, who suggested that it be split among him and three classmates, each of whom had skills useful to the venture. This would fund a feasibility phase for the company, to take the following form:

1. Incorporation, selection of an Internet service provider, and securing of a domain name (the Internet address that identifies the company).
2. Purchase of a laptop computer, the necessary software, and projection equipment to develop Web sites and perform sales demonstrations.
3. Joint development of a "model" Web site to serve as the company's "calling card."
4. Joint development of an Internet seminar, to be offered as part of a seminar series regularly offered by Jerry's company to their clients.

Jerry and the student group bought in to the plan, put up their investments, and pledged their time to the start-up, and DistribNet, Inc. (www.distribnet.com) was born.

THE FEASIBILITY PHASE

Jay bought the computer, a device to display its output on a TV monitor, and Web page development software. Randy worked on the DNi home page, while Jay wrote the seminar presentation. Jerry publicized the seminar to his clients, and the number of confirmed attendees indicated it would be their best-attended seminar ever.

The seminar was very well received, generating a lot of animated discussion. There were 30 people representing 20 companies. None currently had Web sites, though at least half were actively considering them. Three firms asked for follow-up visits to assess their next step.

The partners felt very good about their kick-off seminar. It was decided that Jay would call on the firm that was ready to start the process, and that Jerry would develop some background information and a strategy on the other two. Randy would research Web sites in the industries in which these companies competed, while continuing to develop the DNi site.

Jay soon found out that not everyone shared his sense that every company "needs" a Web site. In 1996, financial justification was hard to come by, and businesspeople seldom are willing to invest for what they see as distant and uncertain future benefits. Because of this uncertainty, there was considerable resistance to the costs involved in building a quality site.

Respondents to DNi's newspaper ad were basically looking for private tutoring in how they might generate business on the Web. Other companies advertised locally, offering Web site design at "penetration" pricing (as low as $400 for a home page). Jay projected that the competition was going to generate a lot of dissatisfied customers, and make it very tough to justify the necessary price differential to provide the quality service that he had hoped would be their competitive advantage.

RETHINKING THE STRATEGY

At the next board meeting, Jay presented a program for the "new" DNi. The company would specialize in building on-line catalogs for electronic commerce. They would then be working on well-funded projects with companies committed to the Web rather than competing with the hordes of self-proclaimed Web designers for $400 contracts.

The proposed new approach was received enthusiastically. Jerry knew of two of his clients

that would be hot prospects, and he would condition them for Jay and Randy to call on. Randy had generated interest in this project among some former colleagues in a financial services business, and said he could raise $20,000 of passive investment for additional software and sales expense. Their next meeting would be in a month, and it would be full speed from then on.

For their next meeting, Jay investigated all the options for a service provider and the necessary software, and drew up a financial plan including a structure for pricing their services. As meeting time neared, he began calling his partners for progress reports, only to find that their enthusiasm had cooled dramatically. Randy had a list of reasons as to why he had not gotten around to making his calls, but said he would begin after reviewing the financial plan. Jerry had yet to contact his two clients, and Jay was not convinced that he ever would.

Jay wondered whether his time frame was too optimistic, whether his concept was faulty, or whether these were the right partners for the challenge.

STUDY QUESTIONS

1. Is Jay too impatient? Are each partner's responsibilities sufficiently clear? Are the partners as committed as he is?

_____

_____

_____

2. What do you think of Jay's vision of the business? Was their initial direction given enough time to succeed? Is the new direction clearly defined?

_____

_____

_____

3. What would you advise Jay to do next?

_____

_____

_____

Notes

1. Dennis Berman. "Increasingly, the Web is for High Rollers," *Business Week Enterprise Online* (December 26, 1997) (www.businessweek.com).

2. Jiri Weiss. "20 Questions about E-commerce" c|net (August 7, 1997) (builder.cnet.com).

3. William M. Bulkeley. "How Can You Make Money from the Web?" *Wall Street Journal* (December 9, 1996): pp. R18.

4. Michael Bragitikos. "Just What Will Take the Net from a Novelty to a Necessity?" *Wall Street Journal Interactive Edition* (December 9, 1996) (www.wsj.com).

5. Bill Sweetman. "Web Site Strategies," *Internet World* vol. 8, no. 3 (March 1997): (www.internetworld.com).

6. Sweetman. "Web Site Strategies".

7. Carol S. Holzberg. "Publicity Ploys," *Internet World* vol. 8, no. 3 (March 1997): (www.internetworld.com).

8. Joel Maloff. "Do Execs Get the Net?" *Internet World* vol. 7, no. 3 (November 1996): (www.internetworld.com).

9. www.travelocity.com

10. Jared Sandberg. "At Last, Main Street.com Is Opening for Business," *Wall Street Journal Interactive Edition* (June 17, 1996) (www.wsj.com).

CHAPTER

Market Research and Analysis

3

Chapter Objectives

After completing this chapter, you should be able to

- Determine market research objectives for a prospective venture.

- Collect meaningful and relevant demographic and market data.

- Apply available information to the current project, recognizing its limitations and adapting it to the current situation.

- Identify market segments, and develop an appropriate marketing plan.

- Consider alternative strategies for entering the market.

MARKET RESEARCH FUNDAMENTALS

Market research can be thought of as a three-part process. First, we determine what we need to know to evaluate the potential of our business idea. Second, we acquire the most current and relevant data available for this evaluation. Third, we apply this available information to our specific business idea and locale.

Data collected from industry sources and journal articles is often referred to as *secondary* data, in that it was collected by others for purposes not directly related to our specific venture. Sometimes this can be sufficient, though we may find the need to fill the gaps with *primary* data, that is, data that we specify and acquire directly. Collection of primary data can be very expensive. It generally consists of conducting market surveys, in person or by telephone, of a statistically significant random sample of our prospective clientele.

A **market** is a group of consumers who have purchasing power and unsatisfied needs. For a venture to be successful, there must be a market for its product or service. Identification and understanding of this market at the planning stage enhances the chances for the success of a new venture. **Market research** is the gathering of information about a market, and the analysis and use of that information to assist in successfully entering the market with a product or service.

The method of market research chosen should be based on what we need to find out, how much accuracy and detail is required to fill that need, and how much time and money is available to complete the research.

Determine What We Need to Know

At this stage, it is important that we clearly define why we are doing the market research. This involves identifying the following:

The specific problem or opportunity addressed by the market research

The business we are entering may still be rather broadly defined at this point, and we may be trying to decide on a specific product or service within that business. We may have a range of products or services in mind, and want to narrow or broaden it based on our sense of the demand and competitive situation in the market. We may have a specific idea, and simply be trying to find the ideal location.

Our objectives, that is, the facts and information we wish to acquire

Within the framework of the problem being addressed, we will almost certainly want to build a profile of our prospective customers and their motivations. Specific information for this profile might include the size of the market and whether it is growing or declining, the competitive situation in terms of consumer options, and any lessons that may be drawn from the successes and failures in that market.

The business and marketing decisions that will be based on the results of the market research

If our primary objective is to establish a location, our emphasis might be on traffic counts and demographics for the most likely areas in which to place the business. Product line decisions might be based more on surveys of the preferences of prospective customers.

Exercise 3.1 What Do We Need to Know?

Answer the following questions for your business idea. Later, compare these answers to the results of your market research.

Who are the customers for our product or service?

_____

_____

Where are they?

_____

_____

How are they best reached?

_____

_____

What are they buying?

_____

_____

From whom? Why?

_____

_____

What are their price expectations?

_____

_____

How big is the market?

_____

_____

How intense is the competition?

_____

_____

What are our competitors' advantages/disadvantages?

_____

_____

How would we answer these questions for our coffee shop idea? Our customers are coffee lovers in our area, and those looking for light meals. Would flyers posted in area office buildings and placed on cars in their parking lots be effective ways to reach our target market? Do you think our best prospects are currently frequenting fast-food places? How can we estimate how much they are currently spending?

As another example of using our basic questions to gain greater focus and insight into a venture, let us consider a case with which the author has been closely acquainted since 1977. This case will be revisited several times within this text to build on the understanding developed, and to investigate the impact over time of the decisions made. Although the case is set in southeastern Louisiana, and the focus is on a wholesale distribution business, the lessons learned are widely applicable.

MINICASE 3.1   Something Is Basically Wrong with Our Market Research

John and Alan Vinturella visited western St. Tammany Parish (WST) in early 1977 to evaluate the feasibility of opening a branch of their family-owned plumbing supply firm based in Metairie, Louisiana (suburban New Orleans). WST, 40 miles north of Metairie across Lake Pontchartrain, was a generally rural area, thought to have the potential to be an exurb of New Orleans in the future.

The parent firm, Southland Plumbing Supply, Inc., headed by John's and Alan's father, J.J., had been serving plumbing contractors in the greater New Orleans area for about 10 years at the time. Neither John nor Alan had ever been involved in a business start-up, or the opening of a branch, before this.

The local phone directory listed only three plumbing contractors, the likeliest constituency for the proposed business. Discussions with principals of the three businesses were not encouraging; each managed to get what they needed delivered by remote supply houses, and local hardware stores stocked enough supplies to get them through an emergency. Only one of the plumbers was aggressively seeking to grow the business.

In Covington, the business center of WST, they visited the hardware store considered to have the best inventory of plumbing supplies, and these items did not appear to be a significant portion of their business. The store was buying from the same suppliers as the plumbers.

Based on their study, John and Alan concluded that it was premature to open now. J.J., however, insisted that the area was promising, and that they should rethink the issue. Further discussion led to a suggestion that what might be wrong is that John and Alan were applying their experience in Metairie to the Covington situation, when the differences rendered much of this experience inapplicable.

A supply house in Metairie, as in most urban markets, served only the trade, that is, licensed plumbing contractors, maintenance people, and public agencies. If end users of plumbing products, or even intermediaries like builders, attempt to buy from a supply house, they would be referred to a tradesperson. In a rural market, with its smaller trade firms and lenient building codes, many people literally built their own homes, and the material was as likely to be bought by the homeowner, builder, or a handyman as by the trade.

In addition, Metairie was a mature market, where new residential construction was a relatively small component of supply house sales; much of the demand was for commercial construction and maintenance materials, as well as repair, replacement, and renovation items for the area's aging housing stock. In contrast, Covington and nearby Mandeville formed a growing bedroom community, and most of the action was in new residential construction.

These observations emphasize that although the "numbers" are useful, they can lead to erroneous conclusions without a good feel for the nature of this type of business, and the characteristics of the specific market under consideration.

With these changes in their thinking, John crafted a new market research approach and continued his feasibility study. The potential sales volume was less a function of current population than of leading indicators, such as the rate of issuance of building permits.

Since permits included an estimated value of the finished house, and norms existed for the percentage attributable to plumbing materials, the dollar volume of plumbing supply sales in the area could be estimated. Applying an estimate of Southland's market share would then yield its expected sales volume. Although the compounding of these estimates would yield a fairly wide range for expected sales, it would be indicative of the area's potential.

The marketing plan was beginning to take shape. The branch would be basically a wholesaling operation, but retail sales would also be made. The customers would not be just plumbers, but everyone building a new home in the Covington-Mandeville area. Its product line would go beyond traditional plumbing items to include related homebuilding materials undersupplied to the area, such as septic tanks and water well equipment.

Pricing would be competitive, but the added value of being a local operation allowed some flexibility. Traditional selling, almost exclusively supply house salespersons meeting with plumbing contractors, would be replaced by advertising in the local "shopper" newspapers. The branch would locate on the main highway between Covington and Mandeville.

Now John could run some numbers to see whether opening the branch made good business sense.

Study Questions

1. What do you think of John's marketing plan? Did he show a good grasp of who the customers are, and what they are looking for? Did he adequately assess the competition?

_____

_____

_____

2. How do you think the pricing strategy in Covington differed from that in Metairie? Would you expect the margin in Covington to be better or worse?

_____

_____

_____

3. Would it have been more prudent to start selling to the area from Metairie, watching its progress, and opening a branch a year later? Was the window of opportunity likely to close before then?

_____

_____

_____

4. What are the longer-term consequences of becoming a wholesale/retail hybrid? Will this enhance or hinder the growth potential of the business? How will it affect the competitive situation? Are they entering a new business?

_____

_____

_____

This example demonstrates the risk of applying a generic approach to a new market before getting to know the particular market better. Had John not reevaluated the answers to the key questions (Who are our customers? How are they best reached?), a promising opportunity could have been missed.

A broader caution is expressed by what Margaret Thorpe, a market development consultant, calls the seven deadly sins of market research:

1. Failure to determine who cares. "Market" is not everyone who has "the problem"; our market is only people who care about the problem. The best market is those who care the most, because they have the most to gain or lose. In our coffee shop example, many area residents feel it would be an asset to the community, but how many would frequent it? People who work nearby are our real prospects.

2. Failure to understand the overall goal of potential customers. Every need nests inside context. Microsoft sees software at the center of the universe. Users see it as one tool to accomplish their jobs, which include everything from writing novels to ensuring that trucks arrive on time. Knowing market needs requires knowing, for example, how people write novels and ship goods. The success of the Quicken software package discussed earlier is an example of an effective reading of market need.

3. Failure to realize that customers seek systems of results. Product developers believe their product will succeed because it's faster, smoother, or sexier. Buyers seek full packages of results. In the previous example, Covington-area plumbing supply consumers already had sources of supply; success of a new store relied on providing not just another source of supply, but on a package of selection, convenience, price, and service.

4. Failure to understand how potential customers do their jobs. Thorpe refers to research on the market for environmentally conscious building materials. Use of these materials required major process changes and increased expense for manufacturers and contractors, the likely prospects, while offering no compensating value in performance or appeal.

5. Failure to understand what competition is. Companies see other firms that offer something similar as competition; however, just because it has the same name doesn't mean it offers the same system of results to the same market. Competition for our coffee shop might include a nearby luncheonette, or "brown-bagging."

6. Failure to understand what drives the market. Markets are systems of interacting elements and participants. Even a cancer cure could not come to market without cooperation between the FDA, third-party payers, hospitals, physicians, and patients. Cynical as it may sound, only patients may seek a cure as the overriding goal.

7. Failure to see how the market does business. A start-up needs to break even before money runs out. Selling to and collecting from clients in decentralized markets such as construction, or bureaucratized ones such as the government, can cause cash flow problems that threaten the survival of fledgling businesses.

With these cautions, we can now take our earlier list of questions to be answered by our market research to another level of detail.

ENTREPRENEURIAL RESOURCE   **Entrepreneurial Edge Online**

Entrepreneurial Edge Online (www.edgeonline.com) is a rich source of information for the prospective entrepreneur. They suggest that our market research answer the following questions:

The Market
- Is my market clearly identifiable? By what methods am I able to reach them?
- How many competitors are in the market? Can the market sustain another player?
- What is the size of the market? How fast is the market growing? Can the market be segmented?
- How do my competitors reach the market? What is required to succeed in this market?

Its Customers
- What factors are most important to buyers when selecting a product/service: price, quality, delivery time, and so on? What are current buyers paying for comparable products/services?
- What types of people buy this product/service?
- What do potential or existing customers like about my competitors' products/services?
- What makes my product/service unique relative to others in the marketplace?
- Does the product/service have limited appeal based on geography?
- Are my competitors making any changes? Are they successful? If yes, why? If no, why not?
- How are my competitors' fees, operations, and marketing structured?

The Industry
- Is the industry growing? What are the current trends within the industry? Who are the leaders within the industry, and why are they successful?
- What type of marketing strategies are prevalent within the industry? Is the industry seasonal?
- Are there regulations that affect the industry? Is the industry sensitive to economic fluctuations?
- Is there customer loyalty within the industry?
- Are there technological changes happening or required in the industry?
- What are the financial characteristics of the industry?

Acquire the Most Current and Relevant Data Available

It is often difficult to convince prospective entrepreneurs to do a thorough job of market research, because they are generally unaware of how useful the information available can be, and they are in a rush to get to market. But doing our homework can improve our chances for success.

The following lists of market research sources were drawn largely from www.edgeonline.com, with some additional sources that I have found particularly useful:

General Information
- Public library. This is the best place to start; many of the following sources are available there.
- Federal and state governments. See following section for details.
- Local and regional chambers of commerce, planning offices, and economic development foundations. They collect information about the community and local businesses and offer most of their services for free.
- Public records. For local market size and trend information, check sales tax collections, building permits, business incorporations, real estate transfers, and utility hookups.
- Local colleges and universities. Many have centers for business and economic research.
- Business publications. Local and national publications, newsletters, and pamphlets exist for every industry imaginable, and for specific geographic areas.
- Magazines and reports. *The Directory of Associations* will show you what trade associations are available for the type of business in which you are interested. Trade associations serve specific industries and are great sources of information.
- Media representatives. This includes advertising space salespeople representing magazines, newspapers, radio stations, and television stations. Many of their companies have extensive research departments, and the information is free. You can call to ask for a media kit.
- *CACI Sourcebook of Demographics and Buying Power for Every County in the USA*. This publication contains useful localized demographics, such as age distribution, education level, employment statistics, housing profile, and purchasing potential profile.
- *Sales and Marketing Management* magazine. This magazine publishes "Survey of Buying Power," a yearly issue. It contains information on every county in the United States and cities with a population over 10,000. This includes the following:
    - Total population.
    - Number of households (products are generally bought to serve a household).
    - Median cash income per household (how affluent a city or county is compared to its neighbors).
    - Population percentage breakdown by income.
    - Total retail sales (how much is spent by customers in retail stores).
    - Total retail sales for each of the following businesses: automotive, drug, food, furniture, general merchandise, and household appliances.

- *American Consumer Lists.* This publication provides actual consumer names and addresses, useful for surveying and marketing, as counts and prospect list, by zip code for groups such as "High-Potential Prospects with Incomes in Excess of $100,000."

- Competitors. Surprisingly, you can learn a lot by going right to your competition and requesting any information, advice, or help they might be able to offer. If you feel awkward directly approaching your competition, contact a business owner located farther away.

   For example, if you publish a magazine, you need to know what competitive publications are charging for advertising space, what their circulation is, and what their reader profile is. You cannot possibly compete unless you know what they are doing and not doing.

- Potential consumers. This is best accomplished via survey. Because it is important to ask the right questions, you will find a detailed method of creating a questionnaire later in a minicase.

- Observation. Pay attention to what customers do in individual businesses. How many people pass by a particular store? What are their reactions? Are they window shopping or going in?

U.S. Government Sources

The U.S. government is a voracious compiler of statistics from which you can reap the benefits.

- *American Statistics Index* (ASI). This is the single best source for locating government statistics and is published annually by the Congressional Information Service of Bethesda, Maryland, with monthly supplements. The ASI provides an index to all the statistical publications of the U.S. government in one location, and its second volume, *ASI Abstracts,* briefly summarizes the actual reports listed in ASI. It lists documents from the U.S. Census Bureau, *Current Industrial Reports* (CIR), the U.S. Bureau of Labor Statistics, and special studies by governmental agencies.

- U.S. Department of Commerce. *The U.S. Industrial Outlook,* published annually each January by the U.S. Department of Commerce, provides a general economic outlook by forecasting growth rates for the coming year and reporting on production in the past year. You may find it a useful reference for anticipating trends in your industry.

- U.S. Census Bureau. The Census Bureau publishes more than 100 Current Industrial Reports on 5,000 manufactured products, accounting for 40 percent of all goods manufactured in the United States. CIRs provide information on production, shipping, inventories, consumption, and the number of firms manufacturing each product.

- *Economic Censuses and Related Statistics.* Published by the U.S. Census Bureau, this publication lists a variety of industries, such as retail trade, service, transportation, and manufacturing. These publications report on monthly sales figures and trends, and information on sales by geographic area, zip code, and merchandise line.

- CENDATA. This is an on-line database offering county business patterns (CBP). It contains industry information organized geographically, and is useful for evaluating the performance and trends of your industry in your target location. The printed version of CBP includes listings for each industry having more than 50 employees in an area, and a computerized version has listings of every Standard Industrial Classification (SIC) category with at least one employee.

Most federal government publications can be ordered from the U.S. Government Printing Office (www.access.gpo.gov). To gain access to government statistics by computer, go to the U.S. Bureau of the Census site (www.census.gov).

MINICASE 3.2   How Many Piano Tuners Can This Place Support?

A piano tuner is considering moving to Buffalo, New York, and would like to assess his business prospects in the area. He plans to estimate how many piano tuners the greater Buffalo area can support, and compare that to the number listed in the phone book.

How do we advise him as to how he should estimate the right number of tuners for the area? One approach is simply to guess. Would it be 1, 10, 50, or 100? Are you comfortable with this approach?

An approach that I would be more comfortable with would be to find data on estimates of how many piano tuners per capita there are in the United States (Is data on this likely to be available?), and apply that ratio to the Buffalo area population. *Test your resourcefulness by trying to fill in the gaps here.*

Assuming that data is not available, we must go to the "some assembly required" approach to estimating, that is, deriving the estimate from available data. This data would then be modified by related local and national data, norms, and rules of thumb.

Although this approach seems so indirect as to be little better than just guessing, it can be a very useful exercise. If nothing else, it causes us to identify some important variables and how they relate to our business of interest. The inaccuracies of compounding estimates can be minimized by working in ranges to give us a ballpark figure.

How can I derive a meaningful estimate from generally available information? It would be interesting to know what percentage of American households own a piano (where might we get such a number?), and how often they get it tuned. If the data are national, we may need to apply some local adjustment factor. If we know the annual number of piano tunings, we can divide that number by the annual capacity of a tuner to determine how many are needed.

I will do an "off-the-top-of-my-head" calculation to illustrate the method, and then leave it to you to provide real values: Buffalo has about 400,000 households (1.3 million population divided by 3 members average); 8 percent of American households own pianos. I can think of no reason to apply any local adjustment to this figure, so we are talking about roughly 32,000 pianos.

My guess is that two-thirds of all pianos are merely furniture (what would your guess be?), so that the remainder of about 11,000 are played regularly and in need of tuning. Tuners recommend that a piano be serviced twice a year, but my guess is that the average is probably once a year for active pianos, or 11,000 tunings per year.

A tuner can service 2 to 4 pianos a day; let us say 3 per day, 5 days a week, 50 weeks a year, or 750 tunings per year per tuner. Buffalo's 11,000 annual tunings, then, would require almost 15 tuners. The phone book lists 9. Sounds promising!

Study Questions

1. Is this a good approach? How many would you have guessed without this analysis? Does the result seem reasonable? Is it enough on which to base the opening of a business?

_____

_____

_____

2. Could it have been done more scientifically? How? Would discussions with piano tuners and music stores have been useful? Are there any journals worth consulting? Any professional organizations? Would a survey have helped?

_____

_____

_____

3. Are there pianos in places other than homes? Are there tuners not listed in the yellow pages?

Trade and Industry Sources

Small businesses, particularly those in retail trade, can locate useful trade references in the *Small Business Sourcebook,* published by Gale Research of Detroit. If your type of business happens to be included, you'll find substantial information, organized for easy accessibility. The book lists trade publications, industry associations, trade shows and conventions, and venture capital firms and consultants active in each business.

For bigger businesses or those not listed in the *Small Business Sourcebook,* try Gale Research's *Encyclopedia of Business Information Sources.* Arranged by industry, this guide lists trade associations and major sources of statistical information, including databases, directories, and major publications in the field.

If you still need help finding information on your industry's sources, consult Gale's *Encyclopedia of Associations* or the *National Trade and Professional Associations of the United States,* published by Columbia Books of Washington, D.C. These two publications offer information on more than 30,000 trade associations and also list the major publications of these associations.

General Business Sources

The following publications are available from most libraries:

- *Standard & Poor's Industry Surveys.* Designed for investors, this can be a source of insight about your overall industry and major competitors. The "Basic Analysis" section gives overviews of trends and issues in the industry. The remaining sections define some basic industry terms, report the latest revenues and earnings of more than 1,000 companies, and occasionally list major reference books and trade associations. When using *Standard & Poor's,* consider the broad industry category under which your business falls, for instance, "Retail" or "Textiles" for an apparel or home furnishings store.

- *Predicasts F & S Forecasts.* This publication provides an index to articles from more than 750 business and trade magazines, newspapers, financial publications, and special reports. The index helps you find interesting and useful stories about new developments and products, mergers and acquisitions, and general sociological and political issues that may affect your business.

  Predicasts is divided into two sections: "Industries and Products" and "Companies." "Industries and Products" is arranged by Standard Industrial Classification (SIC), the number the government has assigned to identify each industry. You will find an alphabetical list of industries with their SICs at the beginning of the book. It will be useful for you to know the SIC number of your business when referring to other documents.

  When consulting *Predicasts'* "Industries and Products" section, look for citations for articles about your industry, product, sales, and market demand. This section includes an index of general economic subjects, including information about the economy, wages, population, and other sociological factors. The "Companies" section will help you find articles about competitors or possible business customers.

- *Business Periodicals Index.* Published by H. W. Wilson Co., of the Bronx, New York, this is an index to articles in major business publications. It is arranged alphabetically and is easier to use than *Predicasts,* but the articles to which it refers are likely to contain fewer details.

- *Consumer's Index.* Published by Thomas Publishing Company of New York, this may be an invaluable source of information as you develop your business. It's a good place to identify suppliers, distributors, potential customers, and competitors.

- *Thomas Register.* There are three sections to the *Register:* "Products and Services," which lists companies according to their products; "Company Profile," an alphabetical listing of companies and their products; and "Catalog File," which has copies of company catalogs. The *Thomas Register* can be particularly useful as you develop the marketing and operations sections of your business plan.

- *Statistical Reference Index* (SRI). For nongovernmental statistics, refer to the SRI, published by the Congressional Information Service of Bethesda, Maryland. The SRI reports statistical studies from major organizations and trade associations. A second volume, *SRI Abstracts,* provides brief summaries of the information included in these reports.

- *Yellow Pages.* An often overlooked source of business information is the yellow pages of your local telephone directory. The yellow pages can give you insight into the nature and scope of your local competition and potential suppliers.

Exercise 3.2 Market Research, Used-Book Store

Assume you are planning to open a store to sell used books. Search business directories for data on firms in the industry. Search computer databases and the Internet for relevant information. List all sources used, whether they proved productive or not.

What is the size of the industry? What are its customer demographics?

_____

_____

_____

You will likely be amazed at the amount of market research information published in widely available sources. Consider the following examples:

Interested in opening a golf equipment store? There are 25 million golfers in the United States; 7 million of them play at least 25 times per year. A recent survey of business executives showed that 61 percent of men and 33 percent of women have either called in sick or left work early to play golf.

Interested in developing software products for children? Over 4 million babies have been born every year since 1989. Sales of educational software increased 66 percent to $243 million in 1993. More than 15 million U.S. homes have school-age children and personal computers; by 1998 that total is expected to double.

The home remodeling industry hit record levels of $114 billion in 1994, according to the National Association of Homebuilders; they project $172 billion by the year 2000. The average age of the 110 million homes in the United States is 28 years. The U.S. population reached 260 million in 1994.

What does this have to do with the business of our choice? Directly, it shows market sizes and trends. Indirectly it can add to our level of sophistication about our industry, objectively confirm what we already knew, or challenge the assumptions on which we were going to base our plans.

We must, of course, factor in the competitive situation in each of these businesses, and local factors, where applicable. For a localized retail business, for example, the *Census of Retail Trade* provides the average number of stores per capita for a variety of retail outlets. Based on their data, we can determine how well our proposed market area is served on a relative basis for the type of business we plan to start.

For example, there is, on average, a stationery store for every 33,000 people; for every 26,000 people there is one bookstore and one nursery and garden supply store. The population can presumably support a barber shop for every 2,200 residents, and a furniture store for every 3,000.

After looking at all the information we have collected from available sources, we need to decide if it is sufficient for our purposes.

Acquire Primary Data, as Needed

Often, as we apply available data to the analysis of our business idea, we determine a need for more specific or more localized information. The process of acquiring primary data can range in complexity from simply seeing how many firms of a certain specialty are listed in the local telephone book, to asking several tradesmen about sources of supplies in their area, to commissioning professional market research firms to conduct a study to our specifications.

Small businesses and start-up ventures seldom have the budgets to commission studies, but a knowledge of the principles of primary research can heighten their awareness of critical factors in measuring the potential of a market. The two most frequently used research methods are *focus groups* and *surveys*.

✓ **Checkpoint:** *Are we satisfied with our market research?*
Answer the following questions for your business idea.

Do we have enough information to make knowledgeable decisions?
If not, what information is missing?

_____

_____

_____

Are there any contradictions or inconsistencies that need further investigation?

_____

_____

_____

What conclusions can we draw from the results?

_____

_____

_____

What business decisions can we make based on these conclusions?

_____

_____

_____ ✓ ✓

Focus groups are generally multiple informal sessions, directed by a moderator, of four to six prospective customers of a particular product. The moderator steers the discussion to identifying participant likes and dislikes about products of the (unknown to participants) sponsor and its competitors, how the products are used, and features desired but not available. The informality and peer support in an effective focus group often generate ideas that are less likely to arise in individual interviews.

Joshua Hyatt, in his article, "Ask and You Shall Receive,"[1] highlighted a company that effectively employed focus groups.

ENTREPRENEURIAL RESOURCE   Focus Groups

How do you find out what customers really want? Using customer input to help develop new products, experts warn, is dangerous. Their advice can take you nowhere, or sometimes lead you catastrophically astray. Think otherwise. After years of new-product failures, the folks at Techsonic Industries decided to listen, employing focus groups. The results may have saved the company.

In 1983, Techsonic Industries' only successful product was the Super 60, or Humminbird, a sonar fish finder. All fish finders work on the same basic principle: A transducer sends out a sound signal to bounce off whatever's below, be it a fish, a log, or a beer can. Techsonic's flasher-style depth sounder interpreted that signal via flashing red lights.

Between 1977 and 1983 the company, based in Eufaula, Alabama, came out with one new product a year, sometimes two. Most of them were disasters, me-too products that blew apart or stopped cold or capably solved a problem nobody seemed to have. After each failure, company managers found themselves again gathered around the Super 60, praying for its eternal health. "Every so often we'd ask ourselves, 'What's going to happen if the Super 60 goes away?'" recalls Al Nunley, now vice president of marketing. "The answer would be 'We're going under. That's what.'"

It was decided that it was time to ask customers what they were looking for in the next generation of fish finders. They hired a marketing researcher from Atlanta named Sue Symons, and gave her a budget of $20,000.

Traveling to Nashville, Atlanta, and Dallas, Symons hired local field services to screen potential subjects. She wanted people, she decided, who owned boats, fished at least 30 times a year, and had been reeling them in since they were kids. They talked about the solitude, about the struggle of man versus fish, about the camaraderie with their buddies. With her nudging, they talked about depth finders: what they liked, how much they spent, where they bought them. Then she had the tapes transcribed and analyzed the contents, searching for oft-repeated verbs and common emotions.

The number-one problem with current fish finders, according to Symons's research, was that fishermen had trouble reading their fish finders in bright sunlight. "We really had no idea how important that was," company president Jim Balkcom says. Complaint number two wasn't exactly peripheral, either: fishermen found their fish finders too complicated. "Our conventional wisdom," Balkcom says, "was that fishermen liked to press buttons." Wrong again.

The distance between having this information and using it is wider than the mouth on the average trophy bass. Techsonic's executives did apply this information, however, using a liquid crystal display for readability, and an automatic mode for simplicity, for their next-generation product.

The product took the industry by surprise. "It was a tremendously big breakthrough," recalls Dave Ellison, editor of *Fishing Tackle Retailer*. "The technology changed overnight." The fortunes of Techsonic also changed overnight, from a struggling company to industry leader.

Whereas focus groups provide qualitative data as to consumer attitudes, survey research can provide statistically significant measures of market size and product acceptance. The usefulness of survey results is heavily dependent on the quantity and method of selection of those to be interviewed (the sample), and proper wording of the questions asked.

Sample selection, questionnaire design, and interview methods are complex topics, and beyond the scope of this treatment. There are many excellent sources of information on these topics. For our current purposes, we will consider an example questionnaire for a fitness center.

Approach the example as an interviewee. Are the questions clear, concise, and unambiguous? Can you see the purpose of each question? Can you see the usefulness of the results?

MINICASE 3.3   Fitness Center Questionnaire

We are considering opening a fitness center in (location). Your response to the following questions would assist us in better serving the needs of the community:

Please check your age group: Under 25__, 26–35__, Over 35__

How far do you live from (location of proposed center)?
    less than 10 miles__, 10–15 miles__, more than 15 miles__

Do you exercise?

If no, please check reasons for not exercising.
        Lack of time__, Lack of motivation__, No convenient fitness centers__,
          Cost__, Medical reasons__

If yes, please check the type of exercise you do:
        Aerobic__, Nautilus__, Free weights__, Running__, Swimming__,
          Other: Please specify _____

Where do you normally exercise?   at home__, fitness center__

Do you think the area needs a fitness center?

_____

Would you be interested in one-on-one training?

_____

Please note any suggestions or comments you might have.

_____

_____

_____

Study Questions

1. If the sample were of sufficient size for statistically significant results, what percentage of exercisers would you consider promising? Are there national norms to compare to?

_____

_____

_____

2. Do you think anyone will be reluctant to answer the age question? Are non-exercisers likely to admit it?

_____

_____

_____

3. Why would anyone say the area does not need a fitness center? Is this response likely to be meaningful?

_____

_____

_____

MARKET SEGMENTATION

From our discussion of small business opportunities, we should have an idea of the general product area in which our business will compete. The next step is to clarify and refine the niche our business will fill, and this process is driven by information gathered on the opportunity.

A basic decision to be made is where in the process of satisfying consumer needs our offering will fall. The product delivery chain may be thought of as consisting of the following:

- Product manufacture, characterized by large competitors, a large initial investment, and the need for an effective distribution system;
- Wholesaling, a function currently undergoing some consolidation, and requiring sources of supply, and a dealer network;
- Retailing, a highly competitive area with a number of specialty niches; and
- Services, generally the easiest types of businesses to start, but the hardest to get to a high level of profitability.

Start-up entrepreneurs with limited access to capital will often gravitate toward niche retailing and service opportunities, which generally require the lowest start-up costs.

Individual businesses are generally identified in one of these categories, even if operating in a manner that falls between two of them, or that combines two or more. Our previous examples have included a wholesale business (Southland), leaning toward a wholesale-retail hybrid (the Covington branch), a retailer (coffee shop), and a service (piano tuning).

Once the decision is made as to where in this spectrum our company will operate, our idea can take on a little more shape, and we can begin to sharpen our target market focus. Within the population of the prospective customers for our product (which could be a service), there are smaller groups, called market segments, with similar needs.

Markets can be segmented along several different dimensions: product-related; geographic; "psychographic" (related to traits, motives, and lifestyles); and demographic, relating to consumer age or income level. As an example of geographic segmentation, let us consider starting a tourist services business for visitors to the Four Corners area of the western United States.

We choose to locate our tourist agency in southwestern Colorado. It is headquartered in Durango, seat of La Plata County. We regularly follow area news, and happen across the following article by Deborah Uroda:[2]

MINICASE 3.4 | **Tourist Services in Durango, Colorado**

DURANGO—Growth in Fort Lewis College enrollment, county population, bank deposits and retail sales were not enough to offset declines in tourism, agriculture and building permits. All these combined to slow economic growth in La Plata County in the third quarter of 1996, reports the School of Business Administration's newsletter the *Econometer.* The *Econometer* index, a composite of local economic indicators, declined 4.5 percent when compared to the same quarter last year. There were significant declines in tourism, with a drop of 10 percent.

Also, there was a 10 percent drop in agriculture hay and cattle prices, a 6.8 percent drop in the value of building permits and a 3.8 percent drop in industrial energy use, reports economic professor Vernon Lynch. Lynch is the director of the office of economic analysis and business research at the business school and compiles the data for the *Econometer.*

Moderate growth in retail sales, employment, population, bank deposits, college enrollment, real estate prices and a strong jump of 17.5 percent for energy prices helped offset the declines to send mixed signals about the county's economic performance. The *Econometer* index jumped 20 percent from the second to third quarter of 1996, illustrating the county's highly seasonal economy. Tourism posted a 67.5 percent increase and retail sales jumped 14 percent from quarter to quarter.

Nationally, the economy grew moderately during the third quarter, with gross domestic product (GDP) showing an annual increase of 2.1 percent. The nation's unemployment rate remained relatively low at 5.2 percent in September. Many economists expect the national economy will continue to grow moderately over the next several months.

The Colorado economy continued to do well in the third quarter. Colorado's non-farm employment increased 3.6 percent through September, with the state unemployment rate sitting at 4.1 percent.

Construction, both residential and commercial, is providing a strong stimulus to the state economy. The legislature's *Colorado Economic Chronicle* gave the state economy an overall good rating.

Here is a sector by sector analysis.

Tourism: The annual drop may be attributed to drought conditions and the national publicity that the Mesa Verde National Park fires generated. Airline passenger emplanements increased moderately from last year.

Retail: Retail sales, after adjustment for inflation, increased 14 percent from the previous quarter and 1.2 percent over last year.

Employment: Employment rates, which dropped slightly (0.8 percent) from the second to third quarter, rose 1.1 percent over last year.

Finance: Bank deposits in the county, after adjustment for inflation, grew by 4.6 percent from quarter to quarter and 5.2 percent from last year.

Construction: Activity increased from the second to third quarters, with the value of building permits jumping 5.1 percent. Annually, the value of building permits declined by 6.8 percent.

Energy prices: The Federal Reserve Energy Price Index declined by more than 3 percent on a quarterly basis, but increased 17.5 percent from last year. La Plata County is a major producer of natural gas, and as a result property owners receive benefits from rents and royalties.

Real estate: The median price for residential property declined 2.3 percent from the second to third quarters, but remained unchanged from the same period last year.

Study Questions

1. Is this news relevant to our plan? Is it encouraging or discouraging? Which statements concern us most? Are these long-term or immediate concerns?

_____

_____

_____

2. What additional information should we gather to put this report into perspective?

_____

_____

_____

3. Is the state of the local economy a factor in projecting tourist traffic? What about the state of the national economy?

_____

_____

_____

Another form of segmentation would be along ethnic lines. Let us say that we want to consider offering financial planning services to the African-American community. Would the following news item help us in crafting a marketing plan?

MINICASE 3.5 | Financial Services to the African-American Community

The following information is excerpted from an article entitled "Profiling the Black Investor," by Olayinka Fadahunsi.[3]

> Recent studies are shedding light on the subject of how African Americans as a group invest and save and just what they expect to reap. A survey commissioned by Chicago-based Ariel Capital Management, the African American investment firm run by John Rogers, focused on American households with annual incomes of $30,000 or more. Working in conjunction with a polling firm, Roper Starch, Ariel found that African Americans are very active in financial planning, with 93% of those polled responding that they had some sort of investment pattern over the last year. That percentage was no different from the slice of all Americans, across racial lines.
>
> While agreeing on the importance of active management of their assets, there remain ethnic differences in implementation. Only 27% of African Americans buy stocks and bonds, compared with 38% of nonblacks. African Americans were also less likely to invest in several other important wealth-building instruments. The percentage of blacks investing in mutual funds was 22%, vs. 35% of non–African Americans; 13% of African Americans invested in money market accounts, vs. 26% of non–African Americans.
>
> The reason may be linked to African Americans' frugal ways. Compared with other Americans, blacks are generally more conservative in their investment choices, choosing to spread their investment portfolio across an average of 3.3 investment

vehicles, as opposed to the 4.1 median for other groups. That pattern has surfaced in other studies as well, as documented in *Black Wealth/White Wealth* by Melvin L. Oliver, a professor at UCLA, and Thomas M. Shapiro of Northeastern University. Citing statistics gathered in 1988, the two found that blacks had more of their overall assets sunk into their homes (63%) than whites (43%), and less in stocks, bonds and other financial stores of wealth.

That's not to say that African Americans are willing to settle for less. Their investments are less diversified, but they expect a larger payoff, with expectations focused on an annual return of 14.6% vs. 11.2% for non–African American investors. African Americans also differ from the country's other ethnic groups in that they are much more concerned about an investment firm's managerial diversity. Race, religion and gender variety in the boardroom were found to carry more weight with blacks than other ethnic groups. The community activities of investment firms were also found to be more important to African American consumers.

Still, the black community shows a fairly uniform idea of the most important factors in selecting a company. A solid reputation (84%), a strong performance record (82%) and a way to easily access money invested (65%) were all major concerns. African Americans have shorter investment horizons, with six years being the longest time frame that investors were willing to wait on average, vs. 7.3 years for non–African Americans.

Study Questions

1. How might the information in this article affect our approach to this market? Even without tangible effect, is the information useful?

   _____

   _____

   _____

2. Are the differences between African-American investment strategies and general investor strategies sufficient on which to base a niche business?

   _____

   _____

   _____

3. How might we test the applicability of these national findings to our local market? Is there any reason to think that the local market might be different?

   _____

   _____

   _____

THE MARKETING PLAN

What Business Are We In?

Many entrepreneurs consider the business they are in to be too obvious to deserve much thought, but it is worthy of serious consideration in the planning stage and frequent review thereafter. In a classic *Harvard Business Review* article, "Marketing

Myopia," Theodore Levitt suggests that had the railroad industry perceived their business as transportation rather than trains and tracks, we might be flying the "friendly skies" of Southern Pacific or Illinois Central.

Our concept of the business we are in establishes the basic character of the business and defines the range of marketing opportunities available. The business concept is often embedded in a mission statement, which identifies our prospective customers, the specific needs of these customers that we wish to service, and the means by which we intend to provide these benefits. This statement further serves to establish guidelines for future growth in light of changing customer needs, actions of competitors, resources available to the business, and changes in environmental factors.

COFFEE SHOP EXAMPLE

As an example, let us consider a mission statement for our coffee shop. Are we simply in the business of selling coffee by the cup? Let me suggest that we are in the business of "providing a comfortable atmosphere for enjoying work breaks, enhanced by premium beverages and snacks." Is this more defining? Is it limiting?

!! Scan the annual reports of some familiar companies for mission statements. Do the statements fit your perception of the companies? Do they help explain some of the companies' actions in the marketplace, such as new products, acquisitions, and so on?

What Is the Competition Like?

Understanding our competition, and how they meet the needs of customers, will help identify our competitors' strengths and weaknesses. The analysis of these strengths and weaknesses will provide us with a mechanism to identify potential

---

3.1 *Expert Opinion*

Management consultant Dheeraj (Raj) Khera suggests we should be able to clearly describe our business in 20 seconds or less:

"I don't mean something like, 'We do programming and system design.' That hardly gives insight into what you do best. I also don't mean, 'We develop software for database management, systems integration, network management, Windows applications, and other custom applications.' Small businesses that do everything under the sun lose credibility. If you wanted a deck built for your house, would you feel more comfortable hiring a general contractor who does all types of construction work or someone who just builds decks?"

Here's a sample of an effective statement for computer consultants: "We develop transaction processing software for insurance companies in the Washington, D.C. metropolitan area." By focusing your business, you can better define your target market and develop the best marketing strategies. People hire consultants as specialists, not generalists. Here's another example: "We provide Novell network administration including on-call support for small businesses in the greater Los Angeles area."

Once the statement is crafted, Khera suggests we memorize it: "With this statement committed to memory, you will be able to tell people what you do clearly, without stumbling."

opportunities or problems for our firm, allowing us to minimize potential competitive disadvantages and maximize competitive advantages. The basic question is what type of competition exists in the market, and what impact that will have on our firm's ability to compete successfully.

The uniqueness of our firm's product or service, the number of competitors, the size of competitors, the overall demand, and the price will all be key factors in gaining a competitive edge. There are three basic forms of competitive structures that differ based upon the number of competitors, the relative ease of market entry, types of products, and knowledge of the market.

Monopoly

A firm with a product or service that has little or no substitute, and has absolute control over the price in our market, is considered a monopoly. Utility companies have traditionally been monopolies, but technology is increasingly opening even these services to competition.

Oligopoly

This structure exists when a few sellers of products or services control the supply of a large proportion of your market. These firms tend to set similar prices and create more difficult barriers for entry into the market. The automobile industry, with its huge capital requirements, is a classic example of an oligopoly.

Competitive

A competitive structure consists of many firms with relatively few barriers to entry; firms competing in this market develop strategies to establish market share. In a perfect competitive structure, individual firms are unable to influence the price or supply of a particular product or service. Agricultural products, and a wide range of services, exemplify nearly perfect competition.

Opportunities for start-ups will almost certainly be in industries that fall somewhere in the competitive spectrum. What is the nature of the competition in the market you would like to enter? Are there larger competitors that set prices (Starbucks, for example, among coffee shops)? Does the current competitive structure leave room for niche strategies (used books, for example, in the bookseller market)?

What Is Our Target Market?

The target of our marketing effort is that portion of the prospective customer population that is the most likely to buy our product or service. Identification of our target market can sharpen our marketing plan in the start-up phase, and give direction to our advertising campaign as the business grows and develops.

The keys to effective target marketing are to (1) define the profile of our potential customer realistically, (2) aggregate the location(s) of these customers with precision, and (3) employ the most cost-effective avenue(s) to connect with these targeted markets.

According to Thomas A. Faulhaber, editor of www.businessforum.com, "Target marketing has been a commercial custom since the bazaars visited or fashioned by the nomadic caravans more than 4,000 years ago. The gift shoppe situated on the main street of a holiday resort and the Hertz car rental facilities at a major airline terminal are present-day models of target marketing. Even the traditional schoolchild's lemonade stand on a hot July afternoon exemplifies target marketing. In fact, all effective marketing has always been targeted."

What is new is the availability of advanced tools to the owner/manager of the smaller business to strengthen its present market position and to exploit additive market opportunities. Some of these basic tools have been around for a long time; the guest book in our store may now be thought of as the data collection resource for our customer database (formerly known as our mailing list). Customer lists can be categorized and indexed in a variety of ways, for example, by size, by geographic location, by specific product interests/needs, by pricing preferences, and/or even by credit status.

A customer database is all too frequently a neglected gold mine. Faulhaber reminds us that "in gold mining, it is commonly necessary to extract and process *two to three tons* of ore in order to obtain *one ounce* of refined gold. Astute management performs a comparable mining operation to extract the gold often hidden in the smaller business's own database."[4]

One way to sharpen our understanding of our target market is through customer surveys. A thoughtfully designed customer survey will give us a much better understanding and factual basis of our customers and their individual needs, dissatisfactions, and expectations. Some survey information may trigger an immediate response to meet a previously unknown customer requirement or to plumb a customer discontent. Smaller businesses are frequently surprised to discover that our perceived profile of present and past customers is no longer valid.

In addition to strengthening our present market position, *target marketing* is a critical tool in exploiting additive market opportunities. This dimension of target marketing seeks to define our potential and as-yet-unknown customers by income, household size, age, ethnicity, affinities, and other variables, and then to locate where these customers tend to be aggregated. Direct mail is often the instrument of this approach, though higher postal rates and mailbox clutter are leading many businesses to other direct marketing strategies. We seem to be nearing the end of the comparable overuse of telemarketing.

However, knowing the location(s) of our potential customers, many other imaginative avenues of connection are available. Until the novelty of the electronic media is totally dissipated, target market communication for business-to-business via facsimile broadcast (fax) or e-mail are attractive. One's own Web site as well as on-line advertising are increasingly effective ways of reaching certain very specific markets. Targeted advertising via community newspapers and cable television is often quite cost-effective. Neighborhood outdoor advertising (billboards), product sample drop-offs, and/or redeemable coupon distribution can be sharply focused communications. Of course, companies such as Avon Products, Inc., continue to flourish employing variants of door-to-door solicitations.

By accurately identifying and analyzing our firm's target market and its relative competition, we can focus on those opportunities that offer the greatest probability of success in selling our product or service. These opportunities, which competitors may have ignored, will provide our firm with the vision to develop a marketing mix that gains us a competitive edge.

What Marketing Mix Should We Offer?

The marketing mix is generally referred to as the "four P's"—product, price, promotion, and place.

Product

What is the product that the market needs? How well positioned are we to provide it? How will we differentiate ourselves from the competition?

COFFEE SHOP EXAMPLE

For our coffee shop, we have determined that the neighborhood needs a premium coffee and light-lunch place. Our cooperative arrangement with the owner of a large office building puts us in a position to offer the service competitively. Our competitive advantage is location.

What brand name and packaging will we use? How wide will our product line be? What will be its features, accessories, and options?

Should we offer retail goods in our coffee shop? We could have our premium coffees labeled with our company name. Have we decided on a name? Might coffee mugs and T-shirts also sell?

Price

Will our price be competition-based or quality-image-based? What is the range of pricing options? How price-sensitive are sales? Can we be low cost *and* high service?

Our coffee shop will definitely be quality-image-based; there are too many fast-food places nearby selling cheap coffee. Still, if our prices are double theirs, we may be limiting sales too much. These are tough decisions!

What will our terms be? What discounts and allowances will we provide?

Would our regular coffee shop customers consider a weekly billing an added convenience? Would a "Buy 9 and Get Your 10th Cup Free" promotion bring additional business?

Promotion

How will we promote the product? What aspects of the product should we stress? How and where will we advertise? What are the most cost-effective media? Can we afford an agency? Are there some nontraditional promotional methods that could be effective? Does our venture lend itself to personal selling over mass marketing and cross-promotions with related products? Are there opportunities for free publicity?

Need we advertise the coffee shop? Would flyers on windshields be enough? Should we call on offices in the area with free samples? Would noncompeting businesses hand out our cards if we did the same for them? Would a press release about our opening be published?

Place

Where and how will we distribute the product? What will the distribution channel look like? Is physical location relevant?

Does the coffee shop location in our friend's building limit us in any way? Is lunch delivery service critical to our success? Should we subcontract delivery? Is there enough profit margin to license vending carts with our products to others?

What Strategy Should We Pursue?

There are four distinct possibilities of strategies: market penetration, market development, product development, and diversification. Start-up firms generally begin in a market penetration mode, progressing quickly into market development. The following are highlights relative to each strategy.

Market Penetration

This is characterized by a firm trying to enter an existing market, or increase sales of an existing product in its present market, through development of an aggressive marketing mix. Methods are to get current users of the product to increase usage with our brand, take customers for the product from our competitors, and create product users of current nonusers. This may be done through creative promotional appeals, or "penetration pricing," that is, short-term pricing low enough to generate notice. Some of the questions we might want to address are:

Why are customers currently buying the product or service?

What might motivate the market to buy more?

How can we persuade our competitors' users to switch to our product or service?

How can we motivate nonusers to try our product or service?

Market Development

This opportunity is characterized by a firm attempting to introduce its products or services to new markets. This could entail opening our business in a new geographic area. It could also take the form of appealing to new customers in our existing area, for example, a hotel catering to business travelers might advertise weekend specials for tourists and the local "in-town vacation" market.

Product Development

Offering new and/or improved products to existing markets addresses product development opportunities. This may mean that the firm improves a product's performance, or it may mean an extending of the product line, such as car dealers offering minivans and sport-utility vehicles.

Diversification

A diversification strategy relies on offering new products to new markets. The new products are often adaptations of the current product line to the new market being pursued. A good example is the Disney organization, which began with cartoons and comics, branched into theme parks, and has now become a broad entertainment company with cruises and movies for all age ranges.

As an example of application of these strategies, let us look at an industry that has had to largely redefine itself due to rapid changes in the employment environment.

MINICASE 3.6   Temporary Employment Business

Fortune magazine reports that the number of temporary workers in the United States has nearly doubled over the past five years from 1.2 million to more than 2 million; this is a record of job creation that beats just about every other industry in the country. While many relate this growth to the corporate downsizing movement, credit must be given to the "temp" industry for developing and implementing strategies that have taken this opportunity and built on it.

The growth and increasing sophistication of the temp industry is creating a national trading floor for talent. "It's a contingency spot market," says Jessica Sweeney, of the Advisory Board Co., a management consulting firm based in Washington, D.C. The industry is becoming a clearinghouse for buyers and sellers of skills; the economic consequence of this phenomenon is a more flexible and efficient job market. It is also creating opportunities for workers and employers.

Many companies are turning to temp agencies to outsource the administration of their temporary workers. Tom O'Halloran, an analyst at Dillon Read, says that five or ten years ago companies would just call a local temp agency and order up workers a la carte. Now that they see how important flexible staffing is to their cost structure, and realize that more and more upscale positions can be filled by contract labor, they're hiring companies to set up on-site and take care of hiring, training, and scheduling.

Employers are also using temporary employment to audition possible full-time hires. Pat Taylor runs her own temp agency in Washington, D.C., which used to specialize in paralegal temps. By 1993, supplying temporary attorneys had also become a significant chunk of her business, as the law firms and government agencies she serviced started running leaner.

Just as companies are using temp assignments as a dress rehearsal before hiring, many workers see temping as a way to sniff around for permanent jobs. According to a survey by the National Association of Temporary Staffing Services (NATSS), three-quarters of respondents said they became temps as a way to look for a full-time position; 40 percent said they'd gotten permanent offers.

Audrey Freedman, an economic consultant based in New York City, can't think of any business that won't be touched by the staffing business. "It's a protean kind of industry," she says. "A client says to them, 'What can you do for me?' and the industry says, 'Whatever you want.'"

Study Questions

1. Relate recent developments fueling the growth in the temporary agency business to the marketing strategies defined earlier. Give examples of application of each of the four strategies.

_____

_____

_____

2. Do all fit clearly within one strategy, or do some overlap?

_____

_____

_____

3. Within this services framework, which of their offerings might be considered a "product"?

_____

_____

_____

Summary

Once a business idea is determined to be worthy of further consideration, we must assess its potential. Often, after we select an approach to the market and do the necessary research, we may detect greater potential in a different approach and have to revise and repeat the research process.

We should first decide what we need to know to make a more informed decision about the feasibility of our business idea, and the optimal way to enter the market. Generally, there is a lot of useful information that is readily available. A good business library is the best starting point. Often our market research objectives must be modified to use available information. In some cases, we may choose to survey the market to acquire data designed specifically to our needs. In every case, we must apply some judgment to the data, since we are trying to project our future prospects.

From the marketing research results, we must refine our marketing plan. What segments of the market will we serve? What do we have to offer the market? Who are our customers? What are they looking for? What is the competitive situation? What is our competitive advantage or distinctive competence? How will we price the product? How will we promote it? How will we distribute it?

With a marketing plan in place, we can begin to make estimates on the tangible factors that allow us to test the feasibility of the venture. How many people will we need? How much will we have to pay them? How much space will we need? What is this space likely to cost? What are our equipment needs? What other operating expenses will there be? What are our sales expectations?

How do expenses vary with the level of sales? What level of sales will it take to break even? How likely are we to achieve this level? How long will it take? We will address these issues in the following chapter.

Review Questions

The following exercises will be helpful for ventures we have discussed, such as the coffee shop and used-book store, and for any other venture you might be considering.

Who are the most likely customers for our venture? What are they buying? What are their price expectations?

_____

_____

_____

What would a good market research strategy be for the venture? What directories, periodicals, and trade publications are available in the area? What on-line search tools are available? How timely is the data? How applicable is it to your venture?

_____

_____

_____

If our start-up budget were to allow for some primary research, what form should it take? Do you feel that the results would justify the cost?

_____

_____

_____

How might we segment the market for our product or service? What is our target market? What is the competitive situation?

_____

_____

_____

How would you describe the business you are in, in 20 seconds or less?

_____

_____

_____

CASE STUDY 3
The Atlantic Brewing Company

Jim Patton and Rush Cumming met at the Boston Brew Club, found out that they lived near each other on the Northshore, and began to carpool to meetings. Jim, a college professor, fancied himself quite the amateur brewmaster, and his home-brewed beers frequently won taste contests at the club. Rush, a self-employed carpenter, was more interested in the tastings than the recipes, but enjoyed the conversations with Jim about the fine art of small-batch brewing.

It was an article of faith among members of such clubs, all over the country, that the products of the large commercial breweries were bland so as not to offend any of their mass clientele. Greater emphasis was thought to be placed on shelf life than on taste.

Seeing a business opportunity in the making, Jim and Rush felt that one did not have to be a member of a brew club to be willing to pay a little extra for a beer with "character." Jim decided it was time to do some marketing research on the microbrewery industry, where the techniques of homebrewing were adapted to a minimal commercial scale. Many of these breweries also operated "brewpubs" where the public could sample their wares, and the term "craft brewing" had arisen to describe both types of operations.

At the library, Jim found an article entitled "U.S. Craft Brewing Totals Surge Again":[5]

Explosive growth of the craft-brewing industry continued last year as production increased 50 percent and market share rose 40 percent over the previous year, the Institute for Brewing Studies (IBS) reports in its latest industry update.

The surging popularity of craft beer also brought another sharp increase in the number of new craft breweries as 100 brewpubs and 62 microbreweries opened during the year. At year's end, there were 543 craft breweries in the United States, the IBS told *Southern Draft.* The latest total represents the largest number of operating breweries in the U.S. since Prohibition, IBS Director David Edgar said. While the craft-beer industry can claim only a fraction of the U.S. beer market dominated by the megabreweries such as Anheuser-Busch and Miller, the specialty brewers' 1.3-percent market share at the end of 1994 represents a 40-percent jump over its 1993 share.

"With a 23-1 opening-to-closing ratio of craft breweries, this industry has proved specialty beers aren't simply a fad, as projected earlier," Edgar said. "This industry is being driven by an ever-increasing number of beer consumers demanding more from their favorite beverage." They are getting more, too, he said, adding that "as the industry continues to grow and flourish, so does the quality and diversity of craft beer."

Another source gave a little more detail from the industry update:

- 100 brewpubs and 62 microbreweries opened during 1994.
- More breweries opened in 1994 than during the industry's entire first 12 years (1977 to 1988).
- Closures decreased 59 percent, as only seven companies ceased production in 1994.
- A record seven microbreweries expanded beyond 15,000 barrels sales to join the regional specialty breweries, now numbering 16.
- The combined total number of operating craft breweries (regional specialty, microbreweries, and brewpubs) increased to over 540. This represents growth of 41 percent in 1994, well above the 29 percent growth enjoyed during 1993.
- Craft-beer production rose in 1994 to 2.5 million barrels, or nearly 78 million gallons.

One industry writer was bold enough to project the industry's direction: "After three years of 35 to 40 percent growth, the craft-brewing industry surged by 50 percent in 1994. The craft-brewing industry can look forward to at least another 40 to 45 percent growth in sales in 1995. It's likely the year will also see another 200 new microbreweries and brewpubs opening for business. It's difficult to make sound projections much further beyond."

Another article reported on a survey from the Midwest: "The typical microbrew drinker has an annual income in excess of $50,000, has at least a college degree (in many cases a postgraduate degree), is married with 0 to 2 children and is a professional between the ages of 25 and 44."

Jim decided it was time to put a venture together. He visited a microbrewery in Pennsylvania, meeting the designer and builder of their equipment, an Englishman named Fred Glick, who had become something of a cult figure in the industry. Fred responded to Jim's interest in starting a microbrewery by roughing out a design that would meet Jim's specifications, and an estimate of the cost of building the state-of-the-art equipment.

On the flight home, Jim developed the outline of a business plan, and a rather detailed estimate of start-up funds required. The funds, on the order of $250,000, were well beyond his means, but he and Rush could provide the seed money to pre-

pare a private placement stock offering and present their story to prospective investors. Jim had already picked out the location of the microbrewery, near his home in Peabody, Massachusetts, and a company name, The Atlantic Brewing Company.

The product was clear in his mind, a beer free of preservatives and made with a locally available spring water. They would produce a lighter brew, "Golden," and a heartier "Amber." Seasonal and specialty beers would also be made as production schedules allowed. Their products would be priced with imported beers, while offering greater quality and freshness. They would appeal to all premium beer drinkers, not just the connoisseurs.

Because the cost of bottling equipment was prohibitive, they would begin by distributing kegs only. This would require competing for tap space at bars and restaurants, initially on the Northshore with its affluent demographic. They would distribute directly, delivering in company trucks.

Jim knew from the brew club that there were at least fifteen microbreweries in greater Boston, with two or three others in the planning stage. He planned to gather data on how and where they marketed their products and whether there might be some geographical niche where competition was not too intense. His initial instinct was to expand north and west from Peabody, avoiding the crowded Boston and southern New England areas.

Once this research was done, he could complete the business plan and begin the search for investors.

STUDY QUESTIONS

1. Where might Jim find regional data comparable to the national data from IBS? Try your suggested sources to see what is available. What do you find?

   _____

   _____

   _____

2. What type of information would support or go against Jim's assumption that his market is to the north and west? Do you expect that secondary data could answer the question, or are primary data required? What might be gained from surveying area beer drinkers? How

might a survey of bar owners help us? What would we ask them?

_____

_____

_____

3. How would you rate the marketing plan? How is Atlantic Brewing differentiated from the competition? What need are they filling? Are we convinced that need exists?

_____

_____

_____

4. Analyze their pricing strategy. What is their greatest competition?

_____

_____

_____

5. Suggest a marketing campaign that emphasizes Atlantic Brewing's strengths. To whom are we trying to appeal? What is the best way to reach them?

_____

_____

_____

Notes

1. Joshua Hyatt. "Ask and You Shall Receive," *Inc.* (September 1989): vol. 11, no. 9, pp. 90(9).

2. Deborah Uroda. "La Plata Economy Slows with a Drop in Tourism," *Four Corners Business Journal* (May 1, 1997): (www.businessjournals.com).

3. Olayinka Fadahunsi. "Profiling the Black Investor," *Black Enterprise Moneywise* vol. 27, no. 11 (June 1997): p. 70(1).

4. www.businessforum.com

5. Sara A. Doersam. "U.S. Craft Brewing Totals Surge Again," *Southern Draft Brew News* (June/July 1995): (southerndraft.com).

CHAPTER

Refining the Venture Idea: Testing "Fit" and Feasibility

4

Chapter Objectives

After completing this chapter, you should be able to

■ Evaluate a prospective venture in terms of its fit with your interests and financial requirements.

■ Develop the product-based venture, by protecting the product idea and evaluating various methods of distribution.

■ Refine the venture idea strategically, planning how you will enter the market and identifying barriers to entry.

■ Analyze the financial prospects for the venture, estimating revenues and expenses and performing a break-even analysis.

■ Consider various legal structures, determining which form best fits the venture at start-up and beyond.

VENTURE SCREENING: OVERVIEW AND PERSONAL FACTORS

Our market research often yields several venture ideas that show promise. Those ideas that make it this far in our consideration must then be subjected to a more rigorous screening process that goes beyond passing interest to serious evaluation. The following approach to such an evaluation is adapted from a model developed in "Feasibility Checklist for Starting a Small Business," available from the Small Business Administration.

The feasibility study often begins with a personal assessment, measuring the requirements of the venture against your skills and expertise, or those of your venture team. The first question concerns the study itself, that is, whether we can afford a meaningful, rigorous, and objective feasibility study. This often depends on whether we can perform the study ourselves, or whether we will require assistance (e.g., marketing, legal, financial).

Venture screening involves analyzing and evaluating information gathered in our market research, with the purpose of determining whether this idea has a significant probability of being developed into a successful business. The product of this analysis is often referred to as a **feasibility study.** The feasibility study often repeats considerations of market segmentation, planning, and strategy issues addressed during the market research phase, but at a greater level of detail and in closer relation to how the venture will be implemented.

✓ *Checkpoint: Often overlooked are issues of the personal "fit" of the venture. What about the venture appeals to you? How well does it fit your career aspirations?*

_____

_____

_____

What do you have to give up to pursue the venture?

_____

_____

_____

Do you have the skills and expertise critical to the success of the project?

_____

_____

_____

Does the venture effectively utilize your skills and abilities?

_____

_____

_____

Do the potential rewards justify the commitment required?

_____

_____

_____ ✓ ✓

ENTREPRENEURIAL PROFILE   Suzanne George[1]

"All of my formal educational training had been in communication and psychology, not in art or handicrafts, so the fact that I now earn money making beautiful shoes by hand is a dream come true for me," says Suzanne George, 34, who launched her San Francisco–based shoemaking business in the summer of 1995. All of George's footwear is custom-made to meet the desires and specifications of individual clients.

"The idea for the business grew out of my knack for envisioning creative, new footwear styles," George explains. "I kept having 'pictures in my head' of innovative shoe designs. My desire to transform those visions into reality led to my interest in making shoes by hand."

Although George first got the idea to start making and selling custom-designed shoes when she was in her early 20s, she sat on the idea for more than a decade because she feared it wasn't a viable career option. "My impression was that you pretty much had to be born into a family of shoemakers in order to acquire the skill," she explains. "As a result, I shied away from pursuing my dream by working in the nonprofit sector, working in banking, and studying counseling psychology in graduate school, instead."

As George moved from one career situation to the next, she found that she couldn't shake her desire to make made-to-order shoes. "The longer I thought about it, the bigger the idea got in my mind, and the scarier it became to reach out and try to attain it," says George. "In my late 20s, though, I decided it was time to give my dream a try. My close friends were sick of hearing me simply talk about it, anyway, so I finally went out and did something about it."

George was accepted by a reputable technical college in England that specializes in shoemaking and saddlery; students there can also learn to make handbags and accessories. She learned of the college from a San Francisco design school's librarian who knew of its reputation. Upon the program's completion, she apprenticed with some shoemakers there before returning to the United States. In all, she was abroad for a bit more than a year. Upon her return, she took part in a six-month training course on how to operate a profitable small business at the San Francisco Renaissance Entrepreneurship Center, a community economic development program established in 1985—one of the first microenterprise-development programs in the nation. She then obtained her business license and focused her attention on her new sole proprietorship, Suzanne George Shoes.

"My favorite thing about the work I do is that I'm preserving a craft and creating high-quality goods in an old-world manner, which is quite rare in this modern era of mass production," says George, who meets with clients at their homes in order to get a sense of their personalities and to allow them to show her many of the footwear and clothing items they prefer. She then works on the shoes at her homebased location, returning with them upon completion to the clients' premises. "I also like the fact that I get to work with people in their own environments and help them to create custom-made footwear that expresses who they really are."

The ideal venture is one in an area where our interests and the needs of the market intersect. More often, some compromise is required. This can take the form of accepting less return in order to be able to do just what we like, or departing a little from our ideal job to earn a more comfortable lifestyle.

As we screen ventures, it can be very useful to have a sense of the relative weight of personal and financial factors. A good starting point is in developing a financial requirements "baseline."

Exercise 4.1 Establishing Personal Financial Requirements

There are no right or wrong answers to the following questions, but their consideration should help you in developing a perspective on the financial effects of an entrepreneurial career.

How much income do you desire? What minimum income do you require?

_____

_____

_____

Are you prepared to earn less income in the first one to three years?

_____

_____

_____

What financial investment will be required for your business?

_____

_____

_____

What is the average return on investment for a business of your type?

_____

_____

_____

How much could you earn by investing this money in another way?

_____

_____

_____

How much could you earn by working for someone else?

_____

_____

_____

Could you earn more by working for someone else and investing your venture money in another way? Are you prepared to forgo this additional income just to be your own boss with only the prospects of more substantial profit/income in future years?

_____

_____

_____

VENTURE SCREENING: MARKET AND STRATEGIC FACTORS

Should the venture idea under consideration pass the first screen—that is, it is a good personal fit with acceptable financial rewards—we then need to assess market and industry factors. For this second level of screening, we are largely firming up many of the options considered in our market research, specifying much of the data that will be used in our later analysis of the financial prospects for the venture, and identifying the keys to the success of the venture.

Venture Specifics

The critical issues to be resolved at this stage relate to the business concept and implementation. It is useful at this point to develop a written prospectus that includes the following:

- A description of the business and a profile of its target customers.
- The products/services offered, including their sources where relevant.
- Major competitors—those who sell or provide like products/services.
- The competitive advantage of the venture, that is, why someone would buy its product/service.

As an example, let us return to our coffee shop venture.

COFFEE SHOP EXAMPLE

The coffee shop concept is beginning to take shape.

Café de l'Est is a coffee shop and light-dining establishment serving fine coffees, pastries, and healthy light entrees in a pleasant atmosphere. Located in the eastern business corridor of the city, we plan to serve area workers, shoppers, and residents a wide variety of international coffees, pastries by a leading local bakery (Gambino's), and taste-tempting salads.

The only direct competition in the target area consists of a Tastee Donut Shop and a Toddle House Diner. Neither has table service or premium coffees, and their selections of sweets leave much to be desired. Light-meal service is available in the food court at the mall, and at a wide variety of fast-food places, but all are noisy and crowded.

The major employer in the area is the hospital, which has a typical hospital cafeteria on site. Though we feel sure that most employees would prefer our offerings, our marketing challenge is to make it worth their while to leave the hospital campus.

Our target customers are those who are looking for quality light fare in a quiet, relaxing atmosphere. We hope to make Café de l'Est *the* place to go for breakfast, lunch, break time, and for meeting friends and business associates.

Product-Based Businesses

Product Development

Some prospective entrepreneurs' interest in starting a business is a product idea. If our market research has indicated a need for the product and, we have determined that its production is feasible, venture refinement focuses on protecting the idea (via patent or trademark) and maximizing its potential.

Many product ideas can be patented. Without a patent, anyone can duplicate your idea and sell it; with it you can stop anyone else from making, using, or selling your idea without your permission.

Although there are many examples of products that have been successful without patent protection, in general, patents add value to an idea. In addition, many companies that you may wish to market to, or license your design to, require that you already have a patent, have filed for one, or can prove that one is attainable.

ENTREPRENEURIAL PROFILE   **Identity Research Corporation**[2]

A very useful Web site for information on patents, trademarks, and copyrights is that of Identity Research. Following is an example of the type of information provided at their site:

IS MY INVENTION PATENTABLE?

An invention can be patented if it is:

Novel or new. The invention cannot be previously known. It must differ physically in some way from the prior art. The physical hardware must be different, or there must be new use. As defined in the patent law, an invention cannot be patented if:

(a) The invention was known or used by others in this country, or patented or described in a printed publication in this or a foreign country, before the invention thereof by the applicant for patent, or

(b) "The invention was patented or described in a printed publication in this or a foreign country or in public use or on sale in this country more than one year prior to the application for patent in the United States."

Unobvious. The invention must be unobvious to someone of common experience in the field of the invention. In general, if a problem has been solved in some unique way, which someone of ordinary skill in the art would not readily consider, the invention is not obvious.

Useful. The invention must have some use or purpose. Virtually any usefulness will suffice, provided that it is functional and not purely aesthetic.

WHAT CANNOT BE PATENTED?

In addition to the statutory requirements of novelty, non-obviousness and usefulness discussed above, there are several categories of information that cannot be patented. These include methods of doing business, inventions for atomic weapons, and inventions used for illegal purposes only.

A trademark is a word, phrase, symbol or design, or combination of words, phrases, symbols or designs used to identify the source and quality of a business product. Registered trademarks can increase your idea's value, giving you the right to bar others from using the trademark.

Does Coca-Cola recognize the value of its trademarks? They have registered the following: "Coca-Cola," "Coke," "Diet Coke," "Diet Coca-Cola," "Coca-Cola Light," "Coke Light," "Cherry Coke," "Cherry Coca-Cola," "Diet Cherry Coca-Cola," "Fanta," "Sprite," "Diet Sprite," "Fresca," and "TAB." Just to be safe, they added a couple of design elements too: the contour bottle design for Coca-Cola, and the dynamic ribbon device.

In an article entitled "Pump Up the Value," Tomima Edmark suggests some additional strategies for turning your good idea into a hot seller.[3]

- A prototype of your idea provides extra value in the eyes of prospective buyers because it allows you to demonstrate your idea and proves it can be reproduced into a tangible form. Obviously, a prototype that looks and works exactly the same way as the eventual marketed product is best because it leaves nothing to the buyer's imagination. On the other hand, a sloppy prototype, poorly painted and held together with duct tape, implies a lazy and unrealistic seller.

- Gaining manufacturing know-how can be complex because you'll probably be researching areas you may be unfamiliar with, learning terms such as injection molding, fabrications and surface mounting. However, this information is very valuable to potential buyers because it reduces their research time and speeds up their purchasing decision.

- Knowing the basic economic factors associated with your idea will not only add value to your idea but will also allow you to negotiate from a position of strength. Determining these factors gives you a better understanding of the costs a potential buyer will be considering.

Basic economic factors can often be estimated using published industry norms for items such as raw material and labor expenses, manufacturing overhead, and shipping costs. Other factors may use norms as a basis, but require tailoring to your venture based on a marketing plan; this would include items such as advertising methods and costs, sales commissions, target markets, and selling price.

Product Life Cycle

As we begin to measure the size of the market in which we will compete, the stage of development of that market can be an important factor. This stage is often described in terms of where a product is perceived to be in its life cycle.

The **product life cycle** describes the sales pattern of a product over time. Generally, the time span begins with product introduction and ends with its obsolescence and replacement. Although the form of the life cycle is fairly standard, it is subject to variations. The concept underlying the premise of product life cycle is that all products pass through **development, growth, maturity,** and **decline.**

The development stage of a product type represents a slow growth period. It is assumed that newly released products require some time to gain market acceptance, so sales in the initial period may be slow. If the product proves to be successful, rapid growth in the market often follows.

It is considerably easier to enter a market in a growth stage than it is to enter a saturated, mature marketplace. Levels of competition in markets experiencing growth are considerably less intense than in mature markets, where competitors are concerned about loss of sales and market share.

If a product enters a market that has already moved into the mature stage, competition is intense because the product must compete for a share of an existing market that is not experiencing growth. Introducing a product into such a market will often prove expensive, and will often result in retaliation from established competitors.

According to the concept of the life cycle, the market for any product is limited. When this limit is approached, the market enters the maturation stage. The life cycle further assumes that each product eventually is replaced by another or that initial rapid growth will end in decline.

Once the market enters decline, new products are not entering the market, and demand levels are falling. At this point, many competitors in the market are working to increase market share to maintain stable sales levels. Others, where the declining market is not significant in their company's marketing mix, may be abandoning the market. A new equilibrium is established in the market, as the market share of departing companies is redistributed.

Thus, the life cycle is vital as a planning tool because profit potential changes during each stage of the cycle. Market factors such as demand and supply are changing constantly as they pertain to your company, market, and industry, so a detailed knowledge of the appropriate product life cycle can make your market strategy more timely and effective. The strategy will have to be modified as the product passes through each stage of the cycle in order to meet the unique demands of that stage.

Let us look at the life cycle concept in a real-world example.

MINICASE 4.1 | Personal Care Products

For immediate release, from Frost & Sullivan, specializing in healthcare markets.

U.S. PERSONAL CARE SALES TO TOP $30 BILLION BY 2001, PACED BY NICHES, "GREYING" POPULATION

MOUNTAIN VIEW, Calif.—Paced by new product introductions targeting emerging niches and increasing demand from a greying population, wholesale revenues from U.S. personal care product sales will grow from $20.8 billion in 1994 to $30.9 billion by the year 2001 at a 6 percent compound annual rate, projects a new study just released by Frost & Sullivan.

In 1994, the share of personal care revenues spent for skin care was 25 percent, hair care 21 percent, cosmetics 15 percent, fragrances 12 percent, oral products 10 percent and soaps 8 percent, according to the report, U.S. Personal Care Product Markets.

Natural ingredients like aloe vera, almond oil, rose-hip oil, tomato extract and other ingredients derived from fruits, vegetables, flowers and herbs are becoming increasingly popular for their beneficial properties and "natural" characteristics as manufacturers respond to increasing buyer "chemophobia."

Multifunctional products are gaining greater market presence. Two- and three-in-one products are proliferating, including shampoos that condition as well as provide intensive treatment, lipsticks with sunscreens, and toothpastes that prevent tartar and plaque build-up along with cleaning teeth.

An increasingly middle-aged population is seeking to keep a healthy, younger look with personal care products that minimize effects of aging. As changing demographics influence research and development, alpha-hydroxy-based products known for their anti-aging properties have become an increasingly important market presence.

African Americans and Hispanics are meanwhile growing in population much faster than majority whites, offering a new world of target marketing for focus on these specialized ethnic groups' demands.

With an already high penetration rate, successful manufacturers offer frequent new product introductions and relaunches. Vendors need to stay ahead of the competition by shortening product cycles. Product improvements and extensions lengthen and revive product life.

Frost & Sullivan, a subsidiary of Market Intelligence, is an international high-technology research firm specializing in healthcare markets. All Frost & Sullivan reports are based on extensive interviews with marketing and technical experts from selected companies in each market segment. Primary research is validated by thorough analysis of available secondary research. Frost & Sullivan is the leading publisher worldwide of high-technology market research reports.

Study Questions

1. Identify three trends in personal care product marketing from the press release.

_____

_____

_____

2. Describe consumer "chemophobia," as used in the press release.

_____

_____

_____

3. Identify how product life cycle considerations mentioned in the press release can affect market planning for manufacturers of personal care products.

_____

_____

_____

4. What types of products might appeal more to the growing African-American and Latino markets than current offerings?

_____

_____

_____

5. Do you see any windows of opportunity in this product area for a start-up?

_____

_____

_____

6. Can you identify new products or franchises that are addressing these trends?

_____

_____

_____

Product Distribution

When our venture involves a product, or line of products, a major concern becomes the manner in which we get the product to the customer or end user. Each of the distribution options, or *channels,* has its own special advantages and disadvantages.

Direct distribution can include a sales force employed by the producer, calling on customers in person or via telemarketing, mail solicitation and catalogs, and sales via the Internet. Direct distribution gives complete control of the sales process, immediate feedback from customers, and the highest margins. The downside is that sales costs tend to be highest by this method, and the product can receive greater exposure by other methods.

A **distribution channel** consists of those individuals or firms involved in the process of making a product (or service) available for use or consumption by consumers or industrial users. Distribution can be direct, where the product source sells directly to the consumer, or can involve intermediaries, who can assist the source in reaching buyers by various means.

A *distributor* buys and inventories your products, as well as products of others, and sells them to a retailer or end user at a markup. This results in less need for inventory at your site, and lower selling costs, since purchases are in bulk to repeat customers.

Additionally, distributors are often more closely in touch with the market. On the other hand, you must sell at a low enough price to leave room for them to profit, and make sure that your product receives a sufficient share of their attention.

Typically, distributors (also called jobbers or wholesalers) aren't interested in carrying a new product unless there is a proven demand. "The best way to do this is to first get a bunch of retail orders yourself, then present them to a distributor," explains Stephen Hall, who is also a contributing editor of *Food Entrepreneur,* an industry trade journal. Without these orders, he says, distributors feel they will have to undertake the "pioneering" of the product, which they may not be willing to do.

Let us say that your product is a great new seasoning mix. You build up some inventory, put up a Web site, and begin to call area grocery stores to schedule a product demonstration. A regional chain allows you to set up a table at one of their stores to give away samples to shoppers. The store manager gets good feedback from the tasters and places a small order.

Sales of your product at the test location go well, and the chain would like the product in all their stores. They buy all their chain-wide nonperishable goods from an area distributor, who buys in bulk for breakdown to individual store quantities. The distributor has a formula for what they will pay based on the retail selling price.

Just because you get a distributor to carry your line, however, doesn't mean you've got it made. In the words of one producer, "Distributors warehouse, deliver, receive orders and do invoices—but they don't sell."

Agents function as a sales force for your products as well as others, but are not on your payroll; agents are paid a percentage of sales volume. This generally results in low sales costs and greater reach than a direct sales force. Like the distributor arrangement, you must share the agent's attention with other vendors.

You discuss your product with a sales agent who sells regional products to various gift shops and gift-basket marketers. She suggests that, for a percentage of sales, she can get your product on the shelves of most of her clients, and do a terrific holiday business with her gift-basket clients.

The *retailer* channel can be sold to directly, but for most "small-ticket" items such as our seasoning mix, the sales costs of doing it this way can be prohibitive. In this situation, a distributor or wholesaler could be our best means of getting the wide exposure needed to succeed. We should still call on retail outlets, however, because of how close retailers are to their market and customers. Comparing various ways in which retailers display the product, and asking store and department managers for suggestions, can be valuable input to refining our marketing plan.

‼ In the process of developing our distribution strategy, trade shows can be very helpful in understanding distribution channels for our product category, in establishing useful contacts, and in finding ideas for new marketing strategies. For listings of regional or national trade shows, consult Tradeshow Week's *Tradeshow Week Data Book* at your library.

"We always get new ideas from shows such as the one put on by the Direct Marketing Association," explains Pud Kearns, who runs Mary of Puddin Hill, a Greenville, Texas, fruitcake company. One new idea for Kearns was to diversify the family business to include off-season mailings for Valentine's Day and Easter, which proved to be good sales boosters.

Another method of direct sales is *mail order*; the key ingredient for mail order success is a good mailing list. Though lists can be leased from various list brokers, finding one that fits your target customers can be difficult. "It's better to put a sign-up list in your store, if you have one, and encourage everyone to sign up," says Kearns, whose family used this method to build their 24-page catalog. "A lot of people also have good luck advertising in magazines—just make sure they are magazines your customers read."

Selling through another company's mail order catalog, such as Williams-Sonoma, is also an option. Because product category leaders are overwhelmed with samples shipped to them from small vendors, you might also consider making contacts with such catalog companies in other ways, such as at trade shows.

4.1   *Expert Opinion: Tales from the Front—Distributing Food Products*

Another place to get a feel for the food products market—and possibly even solicit new orders—is on the Internet. "Food is definitely a very popular topic on the Internet," says Ken McCarthy, president of the San Francisco Internet consulting and production firm E-Media. "You can buy advertising on some sites, or you may get [recognition] if you provide an interesting site with recipes, for example." Specifically, McCarthy recommends checking out sites at http://www.epicurious.com, http://www.starchefs.com, and http: //www.veg.org/veg .

Other venues for marketing a food product include mail order and wholesale clubs. "Rather than go head to head with competitors, look for different ways of bringing your product to market," suggests S.R. Knapp of Tucker-Knapp Integrated Marketing Communications.[4] "Find a less traditional way of reaching your target audience." That could mean a unique kind of packaging—or looking for a different market altogether.

Wholesale and membership clubs, for example, provide plenty of opportunity. "Club stores—with their numerous food sampling tables—are turning into a proving ground for new products," says Knapp. "These stores have become more consumer-friendly, and because they're always looking for ways to differentiate themselves from grocery stores, they're often more willing to work with entrepreneurs."

Market Analysis

The primary objective of a market analysis is to arrive at a realistic projection of sales. This sales estimate, as we will see later in our break-even analysis, is the basis for our projections of the financial performance of the venture.

We continue our feasibility study by gathering the following information:

- The geographical areas from which we can realistically expect to draw customers.
- The population of these areas, and the population trends.
- Demographic information, such as average family size, age distribution, per capita income.
- Consumer shopping and spending patterns relative to our type of business.
- The relative importance of price/service/quality to the target market.
- Whether our appeal is to the entire market, or only to a segment (which segment?).
- Whether the market or market segment is large enough for the venture to be profitable.

Let us continue to refine our coffee shop idea.

MINICASE 4.2 | Café de l'Est

We feel that our venture should be in the commercial center of the area, because its success depends largely on workers and shoppers. In New Orleans East (NOE) this is its Interstate Highway 10 corridor; a five-mile radius around the corridor is home to over 42,000 households and over 122,000 people. Population in the area has been slowly increasing, and family income is on the rise again after several difficult years.

A more specific location in which we are interested is the corner of Lake Forest and Read Boulevards, at NOE's prime I-10 exit. This intersection is in walking distance of many regional facilities, including a shopping center, a hospital and medical offices, the area's largest office building, a library, a high school, and a playground.

We contact the NOE Economic Development Foundation, which has some data from a survey they recently conducted on NOE residents:

> NOE is a racially mixed suburb, with 64% black population. It is also a relatively new suburb; 43% of our sample reported having lived in NOE for ten years or less. The median age of adults in the sample is 39.5, and a majority of the households (54%) report having children under 18. Most are homeowners (64%), and income levels are in the working class to middle class range.
>
> New Orleans East residents like to eat out; a majority reported eating in a sit-down restaurant at least three times in the past month. Residents with family incomes over $26,000 are the most likely to eat out. We asked respondents about what foods they like most when eating out. The most popular types, among those listed, are sandwiches and salads, and grilled chicken and fish.
>
> When asked about specific types of food outlets in New Orleans East, an ice cream parlor elicited a very positive response, as 61% said they would be "very likely" to patronize an ice cream parlor in NOE. A coffee shop with a bakery and a restaurant geared to children are also favored by a majority of respondents. Many respondents observed that New Orleans East needs "nicer" restaurants, or something other than fast food.
>
> There appears to be a clear opportunity for a casual style restaurant to succeed in this area.

Study Questions

1. Do you agree with the "clear opportunity" conclusion? Does our venture fall within the researcher's concept of a casual-style restaurant?

   _____

   _____

   _____

2. Had we acquired primary data, would we have surveyed area residents? How else would you select a sample of our prospective customers? Are the available data sufficient for our purposes? What else do you recommend we do?

   _____

   _____

   _____

3. Do you consider the information we have so far to be favorable to our venture? Does it indicate that our chances might be improved with some minor modifications? What would those modifications be?

_____

_____

_____

Entry Strategies

The market does not necessarily welcome a start-up business with open arms. To existing businesses in the industry we are entering, we are a competitor for their hard-earned customers. To customers, we are an unknown entity that must exhibit some advantage over the firm it currently patronizes to be worth the trouble for them to consider switching.

Business practices or conditions that make it difficult for new firms to enter a market are called **barriers to entry.** These can take the form of ingrained customer habits, cost disadvantages due to some proprietary technology or greater experience on the part of competitors, limited access to materials of production or distribution channels, or high start-up investment required to enter the market.

Our best chance of overcoming barriers to entry is when our venture addresses at least one of the following market shortcomings:

- The product/service/business addresses a presently unserved need.
- The product/service/business serves an existing market in which demand exceeds supply.
- The product/service/business can compete successfully with existing competition because of an "advantageous situation," such as better price, location, and so forth.

Does our café serve an unserved need? There are enough restaurants in the area, but we are targeting customers who are dissatisfied with current choices. Do we have an "advantageous situation"?

✓ **Checkpoint:** *Entry Advantages*

Does the venture you are considering have one or more of the three entry advantages? Could some aspect of the venture be modified to create one of these advantages, or to strengthen an existing advantage? ✓ ✓

Entry strategies depend largely on the competitive situation our venture faces. Among the questions that we should ask ourselves in this phase of the venture screening process are:

- Who are the major competitors? What are their major strengths and weaknesses?
- What are the key components of their strategies?
  - Price structure, location, promotional activities?

- Product lines (quality, breadth, width), sources of supply?
- Image from a consumer's viewpoint?
- What are the gaps in their offerings?
- Have any firms of our type gone out of business lately? If so, why?

Though often difficult to obtain, information on the sales and market share of each competitor would be very useful. In addition to the current situation, we would like to know whether these sales and market shares are increasing, decreasing, or stable, and whether any competitors have expansion plans, or whether there might soon be other entries into the market.

Exercise 4.2 Entry Strategy

For the venture you are considering, or for Café de l'Est, develop an entry strategy.

Highlight where the entry strategy uses one or more of the entry advantages outlined earlier.

_____

_____

_____

Identify and assess barriers to entry for the market. Are any prohibitive?

_____

_____

_____

What are your strengths and weaknesses for developing such a venture?

_____

_____

_____

What are the critical factors for success of the venture?

_____

_____

_____

Before proceeding to the next stage of the screening process, we must also ask ourselves whether the venture idea has any fatal flaws. Are any of the barriers to entry prohibitive? Is the cost of gaining entry into this market greater than the financing within our reach? Can we compete successfully with the established players in the market?

VENTURE SCREENING: FINANCIAL ANALYSIS

If we determine that the working venture idea still shows promise after researching market and industry factors, we can take our first look at the financial prospects for the venture. This requires that we make estimates of our expected sales and the expenses of operating the business. Although this process seems daunting, help is not hard to find.

Typical values for operating and expense relationships, often called norms, are generally available for most businesses from trade and industry associations, government agencies, universities, private companies, and banks. Sources you might wish to investigate include data published by Dun & Bradstreet and Robert Morris Associates.

Internet sites for trade associations and for companies in the industry can provide useful information. Guides to starting specific types of businesses, such as used-book stores and specialty restaurants, are available at many bookstores.

We should try to acquire, for our particular line of business, information on the following:

- The normal markup, that is, percentage of the cost of goods sold (CGS) added to cost to establish selling price, or another way of expressing the same concept.

- Alternatively, the normal margin, that is, percentage of the selling price that represents cost of goods sold.

    For example: We buy a product from our supplier for $1.00, and we sell it for $1.25. This represents a 25 percent markup, or a selling price 25 percent greater than CGS. The margin is 20 percent, that is, 20 percent of the selling price represents a "profit" over CGS.

- Average expenses (other than CGS, normally fixed costs and labor) as a percentage of sales.

- Average net profit (selling price less CGS and expenses) as a percentage of sales.

- Average inventory turnover, that is, the number of times the average inventory is sold each year.

    For example: We have annual sales of $300,000 with a margin of 65 percent. This represents a CGS of 35 percent, low for many businesses, but fairly typical for food service. We therefore sell $105,000 (35 percent of $300,000) per year of goods at cost. Over the course of the year, the value of goods on hand is $17,500. Thus, our average inventory "turns over" six times a year ($105,000/$17,500); some express this factor in terms of number of months of inventory on hand (average inventory/average monthly sales). For this example, average monthly sales are $8,750 ($105,000/12), and inventory on hand is two months' sales ($17,500/$8,750).

Using sales and expense estimates, we can construct a projected income statement for the venture; we can then determine the level of sales required to "break even," that is, show no profit or loss. In practice, this means that the amount of money left over after the cost of goods sold is deducted (or "gross margin," that is, margin percentage converted to dollars) just covers operating expenses.

Although many people are uncomfortable with the guesswork involved in projecting sales and expenses for a prospective business, there are approaches that at least yield informed guesswork, similar to the marketing research estimates earlier. Remember that in any case of predicting future events, there is no right answer, and if we are careful, our judgment is as good as anyone's on our own business concept. Let us now look at the components of break-even analysis.

Estimate Monthly Sales

If possible, it is better to derive a sales estimate than simply to pick one. We may first try to find an estimate of the total demand for our product in our market area; market research will often yield a fairly well founded number for this, or provide norms that can be used. Next, an estimate of what share of that demand our company might reasonably be expected to capture can be multiplied by total demand to give the sales estimate.

For example, we may estimate that a market will support total sales of $60,000 per month and that we can capture 75 percent of those sales. Our estimated monthly sales figure is then 75 percent of $60,000, or $45,000 per month.

4.2 *Expert Opinion*

"Rules of thumb," although less "scientific" than norms, can be very helpful in putting our estimates together. In browsing through books about starting a food and beverage outlet, I picked up the following advice:

- Expect start-up costs of $30,000 to $40,000.
- A good starting store size is 1,000 square feet.
- A successful first year would yield about $300,000 in gross sales.
- Rent and related costs, or mortgage payments, should be budgeted at 8 percent of annual gross sales; other fixed costs should be held to 10 percent.
- Expect payroll costs to be about 35 percent of annual gross.
- Expect food costs to be about 35 percent of annual gross. Margin is thus 65 percent of sales (deduct food cost percentage). Expenses are 53 percent (rent, other fixed, and labor), and net profit (deduct food cost and expenses) is 12 percent.
- Net profit of 12 percent is the norm for coffee shops and small cafés.

Estimate Monthly Expenses

Identify the major expense categories for operating the business; SBA publishes a "Checklist for Going into Business," which contains some helpful worksheets. Estimate how much you would spend in each of those categories each month, distinguishing fixed from variable costs.

Fixed costs are not expected to vary with changes in sales volume within a narrow range of expected sales. Salary costs, for example, would not change as sales vary slightly, but wide changes could cause additional hires or layoffs.

Variable costs are tied directly to sales level, and are often expressed as a percentage of sales. For product sales, these will be cost of goods, shipping expenses, sales commissions, and so forth. For service firms, full-time employees are a fixed cost, hourly or contract employees would represent a variable cost.

MINICASE 4.3   **How Much Do We Have to Sell to Make It Here?**

In February 1977, John Vinturella of Southland Plumbing Supply began to investigate the feasibility of opening a branch of the Metairie, Louisiana, company in Covington, Louisiana, 40 miles to the north. The question was whether the expected sales level of the branch would support profitable operation.

John estimated that he would need two other people to adequately run the branch, a warehouseman and a delivery person. A delivery truck would be leased. Furniture requirements would be minimal, and shelving for inventory could be built inexpensively. Following are his estimates of monthly expenses:

Expenses			*Break-Even Analysis*	
Salaries	John	$2,000	*Expenses*	$8,000/mo rounded
	Others	2,000		
	Benefits (25%)	1,000	From Metairie Experience:	
			Margin: 20% per sales $	
Equipment	Trucks	300		
Leases	Other	60	*Sales needed to generate expense $:*	
			Margin% × Sales = Margin$	
Expenses	Transportation	480	$0.20 \times Sales = \$8,000$ (= *Expenses*)	
	Insurance	360	Sales = $40,000	
	Legal/Acctg	150		
	Utilities	300	*Estimated sales*	
	Supplies	420		
	Advertising	100	Low	$35,000
	Miscellaneous	100		
			Expected	$45,000
Contingency	(10%)	727		
			High	$60,000
TOTAL		$7,997		

Total expenses to operate the branch would be on the order of $8,000 per month. These are all essentially fixed costs, that is, they are relatively constant within the estimated range of sales volume. Variable, or sales-volume-dependent, costs consist of only the cost of goods sold, estimated to be 80 percent of sales, based on the experience in Metairie.

From parish permit information, John estimated the amount of money to be spent on homebuilding and remodeling over the next year. Information from the U.S. Bureau of Labor Statistics allowed him to determine the percentage of that amount to be spent on plumbing materials. BLS data also provided an estimate of repair and replacement expenditures for existing homes.

After estimating the total amount of plumbing material sales in the market area, and analyzing the competitive situation, he assumed a 75 percent market share for the new branch. This yielded an expected sales figure, and from the ranges in his calculations, he decided on pessimistic and optimistic values for monthly sales (see *Break-Even Analysis*).

The level of sales required to break even, then, is that sales volume at which the remaining 20 percent of revenues (margin) generates enough gross profit to pay expenses. In this case that number is $40,000 ($8,000 × 20%). This is below the estimate of the most likely sales volume, so there is a reasonable expectation of this being a profitable venture.

Study Questions

1. How would you rate the quality of the market research used to justify the venture? What would you have done differently? What would you have done additionally?

_____

_____

_____

2. Given the information used in John's analysis, would you have opened the branch? Are they trying to justify opening the branch, no matter what the data showed?

_____

_____

_____

3. Were John's expense estimates too rough? How could they have been refined? Were the expense categories reasonable and complete? Was the market share estimate realistic?

_____

_____

_____

Estimates should always be on the pessimistic side. The natural tendency is to cut too close on expense figures, and the less visible costs such as permits and taxes are frequently overlooked. The above example missed one fairly basic expense. Have you figured out which one it is? How much should it have been? (Remember that these are 1977 dollars.)

Note also in the example that 25 percent is added to the payroll figure for benefits and other costs related to payroll. This might cover sick and vacation time and the employer contribution to federal, state, and unemployment taxes, but little else. If you plan to contribute to hospitalization insurance or educational costs, or other benefits, this figure should be increased accordingly.

The example also includes a figure for "Miscellaneous" expenses and an added "Contingency" of 10 percent of total expenses. Is this enough to account for the omission?

Calculate Break-Even Sales Level

We must establish an expected margin percentage. Then, *profit* (or *loss*) equals gross margin dollars (*sales* times *margin*%) less *expenses*. In mathematical notation: $P = S \times M - E$, where:

$P = 0$ at the break-even sales level (implying that $S \times M = E$, or $S = E/M$), and

P is the amount of profit if greater than zero (margin$ > expenses), and the loss if less than zero.

In the Southland example, experience at another store indicated that a margin of 20 percent could reasonably be expected. If expenses are $8,000 per month, sales of $40,000 (20% of $40,000 yields $8,000 gross margin with which to pay expenses) represents a break-even situation.

Compare and Conclude

Where in our range of estimates does the break-even sales figure fall? If it is above our optimistic estimate, prospects are grim. If it is around our expected figure, we may need to look a bit more closely. If it indicates that we can break even with a sales figure below our pessimistic estimate, or comfortably below our expected sales, it makes the cut.

Break-even analysis is only a screening device, to help us sort out promising ventures from hopeless ones. A more detailed financial planning process will be discussed later.

MINICASE 4.4   **Break-Even Analysis on Café de l'Est**

We have decided to lease a 600-square-foot space in The Plaza, the regional mall in New Orleans East, for our café. We are quoted a rental rate of $20 per square foot per year, which equates to $1,000 per month. We estimate payroll at $7,000 per month, and other fixed costs at $2,000 per month. Our cost of goods sold averages 35 percent of sales.

Verify the monthly rental calculation.

_____

_____

_____

Calculate the break-even sales level.

_____

_____

_____

Calculate the profit at sales of $12,000, $16,000, and $20,000 per month.

_____

_____

_____

If our expected sales figure is $16,000 per month, do you recommend we open?

_____

_____

_____

LEGAL STRUCTURE

There are several legal structures under which we may start and operate our business, each with its advantages and disadvantages for start-up ventures. The most common business structures are sole proprietorships, partnerships, and corporations.

A proprietorship is simply a one-owner business. It is the most prevalent form (about 70 percent of all businesses) because it is the simplest and least expensive to start.

A partnership is basically a proprietorship for multiple owners. Most are general partnerships, where each partner is held liable for the acts of the other partners. A limited partnership allows for general and limited partners; limited partners' liability is limited to their contributed capital.

The corporation is a legal entity, separate from its owners. It is a more secure and better defined form for prospective lenders/investors. Incorporation is perceived as limiting the owner's liability, but personal guarantees are generally required whenever there is liability exposure.

For each of these options, consult with local or state government offices for specific information on the requirements for opening a business, generally including occupational licenses and tax registrations. With any form of organization, be sure to clear the name under which you will do business, generally with the secretary of state or similar office for business affairs in your state.

We will discuss each here to help you become an informed "legal consumer." Much of the following details on these business structures is drawn from the SBA document "Selecting the Legal Structure for Your Business," by Jocelyn West Brittin. When you are ready to start your business, be sure to engage a lawyer who can advise you on the latest business and tax regulations and recommend which form suits your venture best.

Sole Proprietorship

The sole proprietorship is the simplest type of business organization, and is the form usually chosen by the one-person business, although sole proprietorships can have employees. A sole proprietorship may be owned by only one individual; ownership by more than one person creates a partnership. Its primary advantage is its ease of formation; its most important disadvantage is that the owner is individually responsible for all losses of the business.

As owner of a sole proprietorship, you may hire employees to help you manage the business, but you retain legal responsibility for their decisions and unlimited personal responsibility for the liabilities of your business. Insurance may be purchased to cover many of the risks of running a sole proprietorship.

Where uninsured losses occur, business creditors can go against both your business and your personal assets, including your bank account, car, and house. The reverse is also true, that is, your personal creditors can make claims against the assets of your business.

A sole proprietor can freely transfer a business by selling all or a portion of its assets. Otherwise, the proprietorship exists as long as its owner is alive and desires to continue the business. When the owner dies the assets and liabilities of the business become part of the owner's estate.

A sole proprietor is taxed on all income from the business at applicable individual tax rates. The business income, and allowable business expenses, are reflected on the individual tax return.

Advantages: Simple to start, nominal legal expense, low license fees, profits not shared.

Disadvantages: Difficult to raise capital, unlimited liability.

Partnerships

The decision to enter a partnership should be based on whether or not you can do it alone. The main reasons people feel they cannot are lack of money, skills, connections, and confidence. Are there other ways to address these needs?

If you choose to go into business with a partner, be sure to prepare a formal, written partnership agreement that addresses the following:

BUSINESS PARTICULARS

- Name of the partnership, location of offices, fiscal year of the partnership.
- Duration of the partnership, number of years or until dissolved.
- Where the partnership cash is to be deposited and who may sign checks.
- Contracts or agreements affecting the liability or operation of the partnership.
- Prohibition of competitive business activities by partners; period of time in which retiring or withdrawing partners may not engage in a competing business.
- Method of resolution of differences.

DUTIES, RESPONSIBILITIES, AND SPHERE OF ACTIVITIES OF EACH PARTNER

- Capital contribution of each partner, and resulting ownership shares; conditions under which partners may make additional contributions.
- Designation of managing partner; all partners' titles, duties, and commitments.
- Salaries, if any, to be paid to partners; participation of each partner in profits and losses; methods of disclosure and access to financial records.

OPERATIONAL ISSUES

- Procedure for admitting new partners.
- Method of determining the value of goodwill in the business, for valuation as may be needed in ownership changes.
- Provisions for the partners pledging or selling their interest in the partnership to other partners, descendants, or others.
- Method of liquidating the interest of deceased or retiring partner; provisions for mandatory retirement and protracted disability of a partner.
- Basis for expulsion of a partner, method of notification of expulsion, and disposition of any losses that arise from the delinquency of such a partner.

There are two types of partnerships: general partnerships and limited partnerships. A *general partnership* is created when two or more individuals agree to create a business and to jointly own the assets, profits, and losses. In the absence of a formal partnership agreement, all general partners have equal control and equal management rights over the business.

A *limited partnership* consists of one or more general partners who manage and control the business as proprietors, and one or more limited partners who are basically investors with limited liability. General partners are jointly liable for the partnership, that is, all of the partners are liable together and each general partner is individually liable for all of the obligations of the partnership. Limited partners are at risk only to the extent of their contributions to the partnership.

A partnership has characteristics of both a separate legal entity and a group of individuals. For example, it can own property and conduct business as a separate legal entity. Any partner can bind the partnership and the individual partners to contracts or legal obligations, even without the approval of the other partners. This means that a creditor of the partnership could require you individually to pay all the money the creditor is owed. Before joining a general partnership, determine whether your partners can financially afford to share the losses of the partnership.

A partnership exists as long as the partners agree it will and as long as all of the general partners remain in the partnership. The partnership agreement should state whether a partner can sell his or her partnership share, and how a partner will be paid for his or her share of the partnership when he or she leaves or dies. When a general partner leaves a partnership, he or she is entitled to an accounting that will determine his or her share of the assets and profits of the partnership.

A partnership tax return is filed, but for informational purposes only. Each partner must individually pay taxes on his or her share of the business income. The profits and losses "flow down" from the partnership to the individual partners.

> *Advantages*: Simple to start, can be used to raise capital, complementary skills of partners.

> *Disadvantages*: Suitable partners can be hard to find, partnership agreements can be complex and expensive to craft, structure allows for unlimited liability of each partner.

Corporations

A corporation is considered a separate legal entity; because of this, the owners of the corporation (known as its shareholders or stockholders) are not personally responsible for the losses of the business. Although a corporation usually has more than one owner, it is possible for only one individual to create and own 100 percent of a corporation.

Among the issues to be decided by the business owners are the following:

- The name of the business and its corporate address.
- The management structure, that is, who will be the directors and officers of the corporation.
- The number of shares of stock the corporation can sell or issue, known as "authorized shares."
- The number of shares of stock each of the owners will buy, and the amount of money or other property each owner will contribute to buy his or her shares of stock.

Articles of incorporation are generally filed with the secretary of state for the state in which the business is incorporated. The corporation will also need by-laws, that is, a set of rules of procedure by which the corporation is run. These include rules regarding stockholder meetings, director meetings, the number of officers in the corporation, and the responsibilities of each officer. In some states, small businesses are permitted to incorporate without a board of directors or with other differences. Seek professional advice regarding what types of options may be permitted in your state.

In general, the officers of the corporation are responsible for running the day-to-day business of the corporation, while the board of directors is responsible for the major decisions of the corporation and broader issues of policy and focus. Small businesses that are corporations are often owned by a small group of shareholders who all work in the business. Often these shareholders formally agree to certain restrictions on the sale of their shares so that they can control who owns the corporation.

Because the corporation is a legal entity, separate from its owners, creditors of the corporation may look only to the corporation and its business assets for payment. The individual shareholders are not personally liable for the losses of the business if the corporation is properly established and operated within statutory requirements. The shareholders' only risk is their investment in the corporation.

If shareholders "guarantee" the obligations of the corporation in order to borrow money or to rent space, they are legally responsible for the obligations guaranteed. If shareholders make loans to the corporation and the business fails, their loans may be paid off only after the other loans of the corporation are paid.

Ownership of a corporation can be transferred by sale of all or a portion of the stock. Additional owners can be added either by selling stock directly from the corporation or by having the current owners sell some of their stock. Federal or state securities laws often restrict sales of stock to outsiders, and legal advice should be sought in this situation.

There are three major variations of the corporate structure, with differences relating to tax and liability considerations. Let us examine these differences in the context of a start-up venture.

C-Corporation

The traditional form of the corporation is referred to as the C-Corporation. This form is required when the corporation has a large number of stockholders (generally more than 35), and multiple classes of stock (common/preferred, voting/nonvoting).

Of particular interest to us is how the C-Corporation distributes its proceeds. If the corporation is sufficiently profitable, the decision may be made to distribute some of these profits as dividends to stockholders. A dividend must be paid equally to all shares of common stock and is usually expressed as an amount per share. Profits not distributed are retained by the corporation.

Dividends paid to shareholders by the corporation are taxed to each shareholder individually. This is why there is said to be a "double tax" on corporations. The corporation must pay taxes on its profits, and the shareholders must pay taxes on the dividends paid to them from the profits.

> *Advantages:* Familiar form to prospective investors, easy ownership transfer, limited liability.
>
> *Disadvantages:* Legal requirements on reporting and record-keeping, double taxation of dividends.

S-Corporation

In an S-Corporation, income or losses are "passed through" to individual shareholders and reported on their personal tax returns. The income or losses are divided among the shareholders based upon the percentage of stock of the corporation that they own.

Many start-ups elect "S" status since the losses expected in the early years can be claimed as they are incurred. C-Corporations can carry losses forward only until there are offsetting profits. Election of S-Corporation status is subject to restrictions on number and type of shareholders. S-Corporations can be converted to C-Corporations in later years.

> *Advantages*: Eliminates corporation double taxing while keeping limited liability advantage of incorporation, allows pass-through of losses to offset income from other sources.
>
> *Disadvantages*: All profits must be distributed and taxed annually; if in tax bracket exceeding corporate rate, the C-Corporation tax would be less.

Limited Liability Company (LLC)

The LLC is a hybrid entity that may be considered a partnership with corporate protections. In a conventional partnership, there are limitations on who can participate in management decisions, so as to preserve protections on liability. All members of an LLC can participate in the management, without risking loss of liability protection. Moreover, the earnings of an LLC are not subject to corporate taxes; instead, the profits flow through to the owners in proportion to their ownership.

Like a corporation, however, an LLC shields the owners, or "members," as they are known, from personal liability for the organization's debts and liabilities. LLCs also offer pass-through tax advantages similar to an S-Corporation, without the limitations on the number and type of owners.

> *Advantages:* Corporate liability protection, tax advantages of S-Corporation without restriction on number of shareholders.

> *Disadvantages:* Cannot accumulate earnings, may face risks of higher taxes and liability for business done in states other than the one in which formed.

Summary

Our market research often yields several venture ideas that show promise. These ideas must then be put through a screening process that selects one, or possibly more, of these ideas for more detailed study.

Often, the first qualification for a venture is whether it forms a good fit with our interests and skills. The ideal venture is one in an area where our interests and the needs of the market intersect. More often, some compromise is required. This can take the form of accepting less return in order to be able to do just what we like, or departing a little from our ideal job to earn a more comfortable lifestyle.

Where the venture is based on a product or products, some additional issues must be addressed. We may need to patent the design or other unique feature, or register a trademark that we wish to use. We may wish to license or subcontract manufacture of the product rather than make it ourselves. Our marketing plan must be tailored to where the product is in its "life cycle," that is, a new product type, or a product in a growing, mature, or declining marketplace. The method chosen for distributing the product to consumers can be a significant factor in product success.

Knowledge of our prospective customers and the competitive situation are critical to our success. These are the keys to developing an effective strategy for breaking into the market.

With many of the marketing decisions made, we can develop projected financial statements for the operation of the business. A break-even analysis is particularly useful in measuring the probability of financial success.

At this stage, we may want to decide the legal structure under which the company will be organized. This decision can affect taxes and liability, and our ability to raise start-up capital.

Review Questions

1. What questions is the feasibility study designed to answer?

_____

_____

_____

2. What are the major criteria for whether an idea is patentable?

   _____

   _____

   _____

3. What are some strategies for maximizing the potential of a product idea?

   _____

   _____

   _____

4. What is a product distribution channel?

   _____

   _____

   _____

5. What are the basic entry strategies?

   _____

   _____

   _____

6. Define "break-even sales level."

   _____

   _____

   _____

7. Compare and contrast the various legal structures for a start-up venture.

   _____

   _____

   _____

CASE STUDY 4.1
Tammany Supply, Inc. (A)

BACKGROUND

In February 1977, John Vinturella of Southland Plumbing Supply began to investigate the feasibility of opening a branch of the Metairie, Louisiana, company in Covington, Louisiana, 40 miles to the north. The question was whether the expected sales level of the branch would support profitable operation.

The decision was made to proceed, and John selected a location on Highway 190, the main road between Covington and Mandeville and the business thoroughfare for all of western St. Tammany Parish. The site was just across Lake Pontchartrain from Southland's main operation, via the world's longest bridge, the Causeway.

"Buck" Rogers, a good young warehouseman at Southland, was assigned to run the Covington warehouse. John hired a local truck driver in the last week of February, and they began to stock the branch from out of the Metairie inventory. The highly visible location paid off immediately, as several sales were made during the stocking process to passersby.

Sales comfortably exceeded the break-even estimate of $40,000 per month. Operating for essentially 10 months of 1977, sales averaged almost $50,000 per month and seemed to be accelerating before the typical seasonal slowdown from December to February.

ENTREPRENEURSHIP BY DEFAULT

In early 1978, John and his family began to discuss "spinning off" the branch as a separate business, with John trading his partial ownership of Southland for complete ownership of the Covington operation (working title "Tammany Supply"). The branch had been operating quite independently, and family members at each location had become quite detached from one another.

For John, this was not a straightforward decision. While his brothers had never worked anywhere but Southland, John had been with the company just over two years after ten years of working in other fields. After receiving a doctorate in engi-

neering, he had been a college professor and an internal consultant at several corporations.

The position with Southland had begun as an internal consulting assignment also. John's initial charter was to develop a computer-based version of Southland's manual pricing system, and to assist his father in introducing the Kohler plumbing products line to their customers. As these projects were nearing completion, John was expecting to move on when the Covington branch idea arose.

For several years, John had seen an entrepreneurial career in his future, and much of the appeal of opening the Covington branch was the opportunity to start a business from scratch. But the business that John had expected to preside over was a computer consulting firm. A year ago, John had viewed his starting the Covington branch as an entrepreneurship "laboratory"; now it was time to decide whether it would become a long-term commitment.

SCREENING THE VENTURE

John had thoroughly enjoyed his first year in Covington. He had become very active in the local chamber of commerce and the homebuilders association, and had even begun to dabble in local politics. The independence of sole ownership of the business, and his newly acquired community status, gave the prospect of the buyout enough appeal that he decided to look at the long-term financial prospects for the venture to help him make up his mind.

In March 1978, John asked Southland's accountant to develop a 1977 income statement for the Covington branch as if it had been a separate corporation, and to project the value of the Covington assets on June 30, 1978. This marked both the end of Southland's fiscal year and the day the sale would take place. John was comfortable that the Covington branch could operate profitably, and worked on developing estimates of what he could earn with the company as his own, as shown in the following table:

Income Statement	Actual				Projected
	1977	**1978**	**1979**	**1980**	
Sales	$496,486	$660,000	$720,000	$800,000	
Cost of Goods Sold	394,763	528,000	576,000	640,000	
	20.5%	20.0%	20.0%	20.0%	Margin
Total Income	101,723	132,000	144,000	160,000	
		1.33	1.09	1.11	Sales Increase
Expenses		0.98	0.95	0.92	Economies of Scale
Personnel	42,058	54,791	56,784	58,046	
Operations	13,041	16,989	17,607	17,998	
Sales	6,557	8,542	8,853	9,050	
Administration	9,225	12,018	12,455	12,732	
Depreciation	2,074	2,702	2,800	2,862	
Total Expenses	72,955	95,043	98,499	100,687	
					AverageProfit
Profit/Loss BIT	28,768	36,957	45,501	59,313	$47,257

The figures used for margin, sales increase, and economies of scale in the statement represent the assumptions on which the calculations were based. The sales increase row shows a 33 percent increase in the first full year (20 percent due to having 12 rather than 10 sales months), followed by 9 percent and 11 percent gains in subsequent years. With each sales increase, expenses are increased proportionately, "deflated" slightly by the economy-of-scale factor. A 20 percent margin is assumed throughout the three projected years.

John knows of some ways in which expenses would have differed if the branch had been truly independent, and that the proper adjustments would present a more accurate picture of expenses of his company. In particular, Southland charged the branch $2,000 for a clerical assistant's time for things that the Covington staff will now do themselves. In addition, the branch was not charged for supplies, and a small percentage increase in each expense category should be allocated to cover that. With these adjustments, a revised expense section of the income statement would be:

Expenses:	Adjust	1977	1978	1979	1980	
Personnel	−$2,000	$40,058	$52,186	$54,083	$55,285	
Operations	5.0%	13,693	17,839	18,487	18,898	
Sales	2.0%	6,688	8,713	9,030	9,231	
Administration	5.0%	9,686	12,619	13,078	13,368	
Depreciation		2,074	2,702	2,800	2,862	
Total Expenses		$72,199	$94,058	$97,479	$99,645	
						Average Profit
Profit/Loss BIT		29,524	37,942	46,521	60,355	$48,273

CAN HE MUSTER THE RESOURCES TO DO IT?

In round numbers, John was offered the business for $237,000, the value of its assets (see "Attachment: Asset Value," which follows). He would apply his stock in Southland, worth about $65,000, leaving him about $172,000 to put together to make the deal. Southland would finance the inventory for one year, but the remainder of the sale (about $60,000) would have to be cash. John's savings provided about $35,000, and he could borrow the rest from the bank.

John assessed the situation. Everything he owned and had saved would now be in the business. His first year's income, after the $10,000-a-month payment to Southland for inventory, would be minimal. Without Southland's administrative support, the hours would be long. This was not his chosen career, and many of its demands were outside his expertise.

John reasoned that, if he did not like being a "plumbing supply tycoon," he could always sell the business at a profit. It was time to make the move!

John locked the door to Southland's Covington branch at about 10 P.M. on June 30, 1978. At 6:30 A.M. the next day, he would open that same door to Tammany Supply, Inc.

ATTACHMENT: ASSET VALUE

From actual 1978 figures, John estimated $4,000 of accounts receivable to be uncollectible and $6,000 of inventory to be obsolete. Fixed assets of the business were judged to have been depreciated to $8,000 less than their replacement value. Adjusted asset (or "book") value is then:

Assets:	1978	Adjust	Adj 1978
Cash	22,831		22,831
Accounts Receivable	85,800	–4,000	81,800
Collection Days	37.17		37.17
Inventory	118,411	–6,000	112,411
Turns	5.44		5.44
Other Assets	11,733	–8,000	19,733
Total Assets	$238,775		$236,775

STUDY QUESTIONS

1. Is John underestimating the disadvantages of independence: decreased purchasing power, loss of access to the considerably larger inventory in the Metairie warehouse, and management depth and other synergies due to being part of a larger operation?

   _____

   _____

   _____

2. Can John assume that Southland's Covington-area customers will become Tammany's customers? Why would they, or why might they not? Can TSI maintain the service level they had with Southland's resources behind them?

   _____

   _____

   _____

3. John is 35 years old, and knows the administrative side of the business, but not the "pieces and parts"; Buck knows the material, but now, at 20 years old, he has become purchasing agent as well as warehouse manager. Are they in over their heads?

   _____

   _____

   _____

4. Could the final price have been flexible, based on the first few years' performance of TSI? Should John have factored in the cyclical nature of the business, rather than counting on steady growth for the evaluation period?

   _____

   _____

   _____

5. Do you agree with the evaluation process? What might you have done differently? Do you agree with the result? If you were to modify it, in which direction would you go? Should the deal happen? Is it "win-win"?

   _____

   _____

   _____

Notes

1. Kylo-Patrick Hart. "Business Start-Ups Online", *Entrepreneur Magazine Online* (www.entrepreneurmag.com) (June 1997).

2. www.idresearch.com

3. Tomima Edmark. "Pump Up the Value," Entrepreneur Magazine Online (May 1997)(www.entrepreneurmag.com).

4. www.tuckerknapp.com

CHAPTER

Start-up Alternatives: Home-Based, Franchises, and Existing Businesses

Chapter Objectives

After completing this chapter, you should be able to

■ Identify options for starting a business more gradually or on a smaller scale, such as beginning in your home, networking with other companies, and converting current employment to self-employment.

■ Research franchise opportunities and the ability of various franchisors to support and assist you in pursuing these opportunities.

■ Assess the possibility of buying an existing business, establish a meaningful value for a business, and negotiate its purchase.

■ Where business location is not predetermined, evaluate location options and establish criteria for the optimal location.

THE GRADUAL START-UP

Working from Home

Link Resources Corp., a New York research organization, estimates that more than 25 million home-based businesses operate in the United States. Other sources estimate that a new home-based business venture is launched every 11 seconds.

It is essential to realize that "home-based" is not a type of business, but a way of implementing a business idea. Not all businesses lend themselves to being home-based; some do, but soon (with luck) they outgrow a home office. To succeed, your business must represent an opportunity, by the criteria we have been applying, where the home turns out to be a reasonable choice for its location. Often, the desire to work from home dictates the choice of one opportunity over another.

Sometimes, home is where the substantive work of the business, such as software development, is performed. More often, home is where the administrative functions of the business are performed; for example, scheduling service calls to be performed at a customer site, working up price quotations, and doing the bookkeeping for the business.

Where selling and/or delivery of service goes on at the customer site, a storefront is rendered unnecessary, and a home office is entirely appropriate. One example would be kitchen remodeling, where advertising and displaying in home shows generates calls from prospects; you go to their home to estimate a price and, hopefully, make the sale. Another example in home services would be property inspection, for prospective buyers worried about the potential problems in a property.

Other ventures involve services to other businesses in a subcontracting arrangement. An example would be a meal delivery service. Your contact is with restaurants that might wish to provide customer delivery but cannot justify the cost in-house. Another example might be performing bookkeeping or collection services to small businesses.

What's behind the move to the home office? Modern technology. Computers, fax machines, cellular phones, copy machines, color printers, and toll-free phone numbers are now easily accessible and affordable to home-based businesses. The *Wall Street Journal* recently reported that "most home-based businesses—especially start-ups—can stick to the basics and equip themselves for $3,000 to $5,000."

According to Richard Ekstract, chairman of the Home Office Association of America (HOAA), "America is in the midst of an extraordinary workplace transformation. As we head into the new millennium, the number of home offices will skyrocket. The same people who were workaholics and corporate climbers in the 80s now seek personally rewarding and satisfying outlets for their talents. The 'me-first' attitude is being replaced with a more family oriented mentality."

Home-based entrepreneurs also need to be aware of the laws and regulations governing businesses in general, and those governing what types of businesses may operate from a home. In particular, zoning regulations may specifically designate, or specifically prohibit, businesses as home-based.

Most states outlaw the home production of fireworks, drugs, poisons, explosives, sanitary or medical products, and toys. Some states also prohibit home-based businesses from making food, drink, or clothing. Be sure to consult an attorney and the state department of labor to find out which laws and regulations will affect your business.

✓ **Checkpoint:** *Home Office Issues*

Working under the same roof that your family lives under may not prove to be as easy as it seems. It is important that you work in a professional environment. One suggestion is to set up a separate office in your home to create this professional environment. Ask yourself these questions:

- Does our home have adequate and suitable space for a business?
- Will running the business from home cause family friction?
- Will the family respect, and not interfere during, working hours?
- Do I have the self-discipline to maintain schedules?
- Can I deal with the isolation of working from home?
- Am I a self-starter? ✓ ✓

Although home-based businesses can often be started at a fraction of the price that would be required to open other businesses, a strict accounting requires that the entrepreneur include the "opportunity" cost. This is what he or she could be earning in a "regular" job.

Strategic Partnerships and the "Virtual" Company

Ronald Brill is a national authority on changing work trends. In 1988, he founded the Independent Workers Association, a support network for home-based business professionals in the San Francisco Bay area. He suggests growing the small business by forming strategic partnerships, or in his phrase "work-linking."

A **strategic partnership** is an agreement between businesses to operate as a temporary, flexible alliance to offer products or services to the marketplace. Ronald Brill says that "it can be as simple as a cooperative ad or brochure featuring related independent businesses or as complex as a joint venture agreement. Partners may be across town or across the ocean. These ad hoc agreements can be made between two or even more businesses."

In joint ventures, each partner brings skills or facilities to the alliance that would be difficult or prohibitively expensive to acquire otherwise. Cooperative arrangements can create a mutual referral network among collaborating independent businesses. The wide range of possibilities offers a way for smaller businesses to expand while remaining independent.

These alliances broaden the capabilities of each partner without increasing individual overhead, creating the image of a "virtual company" that is more substantial than the actual company. Because partnerships can be added to, or new ones formed, new virtual companies can be created to reach new and different markets. An added benefit is breaking the isolation characteristic of independent work.

Bill Bygrave, director of the entrepreneurial studies department at Babson College, in Wellesley, Massachusetts, believes there's growing awareness of the virtual-corporation model for fundamental reasons relating to today's economy. "Big companies increasingly realize that smaller companies have been doing this all along—and getting higher productivity from it," says Bygrave.

The phenomenon, adds Bygrave, reflects an imperative that companies must increasingly specialize in a more complex and competitive economy. That creates a self-reinforcing dynamic, as the needs of one specialist spawn demand for the skills of others. "Your success is based on keeping tight control over your area of expertise—and then subcontracting everything else out," says Bygrave. "The key is to keep overhead low, own as few resources as possible, and keep productivity high."

The following profile describes the ultimate "virtual corporation": one employee, a network of suppliers and retailers, and real growth potential.

"VIRTUAL" COMPANY PROFILE   Walden Paddlers

In the August 1993 issue of *Inc.* magazine, in an article entitled "Virtual Realities," Edward O. Welles discusses Walden Paddlers, a kayak-maker located in Acton, Massachusetts.[1]

The company's founder, Paul Farrow, has led the design, production, and marketing of a technically sophisticated kayak fashioned from recycled plastic, one that significantly undercuts its competition on price and outmaneuvers it in performance. Moreover, Farrow has done all that with just one employee—himself.

Farrow deliberately set out to weave a web of strategic partnerships around Walden to avoid building a costly, cumbersome, slow-footed organization. Farrow sought, instead, to leverage as much as possible the skills of creative outsiders and dedicated specialists like himself to share risk, reduce development time, and save money, while hitting a broad slice of the market as fast as he could. Walden Paddlers is what is known in today's fast-paced economy as a "virtual corporation," a company that outsources just about everything in the pursuit of eternal flexibility, low overhead, and the leading edge.

Farrow's market research told him that 70 percent of the kayak market is controlled by just three large manufacturers. At the same time, there are no significant distributors standing between those manufacturers and retailers. The kayak market is very open. Manufacturers, perhaps because of their enthusiasm for the sport, often readily share information. When Farrow wrote to them and asked for their dealer lists, they obliged.

All used pretty much the same dealers—a meaningful nationwide universe of only about 300. And a relative handful of those dealers—75—sold 80 percent of the units, offering Walden the potential of substantial penetration, provided Farrow could come up with an appealing product.

Finally, Farrow perceived an underserved market. There are 280 million people in the United States and Canada combined, but no more than 30,000 kayaks are sold each year. All the available research told Farrow a lot more people would participate in the sport if they felt less intimidated by the cost and the technology.

Alliance 1: The Manufacturer

Farrow knew, given his limited resources, that building a full-blown manufacturing and marketing organization would prove slow, costly, and near impossible. He estimated that building a single organization that would design, manufacture, and market kayaks would cost in excess of $1 million—money he most assuredly lacked.

Farrow knew the key link would be the molder who would actually make his kayak. He contacted Hardigg Industries, in nearby South Deerfield, Massachusetts. It happened that Jamie Hardigg, son of the company's founder and its director of marketing, was a serious white-water kayaker who had ventured all over the world to pursue the sport. Farrow was referred to the person in charge of Hardigg's custom fabrication business, Joe Strzegowski.

Instead of just quoting Farrow a price, Strzegowski negotiated an agreement in which Hardigg, in effect, agreed to share the start-up cost with Farrow. Rather than charging a prohibitive sum for the first kayak out of the mold and having the cost of subsequent units tail off sharply from there, which would probably have killed the deal, Strzegowski agreed to spread the cost over the life of the project, lowering Farrow's barrier to entry.

"We thought—briefly—about getting into the kayak business ourselves," Strzegowski also notes, "but we're a manufacturing company. We don't have a marketing mechanism to make that work." In fact, he says, for Hardigg there is more to be gained—and learned—by working with a committed outsider like Farrow than there is in trying to emulate him.

For example, Farrow has pushed Strzegowski on the applications for recycled plastics, something Hardigg has not done much work on up to now, but knows it must. Farrow's project also introduced the company to a technique known as rotomolding.

Farrow describes their agreement as "a letter written by one businessman to another." It's three pages long, and though it was given the once-over by Farrow's lawyer, it is largely devoid of legalese. It gives each party an escape clause should Farrow not realize his anticipated volume. Should the parties split up, each is barred for two years from entering the other's business.

Alliance 2: The Designer

For design expertise, Farrow was referred to Jeff Allott at General Composites in Clifton Park, New York. Allott spends his weekends racing canoes in northern New York State and New England. Allott was trying to reposition General Composites away from the sagging fortunes of defense and aerospace—which the previous year accounted for 70 percent of their revenues—and more toward the realm of sporting-goods development.

Their contract spread Farrow's payments out over the eight months from design to final production. Two-thirds of the payment was pegged to milestones such as the design of the first and second prototypes and approval of the first article out of the mold.

With this approach, Farrow is ensured that Allott is wired into the entire process all the way through to production and that he does not simply produce a design and is never to be heard from again. Allott will get, as the final third of his payment, a percentage of each boat sold, again to ensure that he will have a vested interest in consistent production and even marketing, not simply in the execution of a design.

Allott further agreed to act as a representative for Walden in upstate New York and Vermont—a natural fit, as Allott is plugged into the local white-water racing scene in those regions. "What better person to have peddle your boat than the guy who designed it?" Allott reasons. If all goes well, Walden will also produce succeeding generations of boats. They will be principally designed by Allott—and again he will take some of his compensation as a percentage of sales.

Alliance 3: The Dealers

During product development, Farrow had visited key dealers, explaining his product and how it might fit into their lines. They seemed receptive, hoping that kayaking would serve as a follow-on sport to backpacking for the baby-boom market. Even though a kayak, like a bicycle or a backpack, is not a high-margin product, it is a solid core offering around which a dealer can sell higher-margin accessories. They were also attracted to the 40 percent margins with the Walden product, compared to the 30 percent that was typical in the industry.

Farrow's marketing approach was to give dealers demo boats for 30 days. They could do whatever they wanted with them—paddle them, sell them, or take them apart. All Farrow asked was that after 30 days each dealer either paid him for the boat or returned it. He figured that putting a lot of kayaks into the hands of people who love kayaks for 30 days would earn him not just distribution but also plenty of free advice.

Eastern Mountain Sports (EMS), a major outdoor retailer with 47 stores in the eastern United States, showed immediate interest after receiving a demo boat. Before long Farrow was making plans to head out to Seattle to talk to Recreational Equipment Inc. (REI), which is, with 36 retail stores mostly in the West, the West Coast equivalent of EMS. Farrow figured that if he could land those two accounts, he would be immediately addressing 20 percent of the market, and that between them, those two outlets could sell 3,000 units in 1994.

Farrow also hit a local hotbed of kayaking, Charles River Canoe and Kayak, in Newton, Massachusetts. "He's interested in using us as a trial location. Things he may not see about either the boat's performance or the market's reaction to it would be accessible to us," says Dave Jacques, Charles River's co-owner, who was very impressed with the boat. Jacques and his partner, Larry Smith, agreed to have input in the design of future hulls coming out of Walden.

Planning for Growth

Farrow says that three years from now, if all goes well, he'd like to forge a distribution deal with a major national company that has marketing experience in the leisure and sporting-goods industry. Such a deal would include advertising in national media to reach a more general audience, and contribute to establishing some equity in the company. "I'm convinced that a good distributor adds a lot of value," says Farrow. The key, he adds, is for the entrepreneur to be egoless enough to give up something of value to create, in turn, something of more enduring worth.

Using One's Current Position as a Springboard

Many larger companies, seeing advantages to becoming a little more "virtual" themselves, are finding that they can save money or get a better result by having some defined project done by outside specialists rather than by company employees. Many entrepreneurs are forming businesses to serve this growing movement, commonly referred to as "outsourcing."

Often, current employees leave the firm to provide services to their former employer. "It's going on all over the place," says Zenas Block, a professor at New York University's Stern School of Business. People are leaving corporations to start new ventures, only to turn right around and sell back to their former bosses.

Not that all such arrangements are 100 percent voluntary. Downsizing, or just the threat of it, often plays a coercive role. Block cites the case of McGraw-Hill, which, after closing its market-research department, hired back some laid-off employees who had started their own market-research firm—at a higher hourly rate. The publishing giant still saved money by paying for services only as needed.

Frank Casale, executive director of the Outsourcing Institute, in New York City, has studied the economics from the employee's standpoint. "The typical multiple is, if you're making $50,000 working for an organization, you can make anywhere from 20% to 50% more by selling the same services to that organization as an outside contractor."

MINICASE 5.1   **Dinardo Design**

In an Internet article, "Start-ups Target Old Bosses as New Customers," Jerry Useem describes a "springboard" opportunity:[2]

When Jeff Dinardo's huge corporate employer, Houghton Mifflin Co., put him in charge of farming out design work to outside studios, he got jealous. Those independent businesses, he realized, were making enviable sums off Houghton's outsourced work and were "having a lot more fun than I was in-house."

Perhaps it was inevitable, then, that he decided to join their ranks, resigning from the Boston-based publisher in 1992 to set up Dinardo Design, in Carlisle,

Massachusetts. Today one-third of his business comes from Houghton Mifflin. Adds Dinardo, "I think Houghton Mifflin uses us because we already know how they need things done, almost as if we're a little satellite office of theirs."

It took a while for Dinardo's former colleagues to take his upstart studio seriously. "For a long time, they thought of me as Jeff-who-left-the-company, not as a viable outside studio," he says. "It took a few years before I started getting work from my old division."

Study Questions

1. Does your current position lend itself to a similar arrangement with a current employer? Is there some specialty that you have that could generate an outsourcing opportunity?

_____

_____

_____

2. What do you think of Dinardo's reasons for starting up a company? Why do you think it took a while for his former colleagues to give him work? Would he have had the same problem with other divisions of the company?

_____

_____

_____

3. What problems can you foresee in serving a former employer? Is there any potential for conflicts of interest? Are former competitors likely prospects?

_____

_____

_____

FRANCHISING

Overview

A franchise is a continuing relationship between a franchisor and a franchisee in which the franchisor's knowledge, image, success, manufacturing, and marketing techniques are supplied to the franchisee for a consideration. This consideration usually consists of a high "up-front" fee and a significant royalty percentage, which generally require a fairly long time to recover.

About 10 percent of the 20 million U.S. businesses operate under some kind of franchise agreement. About 3,000 companies sell franchises to on the order of 25,000 new buyers each year, or about one every 20 minutes. Franchises account for over a third of all retail sales; John Naisbitt, author of *Megatrends,* predicts that this will rise to 50 percent by the year 2000.

Franchising offers those who lack business experience (but do not lack capital) a business with a good probability of success. It is a ready-made business, with all the incentives of a small business combined with the management skills of a large one. It is a way to be "in business for yourself, not by yourself."

Franchises take many forms. Some are simply trade-name licensing arrangements, such as TrueValue Hardware, where the franchisee is provided product access and participation in an advertising cooperative. Some trade-name licenses, particularly in skin-care products, are part of a multilevel marketing system, where a franchisee can designate subfranchisees and benefit from their efforts.

Others might be distributorships, or manufacturer's representative arrangements, such as automobile dealerships or gasoline stations. It could be Jane's Cadillac or Fred's Texaco; the product is supplied by the franchisor, but the franchisee has a fair amount of latitude in how the business is located, designed, and run. The franchisor will frequently specify showroom requirements and inventory-level criteria, and could grant either exclusive or nonexclusive franchise areas.

The most familiar type of franchise, however, is probably the "total concept" store such as McDonald's. Pay your franchise fee, and they will "roll out" a store for you to operate. The advantages can be considerable.

The franchise fee buys instant product recognition built and maintained by sophisticated advertising and marketing programs. The franchisor's management experience and depth assists the franchisee by providing employee guidelines, policies and procedures, operating experience, and sometimes even financial assistance. They provide proven methods for determining promising locations, and a successful store design and equipment configuration. Centralized purchasing gives large-buyer clout to each location.

While the purchase of a franchise offers significant advantages, the large initial cost can be difficult to raise. Some entrepreneurs find the highly structured environment to be more limiting than it is reassuring. Continuing royalty costs take a significant portion of profits. Still, for many types of businesses, a franchise frequently offers the best chance of entrepreneurial success.

Selecting a Franchise

How do you choose among all the available franchises? Does it complement your interests? Is the name well known? If not, what are you paying for? Is the fee structure reasonable, and are all costs clearly described? Is the franchisor professional? Evaluate the clarity of the franchise agreement, and how well your rights are protected, the strength of their training and support program, and their commitment to your success.

Be sure to talk to current franchisees about their experiences. Beware of a franchisor commited to a rate of growth that exceeds their ability to manage; they may not be sufficiently interested in the sales they have already made. Even if you hire someone to manage the business, expect to spend a lot of time with the operation.

Exercise 5.1 Is There a Franchise in Your Future?

Based on articles found at the newsstand, library, or on the Internet, list some of the current "hot" franchises. Pick one of interest to you to report on. The report should analyze the following:

- the industry in which the franchise operates;
- the competitive balance between large companies, franchises, and independent companies; and
- a comparison of available franchisors serving the market.

Carefully review the franchise agreement. When the company receives a large portion of its fees up front, it has less incentive to maintain an interest in your long-term success. Regardless of how the fees are paid, you should compare them with other franchises for reasonableness.

Other key information in the franchise agreement includes the term of the agreement (generally five to seven years), and automatic renewal options. You should examine closely the company's right to require alterations or improvements to your business prior to renewal and allowable reasons for termination. Another important consideration can be the conditions governing how the franchise can be transferred if the franchisee dies or wants to sell.

Check closely for possible hidden costs (accounting fees, lease location expenses, construction supervision, etc.) and other revenue sources to the company arising out of the franchise (rebates on supplies, rent, etc.).

The Federal Trade Commission requires that all franchisors disclose certain information to a franchisee before sale. Read all of this information carefully. If you have doubts about the information it provides, you may want to investigate further by writing to the FTC or the regulatory agency of the state where the franchisor is registered, if applicable. To see if a company has been investigated by the FTC for disclosure violations, you can write to their Information Services Division (FTC, Washington, D.C. 20580).

ENTREPRENEURIAL RESOURCE · Franchise Handbook: On-Line

In an article on *Franchise Handbook: On-Line,* Gerald A. Marks suggests "Seven Criteria for Franchise Selection":[3]

1. The franchisor is primarily interested in distributing quality goods and services.

   Although most franchisors comfortably meet this criterion, some are more motivated by the desire to sell franchises than to sell products or services. For example, in papers filed in connection with a court action involving an automotive brake franchise, a former franchise director for the company stated under oath that the main policy of the franchisor was to sell franchises, without regard to the location's viability and without any concern as to whether adequate training would be given to franchisees.

2. The franchisor is dedicated to its franchise system as the primary channel of product or service distribution.

   A franchisor should also be dedicated to providing ongoing support and guidance to its network of franchisees. Many franchisors maintain one or more company-owned stores, to remain in constant touch with the needs of the general consuming public. On the other hand, caution must be exercised to insure that the franchisor's concern for its own stores not supersede the needs of franchisees.

3. There is an established market demand for the franchised product or service.

   Be sure that the product or service being offered is not in the nature of a fad, and that it is in a field where independent delivery of that product or service has been fully accepted by the consuming public. For example, franchises offering Chinese and Italian food have generally succeeded only on the take-out side of the business. Consumers seem to prefer independent local Chinese and Italian restaurants for eat-in, sit-down dining.

4. The franchisor or its trademark is well known and enjoys a good reputation.

   Buying an established franchise provides a prospective franchisee with a running start because the franchise name and trademark are already known to the consuming public. The prospective franchisee thereby obtains an immediate market because the reputation and market recognition of the franchisor creates a ready customer base.

5. The franchisor offers franchisees full initial training, on-going support and an effective marketing plan.

>One of the primary reasons for selecting a franchise business opportunity is to buy a proven method of doing business. A successful franchise system, as part of its initial training and ongoing support, will help you operate as efficiently as possible. A simple method of determining whether training and support provided by a franchisor are satisfactory is to ask existing franchisees.

6. The franchisor has developed good relations with its franchisees.

>Good relations generally indicate the existence of a supportive franchisor that is genuinely interested in the success of the entire franchise system. Another, and potentially more revealing, method is to check those sections of the Uniform Franchise Offering Circular that list all lawsuits against the franchisor. Those sections also include the names of former franchisees who have been terminated or have voluntarily ceased being involved with the franchise chain. Such individuals will likely give you a negative, but insightful, portrait of the franchisor.

7. The franchisor is willing to disclose the economic performance of its company-owned stores or that of its franchisees.

>Beware of any franchisor that tells you it is prohibited by law from giving you sales and earnings projections. Franchisors are permitted to give prospective franchisees past sales performances, as long as they properly qualify them as being representative of the earnings of a particular franchisee located in a certain area having a particular population density and socio-economic level.

Attorney Joseph F. Chvasta, Jr., also in *Franchise Handbook: On-Line,* advises: "A key part of researching the franchisor is to visit its corporate headquarters. You want to find out if the corporate staff is a professional organization, or if it is dependent on the one or two persons who founded it—and who may want to walk away from it later on. Moreover, you have to feel comfortable with the corporate staff. Are these people with whom you want to do business? Only by visiting the company can you answer these concerns."

Chvasta reinforces the importance of talking with former and existing franchisees, and not just the franchisees with whom the franchisor would like you to speak. He further suggests visiting several franchisees to see how their operations are run and to talk to their customers, including asking them how they found out about the business and why they patronize it.

Since location is so important to most franchise businesses, ask for a marketing study and traffic analysis of the proposed site. If the company does not provide it, do it yourself. The franchise agreement will also address what are your management responsibilities and what are the franchisor's.

Is a franchise a sure thing? Is it the only hope for independent firms in today's market? Can Jerry's Quick Oil Change compete with SpeeDee? Does the franchise deliver business that we might not have gotten anyway? Does this added business justify the initial cost of the franchise?

While franchising is often billed as a safe path to riches, an increasingly vocal group of critics, including several franchisee associations, are warning prospective franchisees to beware. "The problem isn't that franchising is a bad concept," said Robert Purvin, chairman of the American Association of Franchisees and Dealers. "It's that franchising has become such a seller's market that many people are buying into bad systems."

CASE STUDY 5.1
SpeeDee Oil Change of St. Charles Avenue

BACKGROUND

Gary Copp and Kevin Bennett met at Loyola University in the early 1970s as each pursued a business degree and considered future prospects. Both wanted to start a business at some point in the near future, and they kept in touch as each took a sales job on graduation.

Their get-togethers were largely spent brainstorming about business possibilities. Staying close to their personal interests, they discussed opportunities related to automobiles or sports. As their ideas began to become more tangible, their attention was focusing more and more on servicing cars.

Kevin's uncle owned a service station on a busy corner in Metairie, Louisiana (suburban New Orleans), and had extra space that was offered to them for a related use. G&K Enterprises was formed to operate a car wash on the site, as a "pilot project" for what they might want to do ultimately.

Gary and Kevin hired employees for the new business so that they could keep their day jobs. Each day, after those jobs, a considerable amount of time was spent by both at the car wash, supervising, doing bookkeeping work, and watching and listening.

Though this venture consumed most of their spare time, they knew they were on the right track. At the same time, the "service" in auto service stations was undergoing a dramatic transformation; many stations were converting a gasoline island, or the entire station, to self-service. Few stations had attendants to check under the hood and tell you when your oil was dirty, or remind you that it was time for some regular or seasonal service. Automobile warranties were getting longer, but requiring documentation that maintenance services were performed at prescribed intervals.

A market need had been created, and at the time, there was only one company with national aspirations performing the services that the gasoline stations had abandoned. Jiffy Lube had begun in the northeastern United States and was setting the standard for the industry that G&K would enter. Jiffy offered these services with the added benefit of a 10-minute guarantee for an oil change, lubrication, and maintenance check. Based on owner's manual specifications, they would remind you of service intervals and requirements, and suggest other indicated maintenance procedures.

G&K sensed that it was still early enough for them to seize a leadership position in the industry. They converted their car wash into a quick oil change facility. A rolling-oil can logo was developed and the name "SpeeDee" was chosen. Kevin still jokes that their nine-minute guarantee was not to one-up Jiffy, but to save SpeeDee money on a sign that was priced by the letter.

Their prototype was an instant success, and by the time they had opened three more outlets in the New Orleans area they realized they had a winner. Their profits allowed them to become full-time employees of the venture, and to package the SpeeDee Oil Change System (SOCS) for franchising.

GROWING PAINS

The company decided that franchise stores would all be new locations built to national specifications. This contrasted with the approach of their major competitor, Jiffy Lube, which achieved rapid growth by acquiring existing independent service outlets.

They then began to sell regional rights to subfranchisors around the United States while maintaining the Gulf South region for themselves. Regional owners could then open stores or license franchisees throughout their franchise areas. Early regions, based on the availability of interested investors, included New England, eastern Texas, and greater Los Angeles.

The SOCS strategy was to create a strong layer of coentrepreneurs, the region owners, to become a national company in a short amount of time. By the late 1980s this strategy was beginning to take hold, but the cash demands of conducting a national sales campaign exceeded their expectations. They decided that they needed to direct more of their attention to developing their own region, the Gulf Coast, to improve their cash flow before returning to their national rollout.

SPEEDEE ON THE AVENUE

There was one location in New Orleans that Kevin had always coveted for a SpeeDee outlet, St. Charles Avenue. To locals it is reverently referred to as "The Avenue"; a ride on the St. Charles streetcar is a recommended tourist attraction. In 1988, a location became available with the planned demolition of a seedy convenience store.

Unable to finance a company-owned shop at the site, Kevin offered a franchise on the property to a friend named Al Serio. Al ran a very successful hardware store with his younger brother George, and was sufficiently well-heeled to finance the deal. Al asked Kevin for some time to discuss it with George and with their older brother Jerry, a successful computer consultant.

Al was not a very effective salesman in the meeting with his brothers. He could do it only if they joined him; he did not have the time or that much interest, but he felt obliged to Kevin. Jerry, whose schedule was a bit more flexible, said he would help if the others were interested, but it would not be his choice.

George surprised his brothers by saying that he was a bit frustrated at being second in command at the hardware store, and that this might give him the opportunity to show his talents by being in charge of something. George's comments changed the conversation from why they should not purchase the franchise to discussing the details of how they would run it.

Al found out from his banker that their strong financial position would allow them to "borrow out," or finance the project entirely with debt. They would lease the land for $2,500 per month, borrow $200,000 secured by the building and equipment, and get a $100,000 credit line for franchise and start-up fees, and for working capital.

PLANNING FOR SUCCESS

Kevin provided expense information on the operation of a franchise. Jerry then factored in the financing details and developed *pro-forma* income statements for scenarios representing break-even,

expected, and optimistic situations suggested by Kevin (see table: "Pro-Forma Monthly Income Statement" for SpeeDee Oil Change of St. Charles Avenue).

The key income variables in the operation of the franchise are the number of cars serviced per day (called "rolls"), and the average invoice amount. The oil change is basically a break-even proposition generating about a $25 ticket. To succeed, an operator has to generate enough add-on sales, such as tune-ups and radiator flushes, to double the average ticket.

The key expense variable is payroll cost, viewed as a percentage of sales. This is controlled not by paying low salaries, but by keeping the shop busy, thereby spreading a basically fixed cost over a larger sales figure. The more successful outlets kept their payroll costs on the order of 20 percent.

The general practice in the industry was to close only on Sundays; estimates were based on 26 sales days per month. Many outlets did as much business on Saturdays as on two weekdays.

The traffic count for the location was excellent, about 50 percent higher than what was considered the threshold for a SpeeDee outlet. This suggested that they should have little trouble meeting a target of 40 rolls per day.

The location is in the commuting pattern for the prosperous uptown part of the city, about three-quarters of the way downtown. The surroundings were a moderately busy commercial area on St. Charles, with generally low-income housing off The Avenue.

Al suggested a business acquaintance looking to change jobs as store manager, under George's supervision. SpeeDee provided candidates for shop workers.

STUDY QUESTIONS

1. Have the Serios gathered enough information to make an informed decision? What else would you like to know to be more comfortable about the shop's chance for success?

   _____

   _____

   _____

2. What do you think of the financial data? Does it seem realistic? What could you do to be

more comfortable with the estimates? Do you like the idea of borrowing out?

_____

_____

_____

3. What do you think of the Serios' plan for staffing and managing the shop? Are they sufficiently motivated? When and how might trouble arise?

_____

_____

_____

4. Can it be this easy to make $6,500 per month with other people's money? Are there economies of scale to having multiple outlets?

_____

_____

_____

5. Are there any threats to the quick oil-change industry? What is their major competition? How can the concept be improved upon?

_____

_____

_____

Pro-Forma Monthly Income Statement for SpeeDee Oil Change of St. Charles Avenue				
Days		26	26	26
Cars/Day		36	40	45
AvgInvoice		$41.82	$50.00	$52.00
		BrkEven	*Expected*	*Optimistic*
Net Sales		$39,144	$52,000	$60,840
Cost of Sales	25.0%	$9,786	$13,000	$15,210
GROSS MARGIN		$29,358	$39,000	$45,630
Payroll w/Taxes (% of Sales)		26.6%	22.0%	19.0%
		$10,425	$11,440	$11,560
Occupancy (Land/Bldg/Tax)		$5,075	$5,075	$5,075
Franchise Costs		$5,872	$7,800	$9,126
Advertising	10.0%	$3,914	$5,200	$6,084
Royalties	5.0%	$1,957	$2,600	$3,042
Insurance		$1,156	$1,220	$1,264
Garage/General/WkComp		$960	$960	$960
Damage Claims	0.5%	$196	$260	$304
Services		$2,052	$2,168	$2,248
Bank, Misc. Fees		$700	$700	$700
CredCd Discount	0.9%	$352	$468	$548
Shop Services		$1,000	$1,000	$1,000
Office Expense		$955	$955	$955
Shop Expense		$900	$900	$900
Debt Service		$2,923	$2,923	$2,923
TOTAL EXPENSES		$29,358	$32,481	$34,050
PROFIT/LOSS		$0	$6,519	$11,580

BUYING AN EXISTING BUSINESS

Overview

If a franchise for our chosen opportunity is not feasible, our other alternative to starting a business is to buy an existing business. To some extent, buying a business is less risky because its operating history provides meaningful data on its chances of success under our concept. We must, however, balance the acquisition cost against what the cost of a start-up might have been.

One important factor is the seller's reasons for offering the business for sale. Often these are for personal and career reasons, such as a readiness to retire with the absence of a successor, or another opportunity perceived as a better fit. Where there are business reasons for selling, such as personnel problems, or inability to stand up to the competition, we must decide whether all that is missing is a quality of management that we can provide, or that there are some changes we can make in the way the business is operated that will make the difference.

Due diligence must be performed before a binding offer is made. Is the company's history and network of business relationships clear? Are their financial statements representative? What do they say about the business? Are there any unstated dangers or risks? Are there any hidden liabilities? Often, a review of the financials by our banker and accountant can be valuable.

How good an organization is it? How is it perceived by its customers and suppliers? If we do not buy it, how tough a competitor will it be? What will be the effect of an ownership change on the customer base, supplier relations, and so on? How much customer loyalty is to the business, and how much to the current owner? Does the company have a niche? Is it the one in which you want to operate? Is there a competitive advantage to the operation that is sustainable? Are its assets useful to you? Will key personnel remain with the business?

If the decision is made that purchase of an existing business could improve our chances for success, we must then evaluate existing businesses to determine whether any are available at a price that is economically more favorable than a new venture. How do we value a business?

Before examining specific techniques for business evaluation, it must be emphasized that there is no one correct value for a business. Any valuation is based on assumptions, and projections of future performance. As in our break-even analysis discussion, discomfort about basing financial decisions on assumptions and projections is natural. Entrepreneurship requires exploring uncharted territory and operating in an environment of uncertainty. Success depends on applying our best judgment to reducing that uncertainty.

MINICASE 5.2 — Are Personal Computers Just a Passing Fad?

When Clay Olson opened a retail computer store in Charlotte, North Carolina, in 1983, he was a bit ahead of his time. All he could sell were Commodore VIC-20s and Atari computers that he purchased from an appliance wholesaler, and the public was not yet convinced of their utility. His furniture business could absorb the losses incurred then, but this time he would do it differently.

His retail computer store now, in 1988, would be a separate company, well-staffed, and well-stocked with the best lines. He would now be operating in an industry that had matured so much since his previous venture that even IBM, his former employer, had entered.

His inclination was to buy an existing store, and one day an ad in the newspaper's "Business-to-Business" listings caught his eye. A small computer retailer/assembler was listed by a local business broker. Clay read the package given him by the broker, and requested a meeting with the owner to discuss the business in greater detail.

Clay found the owner, Sam Romer, difficult to read. Sam was an interesting character, 30-ish with a hint of a foreign accent and a know-it-all demeanor. By his account, he had the buying connections to purchase high-quality components from little-known manufacturers, and that he and his technician would then assemble and fine-tune them. Their competitive advantage was then that they could sell high-performance computers for the price of off-the-shelf mediocrities.

The customer list, oriented toward university and government users, was very impressive. Many of their sales were attained by competitive bid, generally several units at a time with small profit margins. There was no established marketing program and little company recognition outside the customer list.

Financial records were very disorganized, and Clay noticed that the company, which had earlier been incorporated as ByteWyse, Inc., in a rather unusual move, had recently been unincorporated. He assumed that it was done for tax reasons, but recognized that, by merging Sam's personal and business accounts, this would make a detailed business valuation a bit more difficult.

Sam seemed to have a good grasp of the technical aspects of the business, and a confidence-building if not completely likable sales manner. He offered as his reason for selling that he wanted to return to graduate school, and that he could continue to sell for the buyers on a commission basis. If Clay chose not to use him, Sam would sign a one-year noncompete agreement. The technician, a real "hacker," was willing to stay on to do purchasing and system assembly for the new owners.

The sale price was $75,000; Sam valued the equipment and inventory at about two-thirds of that. The equipment seemed to be current and well-kept, and the inventory was well-organized. Clay would then be paying about $25,000 for the customer list and purchasing relationships. He asked Sam for about a week to think about it before returning for further discussion.

Study Questions

1. Does Clay have enough information to make an offer? What else should he do? Is there anyone with whom he should consult for advice?

_____

_____

_____

2. How do you feel about the intangibles? Are you satisfied with Sam's reasons for selling the business? How do you feel about keeping him on as a salesman?

_____

_____

_____

3. What exactly is Clay buying? Is he likely to retain existing customers? Could he not establish similar buying relationships anyway? Should he keep the technician?

_____

_____

_____

4. Does the company give Clay a "running start" in the business? Does it offer a better foundation for growth than a start-up? Is it limiting in any way?

_____

_____

_____

5. Should Clay make a lower offer? Based on what? For how much? What should his negotiating strategy be?

_____

_____

_____

Valuing the Smaller Business

Small-business sales are generally (on the order of 94%) sales of assets, with no assumption of liabilities; the remainder are sales of company stock.

Often the seller finances part of the purchase (see Figure 5.1); typically the buyer makes a down payment on the order of one-third of the sales price, with repayment terms of five years at market rates. Do you see any risk in a seller financing the sale?

The most difficult issue in small-business sales is establishing a selling price. It is an inexact science, characterized by a seller's too-high expectations and an overly skeptical prospective buyer. Business valuation may be considered an appraisal of what a business is worth as of a specific point in time.

For tax purposes, a valuation is generally performed under the concept of "fair market value." The IRS has defined this as the amount that a hypothetical willing buyer will pay to a willing seller. Other terms used include "fair value," "investment value," "book value," and "liquidation value."

The basic premise upon which valuations are based is that the value of the business equals the present value of the future stream of cash returns or other benefits of owning the business. Since no one can predict the future with any degree

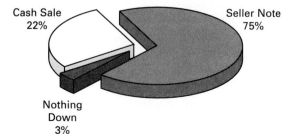

FIGURE 5.1: Small Business Sales—Methods of Financing

of certainty, such future benefits need to be evaluated in light of the degree of risk associated with their attainment.

We will consider three methods of evaluating a business: market, earnings, and book value approaches.

The Market Approach and Considerations Related to Smaller Businesses

The market approach is the simplest method, basing the value of the business on projections of earnings multiplied by a typical price/earnings ratio for the industry. While this technique is often applied to transactions involving publicly traded companies, it is seldom applicable to the small closely held company. There is a ready market for a few shares of a public company, but small businesses are not so easy to turn over.

Size is a major factor in valuing a business. Smaller businesses generally have less market clout and more limited access to debt and equity capital than larger ones. Smaller companies often exhibit a heavy reliance on one or several key persons. These and other factors contribute to a greater perception of the risk associated with smaller companies by investors.

This greater risk is reflected in a discounting of valuations compared to larger companies with similar rates of return. Another way of looking at the same issue is that most buyers would require a higher rate of return on a smaller business.

The small or mid-sized private company is often heavily dependent on one or several key leaders on which much of the fortunes of the business rise or fall. The leader is often the original founder, an entrepreneur who seized an idea, scrounged for capital and customers, and often worked very long hours at great personal sacrifice. The leader has long personal relationships with key customers that made the company a success and on whom the business is still heavily dependent.

Similarly, such an individual has strong ties with key suppliers and oversees manufacturing, personnel, and many of the essential aspects of the business. In addition, the company banker took a risk lending the company money on the strength of the current owner's vision and integrity, and may not look as favorably toward funding a new owner.

On the other hand, at some point in a company's life cycle the key person actually can become the problem. Because the company is her or his baby, the individual is often reluctant to delegate responsibility, even though the business may be too big for one person to manage effectively. While competitors are innovating and the needs of suppliers and customers are evolving, the leader may become bogged down in handling day-to-day details and may lose sight of opportunities or threats to the business. While public company leaders can make the same mistakes, it is the privately held owner's emotional tie to the business that can prevent sight of the chance to take appropriate action.

In using the market approach, the business valuator must recognize and accurately quantify risk from sources that may not be present in similar public companies, even companies of similar size. Although public companies can and should be used where appropriate as comparables, important risk differentials need to be recognized.

The Earnings Approach and Rates of Return

The earnings approach to valuing a business views the business as one more option for investing our money; that is, given our assessment of the risk involved, we have a certain expectation of return. We would certainly expect a greater return a business than on securities backed by the U.S. Treasury, but would possibly accept a lesser return than on a highly speculative venture.

Let us say, for example, that we have an opportunity to buy a business for $240,000 that projects average annual earnings over the next three years of a little over $43,000. This is an annual return on investment of about 18 percent, based on the owner's projections. Let us say further that it is a stable, mature business with a clear financial history and relatively little risk. Is 18 percent return satisfactory? It depends largely on the quality of the projections, and alternative investment possibilities.

Is the owner's projection of future earnings likely to be objective? What are alternative methods of projecting earnings? Are economic conditions consistent enough for a historical average to be meaningful? Are there any "dark clouds on the horizon" for the market area, or for the industry?

What is the competitive situation? How is the market share of the business? What are the long-term prospects for a small independent company in this industry?

Are last year's earnings a good indicator of earnings for the next few years? Were there any unusual circumstances? Are they likely to be repeated? Can we make a better estimate? What will we base it on? What is the quality of the financial records? Are there useful trade sources?

Could earnings be improved when we take over? Do we see waste, overpayment for materials or services, excess or excessively paid employees? How does the owner's pay and perquisites compare to our "opportunity cost," that is, the amount we could earn elsewhere?

Could earnings not be as good as they seem? Is equipment in disrepair, or space insufficient? Will key employees leave the company? Will they be committed to a new owner? Will a major customer be lost? Are key buying relationships assured? Is company reputation an asset or a liability?

Inconsistencies in accounting practices of smaller businesses cause most business valuators to recast the financial statements of closely held companies. For many of these firms, earnings are understated; whereas larger firms try to maximize profits, the objective of most smaller firms is to minimize taxes. Although the vast majority of small businesses use aggressive but ethical methods, opportunities exist for abuse.

The abusive (and illegal) methods can take many forms. Owners can manipulate family member salaries based on the relative advantages of paying personal versus corporate taxes. They can pay family members who do not really work there. Personal expenses could be charged to a company account. Assets could be understated, and/or liabilities overstated. In businesses that make a lot of cash sales, some could be made without invoices, with the owner pocketing the proceeds.

Once we are comfortable that the projections of future income have taken all of these factors into account, we must then relate this anticipated income to a value if purchased today. In Tammany Supply Case "A" (Case Study 4.1) we used three-year averages, making no distinction between the value of today's dollars and the dollars of the year after next.

A more rigorous approach would recognize the diminishing value of the dollar with time. One such approach is referred to as the discounted future income (or cash flow) method. Discounted future income involves making discrete year-by-year forecasts of income, typically for five or seven years, which are then discounted back to their present value today at an appropriate rate of return (often called "discount rate").

A variation on this method assigns a "terminal value" to the final projection year that represents the estimated value for the sale of the company at that time. The terminal value is then added to the present value of income for the projected years to obtain fair market value. In most cases, however, the additional investment in the business to maintain adequate return is assumed to cancel out any terminal value.

MINICASE 5.3   Buying the Covington Branch of Tammany Supply, Inc.

Case Study 4.1 introduced us to valuing a business. We used an earnings method, without discounting future income, and compared the result to asset value. That analysis was done rather informally, since it was an intrafamily transaction.

Assuming that these were "arm's-length" estimates through future year 3, let us return to the accountant for earning estimates for years 4 and 5. For the purposes of this example, we will say that she returned estimates of $70,000 and $80,000, respectively. Projected earnings are summarized in the first row of the following table, using an annual discount rate of 18 percent.

Year	1	2	3	4	5	
Earnings projected	$36,957	$45,501	$59,313	$70,000	$80,000	
Discount rate*	1.18	1.3924	1.643	1.9388	2.2878	
Present value	$31,319	$32,678	$36,100	$36,105	$34,969	
TOTAL (of Present value)						$171,171

*The cumulative discount rate is determined according to the following formula: *Cumulative Discount Rate in Year N = (1 + Annual Discount Rate) to the Nth power*

Let us relate the mathematics of this analysis to the more tangible aspects of valuing a business. First of all, it is assumed that the earnings are available to the business owner on the last day of the year. Thus, at 18 percent annual return, a buyer would expect $1.18 a year from now for $1 invested today. Similarly, as we move across the discount rate row of the table, this return compounds. Thus, a buyer would expect $1.39+ two years from now for $1 invested today.

By dividing the projected earnings by the discount rate, we get today's value of each year's future earnings. For example, earnings of $80,000 five years from now should be generated, at 18 percent return, by an investment today (or "present value") of $34,969. Summing the five years present values, we get an evaluation of $171,171. This is substantially less than our previously agreed upon figure of $240,000, and warrants further consideration.

Study Questions

1. What does this analysis say about the earnings projections? Should we adjust them upward? Should we renegotiate the selling price downward?

_____

_____

_____

2. What effect would it have if sales in later years had been projected in today's dollars, while inflation was averaging 3 percent? How would this change our valuation?

_____

_____

_____

3. Would it be fair now to offer $200,000 when we would be buying almost $240,000 in assets (see Balance Sheet in Case Study 4.1)? Should we ignore the earnings method here, and pay asset value?

Even after answering the questions related to business valuation, we sometimes need to answer more basic questions. Are there better investments available, without the everyday worries of business ownership? Do we prefer the business-owner lifestyle to passive investment?

Asset, or "Book," Value

The book value of a corporation is generally shown on its balance sheet as "Net Worth" or "Owner's Equity." It represents the excess value of the company's assets over its liabilities. What is implied in accepting this value as a sales price is that all components of the balance sheet are fairly valued, and that the assets are useful to the new owner's mission.

Book-value sales are usually based on some adjustments to the balance sheet, reflecting differences between the accounting value of items and their usefulness for business purposes. Balance sheet items that are generally deserving of this type of analysis include the following:

Current Assets
- *Accounts Receivable:* How current are they? Values should be discounted based on their age. Sometimes the seller retains responsibility for accounts receivables, receiving collections against them for the first 90 days under the new owner.
- *Notes Receivable:* How collectable are they? What are the payment terms? Should they be converted to notes owed personally to the seller?
- *Inventory:* Generally, quantities are verified by a physical count on the day ownership changes hands. What cost basis will be used (purchase cost, replacement, other)? Is allowance made for overstock and obsolete items?
- *Other Assets:* Will the seller retain any current assets, such as some portion of cash, certificates of deposit, and so on?

Long-Term Assets

Remember that depreciation is a tax device, applied as aggressively as the law allows. This causes many long-term assets to be undervalued. For example, delivery trucks may be depreciated to zero while they still have considerable utility to the buyer. It is generally in the seller's best interest to revalue assets in their current state, based on market or replacement value. In addition, the seller may want to keep certain assets, such as a company car, and the buyer may not want to buy some assets.

How do we verify the adjustments? We may need to participate in the physical inventory and to have professional appraisals of other assets. This is not to say that the conscientious buyer cannot sometimes still be misled.

In many cases, the selling price can be some combination of earnings and book values. For example, the buyer might pay adjusted book value plus two or three years' earnings. The selling price often varies depending on sale terms, such as the amount of seller financing, years to repay, and interest rate.

Should We Use a Professional Evaluator?

Business valuation is becoming increasingly specialized, with guidelines, case law, and techniques impacting valuations for different purposes, and with continuing advances in the state of the art. However, business valuation is also an "easy entry" profession, with a wide degree of variability in the background, training, and experience of practitioners, ranging from experts to part-timers to complete novices.

Therefore, before contracting with a business valuator, we must ensure that they have the requisite qualifications, skills, training, and experience. The American Society of Appraisers (ASA), one of the nation's oldest multidisciplinary appraisal societies, is the leading accrediting body of business valuation professionals. The ASA has established comprehensive requirements for certifying business valuators. The ASA has also developed standards for appropriate valuation content. Most major business valuation firms now require their staffs to attain ASA accreditation.

George B. Hawkins, president of Banister Financial, Inc., suggests that "a well written business valuation provides a clear roadmap to the reader to follow the various steps taken in arriving at the final estimate of value. It should be the product of a qualified and independent mind, prepared properly for the purpose at hand, and should reach sound, logical and defensible conclusions in the context of current market forces."

Because every company is unique, the potential risks and issues relating to the purchase of a business can vary substantially. Numbers only scratch the surface of the numerous elements, many of them nonfinancial, which have an impact on company risk and value. This is why many prospective buyers seek the assistance of professional valuators.

Negotiating the Sale

Determining the value of a business is not necessarily the same as setting a purchase price. Business evaluations rest so heavily on earnings projections, which in turn are so affected by the widely differing perceptions of buyer and seller, that complete acceptance of a firm value is extremely difficult to achieve.

According to Shannon Pratt, a business evaluation expert, the following are intangible market factors that can contribute to the bargaining positions of the negotiators:

- A strong recent profit history puts the seller in a more favorable position.
- Favorable economic conditions (cost and availability of capital, industry health) create a seller's market.
- "Goodwill" created by a favorable company reputation might increase the selling price.
- A lackluster condition of the company (its facilities, completeness and accuracy of books and records, employee morale) gives the buyer additional leverage.
- If market demand for the product or service of the business is shrinking, so might the selling price.

Special circumstances, such as a seller who wants to unload the business quickly, might lower the sale price. A buyer for whom the business creates a particularly good personal or strategic fit may be willing to pay a little more.

Once a purchase price is agreed upon, the terms and/or structure of the purchase can affect its favorability or unfavorability to one or both parties.

If seller and buyer cannot meet on price, perhaps concessions on payment terms could make up the difference. The seller might accept a small down payment and finance the remainder to hold to the asking price. For instance, the buyer might make a down payment of 25 percent of the total purchase price with the rest paid by a note, secured by the assets of the business, with an interest rate of 9 percent over a period of 15 years.

Other variations in terms that could affect selling price would include the following:

- A portion or all of the down payment could be deducted from initial month's revenues.
- Payment in other than cash could be accepted (e.g., real estate, a marketable security, and so on).
- The seller could sell some of the business assets, such as equipment and machinery, separately, thus reducing the overall value (i.e., price) of the business. For instance, there may be a portion of the business in which the buyer is not interested. The owner could sell those unwanted assets to another party and receive payment for the rest from the buyer.
- A graduated payment schedule might help the buyer with monthly payments on the debt incurred, with higher payments occurring in later years. For example, payments could be $1,000 a month in year one, $1,500 a month in year two, $2,000 a month in years three through five.

If the structure of the sale eases the tax burden for either party, that party is likely to make price concessions. One such issue relates to the choice between buying the assets or the stock of the business.

In the asset method, the buyer buys all of the assets except cash and accounts receivable. The seller uses this money to pay off all liabilities. This protects the buyer from assuming any liabilities that may not have been disclosed.

The stock method, however, calls for all assets, liabilities, and stock to be transferred to the buyer. This minimizes the amount of changes that need to take place (e.g., supplier contracts, lease agreements, and so on). The risk of assuming undisclosed liabilities can be reduced by including in the agreement of sale a provision for deducting the amount of these undisclosed liabilities from payments to the seller.

As we get closer to structuring the deal, we should decide on a bargaining range before we go into the final negotiating session. We should know the tax and legal consequences of our options. If the discussion takes us outside our range, we should schedule another session and reanalyze the data. We must allow for the possibility that the deal cannot be made.

Ultimately we must decide whether the purchase, at a price that the seller will accept, gives us a better chance of success than starting from scratch in competition with the seller's business. Perhaps the seller's errors would start us in a deficit position; we might prefer creating our own corporate culture and customer relationships; maybe we can find a better location, facility, newer equipment, and so forth. On the other hand, the cost of taking sufficient business away from existing firms could be ruinous.

LOCATION CONSIDERATIONS

When basing our business at home, or buying an existing business, location is generally not an issue. Other start-up alternatives, however, often force us to choose a location early in the planning process. Franchisors generally have rather sophisticated systems for identifying where our business should be, but if we are setting up an independent business, our resources are probably more limited.

The impact of the choice of location for a business on sales and expenses is often underestimated. Too often the location decision depends on factors more closely related to the entrepreneur's preferences than to business requirements.

Sometimes initial price and space availability at the time of the search take on inordinate importance. The location decision deserves demographic research and thorough investigation of alternatives.

What should a location decision involve, and why is it so important? To understand this, we need to classify businesses as to the following four location requirements:

1. Home-delivered merchandise, and on-site service, where *business location is irrelevant.*
2. Retail, and many forms of service, where the customer comes to the business.
3. Wholesale, where the business is generally transacted at the customer site.
4. Manufacturing, where distance from raw materials sources and distances to distribution outlets must be balanced.

Retail Location Requirements

For a *retail* business, where customers come to the business location to buy, calculate the value to your business of a good location by considering the following major points.

Traffic of Potential Customers Past Your Display and Entrance

Traffic is the most important factor in choosing a retail location. The more traffic past the site, the more exposure to potential customers, and the more opportunities you have to lure these potential customers into the business.

Customer Convenience

How easy is it to find the business? How visible is the signage from each direction?

Is it easy to identify the business and what it sells?

Is it close to long-established businesses with return customers?

Is there plenty of convenient parking for customers?

Is the building attractive and well-kept?

Total Cost

In addition to lease payments, must we pay a percentage of sales?

Who pays building and ground maintenance and utilities?

In comparing, be sure to balance costs against potential sales volume from that location.

Exercise 5.2 Picking a Retail Site
The following listings are from the same market area. Recognizing the limitations of their brevity, how does each listing address our retail location criteria?

_____

_____

_____

Which might serve as the best location for our next coffee shop? Why?

_____

_____

_____

What additional information would you ask of the listing real estate agent to help you decide?

_____

_____

_____

1. 850–26,000 sq. ft., Centreville Square I & II: 300,000 sq. ft. center with 75,000 traffic count.
2. 1,928 sq. ft. in single story building. The best location on Rt. 55 entering town.
3. 2,000–6,982 sq. ft. RETAIL SPACE AVAILABLE! Fronts Route 1 near Outlet Mall.
4. 2,000 sq. ft. Retail or Offices. Growing business area, high traffic count.
5. 2,000 sq. ft., Corner Space 40' × 50' at Traffic Light.

Management advisor Bill Ransom suggests that the location decision should not be considered final. The demographic of a business location is continually changing. Keep the data file used to choose your location and review the information in this file at least every five years. It is a good idea to review it whenever you experience an unexplained drop in sales. Ask continuously: "Is my location an asset?" If it is not an asset, it is a liability. Do something about it!

Wholesale Location Requirements

For a *wholesale* business, where you go to the customer's location to sell or service that customer, the best location is often that which is nearest the center of your customer base. This results in less travel time for customers that do visit, and for your sales and service people. Visibility to traffic is generally less important, so wholesalers seldom need to pay the high rental rates of retail businesses.

Manufacturing Location Requirements

For a *manufacturing* business, the primary decision on location depends on the cost of transporting raw materials to the plant versus the cost of transporting finished goods to the market. Other factors that can have an impact on the decision include local labor availability and rates, taxes and tax incentives, union or nonunion environment, suitable land availability at an affordable price, quality of life, required infrastructure improvements, weather, and zoning. For smaller manufacturing sites, an industrial park offers the advantages of a planned and appropriately zoned site with infrastructure and support facilities installed. Financing and tax abatements also may be advantages of these locations.

Summary

Once we have identified a promising venture, we must consider the alternative ways to seize the opportunity. In many cases, personal or financial limitations force us to pursue a gradual buildup to our business objectives. For many businesses, start-up costs can be reduced by beginning the business in the home. Networking with supportive but noncompeting businesses can improve our early reach. Sometimes work contracted from our current employer can give us the necessary boost.

Alternatives to starting a new business from scratch include the acquisition of a franchise and the purchase of an existing business. The cost of bringing a new business to profitability must be compared to the higher expenses related to franchising, with its statistically higher success rate, and the purchase price and potential of an existing business.

Establishing the purchase price of a "going concern" can be particularly difficult. While there are alternative methods to quantifying a value from available data on the firm, the quality of that data is often suspect because it is provided by the seller. Professional evaluators are available to assist with the process. After establishing a value for purchasing an existing business, the terms or structure of a deal can often create opportunities to meet our special circumstances.

Depending on the type of business undertaken, the choice of location can be a significant factor. Base the decision on business considerations, rather than personal preferences. Take the long-range view, and periodically consider whether a move might enhance the business.

Review Questions

1. What types of businesses lend themselves best to being based in the home? What personal and family factors must be considered before starting a home-based business?

    _____

    _____

    _____

2. How can networking, or "work-linking," be used to leverage a business? What are the major benefits of this approach?

    _____

    _____

    _____

3. Why are many corporations beginning to outsource projects? What types of skills are they generally looking for?

    _____

    _____

    _____

4. What are the major benefits of operating as a franchise? What are the keys to selecting the proper franchise?

    _____

    _____

    _____

5. What conditions might make purchase of an existing business preferable to starting our own similar business? What are the major approaches to determining a fair market value for such a purchase?

_____

_____

_____

6. What criteria would you apply to our choice of location for the coffee shop? What factors would you follow for a possible move at some later time?

_____

_____

_____

CASE STUDY 5.2
Tammany Supply, Inc. (B)

INTRODUCTION

Based on evaluations done by Southland Plumbing Supply, then verified and fine-tuned by John Vinturella, John bought the assets of Southland's Covington, Louisiana, branch from his father and two brothers in mid-1978. Tammany Supply was incorporated in June 1978, to begin operating on July 1, the effective date of the sale.

The branch had opened in early 1977 (see Case Study 4.1), and had moderately exceeded expectations. In the spring of 1978 the branch was evaluated as a stand-alone business, and a consensus was reached on a selling price of $240,000. John had liquidated his investments, and sold his house in Metairie, netting about $75,000, so some creative financing would be required for the remainder. Down payment on a house in Covington reduced available cash to about $60,000.

The terms of the sale considered the assets in two groups, each worth half the sale value, or $120,000. First was the branch's inventory, for which John would apply his stock in the parent company (valued at $65,000), and Southland would finance the remaining $55,000 over two years at a market interest rate.

For the other half of the sale value, John would pay $35,000 cash and pledge the $85,000 in accounts receivable to Southland. This would be paid monthly, as collected, with the remainder paid out in full at the end of the third month, collected or not. John then loaned his remaining cash ($25,000) to TSI for working capital.

While the terms may seem complicated, this structure was necessary to allow John to make the purchase without having to secure financing outside the family. At 35 years old, John was risking all the assets he had accumulated in 12 years of working and investing, as well as any future inheritance (cashing in his Southland stock) on the success of TSI.

John's only other significant asset was his one-third ownership in the building in which TSI would operate. It was a former truck-repair garage that had been foreclosed on by an area bank. The bank offered an attractive purchase price to Southland when they opened the branch in 1977; John and his brothers decided, for tax reasons, to form a partnership to buy it outside the corporation.

After receiving assurance from the bank that his credit history and the equity in the building supported his assuming the entire loan, John approached his brothers about a buyout. The building had appreciated some and was generating some income, requiring compensation in addition to assuming their share of the loan. They agreed on an amount, and with its payment John was now the sole owner of the building and its accompanying loan.

John unlocked the doors of TSI at 7 A.M. on July 1, 1978. He was in debt a half-million dollars, and his only chance of ever climbing out was to sell a lot of pipe and fittings.

START-UP TRAUMA

Even though John took over an existing business, the loss of Southland's administrative support made TSI feel like a start-up. The long workweek required in serving the building trades was made even longer by having to catch up the administrative backlog after hours. For ten hours a day during the week and Saturday mornings, John was selling, serving customers, and directing warehouse and delivery operations. After hours, on Saturday afternoons, and frequently on Sundays, he was making bank deposits, paying bills, billing customers and making collection calls, writing purchase orders, and analyzing what was happening.

As the business grew, John next hired a salesman but found he needed operations help more. The salesman, Bill Meyer, made the transition nicely, taking over purchasing as well as supervising the warehousemen. Bill would occasionally make outside sales calls, but increasing sales volume was less of a problem than servicing the customers that had already come to rely on TSI. Soon after, John hired Harry O'Reilly to help with counter sales and bookkeeping.

TSI became a distributor of Kohler plumbing products, the best in the industry (they had been buying Kohler indirectly through Southland before then). Soon after, they began to use a Radio Shack TRS-80, an early personal computer, for their billing, accounts receivable, and inventory control functions.

By 1980, John found it necessary to expand and improve TSI's space. Building economies of scale were such that he tripled the size of the building, bringing in tenant companies in related but noncompetitive businesses (carpeting, paint, appliances). TSI built a state-of-the-art showroom, and began to advertise on local television. The warehouse was remodeled, and a mezzanine added. A forklift and new truck were purchased. The rapid growth in the population of St. Tammany Parish was causing a homebuilding boom, and TSI was gearing up to service that boom.

FIRST THREE YEARS

As shown in the accompanying figure, sales comfortably exceeded expectations for the first three years doing business as TSI.

By the end of 1980, John had paid off TSI's debts to Southland and to himself, and was beginning to draw a good salary. The size of the staff had doubled since opening in 1978, and they formed a hardworking and harmonious team. TSI was exceeding all the performance norms for the industry.

The following is a summary of financial performance for the period:

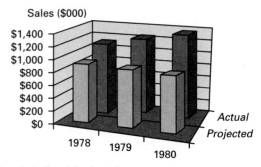

Sales, Actual and Projected
Tammany Supply, Inc.

The company had decided on a March 31 fiscal year end, so income for 1978 has been annualized (it was a nine-month fiscal year). This year-end was chosen to coincide with the end of a traditionally slow period, greatly simplifying taking physical inventory on over 6,000 items. For each year indicated, then, fiscal year-end actually includes the first quarter of the following calendar year.

The performance improvements over projections were due largely to TSI's broadening its concept of the plumbing supply customer; sales were aimed not only toward plumbing contractors but also toward the general public. Direct-to-user

	Income, 1978–1980		*Balance Sheet, End of 1980*	
			Assets: Current	$307,576
	TOTAL	PROJECTED	Assets: Other	$102,327
			TOTAL ASSETS	$409,903
Sales	$3,727,486	$2,180,000		
Gross profit	$943,094	$436,000	Liability: Current	$84,689
As % of sales	25.3%	20.0%	Liability: Long-Term	$60,133
Pretax income	$266,501	$144,818	Equity	**$265,081**
As % of sales	7.1	6.6%	TOTAL LIAB/EQ	$409,903

(DTU) sales are unpopular with contractors, but to a supply house, improved sales volume and the higher margins of retail sales make them worth the criticism.

MOVING TO THE NEXT LEVEL

In the spring of 1981, as preparations began for another busy summer selling season, it was time to assess where the business was headed and the best way to get there. John also had to make some decisions about his relationship to the business, since he had not taken a real vacation since starting TSI. He was having the time of his life professionally, and the financial rewards were considerable, but he knew that adjustments in his work style to avoid burnout were overdue.

A rapidly growing regional plumbing supply chain offered to buy the business, telling John they would locate in Covington and compete with him if he did not sell. The offer was for book value (equivalent to "Equity" in the balance sheet above, or $265,000+) plus a goodwill payment of $100,000. While the offer was gratifying, John figured that at the current rate of earnings ($266,000+ in pretax income over three years), the goodwill payment represented just over one year's profits.

John flirted briefly with the offer before declining, bracing for his first direct local competition. The other company did open a small Covington branch, but it barely lasted a year.

STUDY QUESTIONS

1. Was the purchase agreement with Southland really at "arm's length," or were concessions made to John that might not have been made to an outsider? Did the terms lower the effective selling price? Was Southland continuing to bear some of the risk of TSI's success?

2. Was John overreaching his financial resources when he purchased the business? Should he have postponed the deal a year? Should he have retained the partnership in the building with his brothers? Did he leave himself any financial "cushion"? Would you have done the same?

3. How do you explain the way in which performance exceeded projections? Was one year of operating experience enough to project sales for the next three years? Did John "lowball" his sales estimates to Southland?

4. Should John offer a supplemental payment to Southland? Could the difference in performance have been related to John's managing differently as a business owner than he had as a partner when the store was a branch of Southland?

5. Are two years of growth and success (mid-1978 to mid-1980) enough to justify the large additional investment made in 1980? Should it have been done in more gradual stages?

_____

_____

_____

6. Is the observed growth rate sustainable? What are the consequences of it not being sustainable? Discuss in terms of company investment, and John's personal investment (building expansion).

_____

_____

_____

7. What are the implications of the competition "discovering" the Covington market? Have any barriers to entry been erected? Why could TSI drive a larger competitor out of the market? After they left, do you think they had given up on the market entirely?

_____

_____

_____

Notes

1. Edward O. Welles. "Virtual Realities," *Inc.* vol. 15, no. 8 (August 1993): pp. 50(8).

2. Jerry Useem. "Start-ups Target Old Bosses as New Customers" *Inc.* vol. 19, no. 5 (May 1997): p. 21(1).

3. Gerald A. Marks. "Seven Criteria for Franchise Selection," *Franchise Handbook: On-Line* (www.franchise1.com/articles/7crit.html).

CHAPTER

Building a Successful Business Plan

6

Chapter Objectives

After completing this chapter, you should be able to

■ Define a business opportunity in the widely accepted and easily recognized business plan format.

■ Use the preparation of the plan to refine the concept, detect gaps and weaknesses, and anticipate the questions of prospective stakeholders.

■ Produce a highly professional and meaningful plan that can serve to guide the implementation process.

■ Understand some of the ways in which a business plan can fail, and methods by which we can avoid these pitfalls.

■ Consider approaches that generate enthusiasm and excitement for the project among readers of the plan.

■ Develop a convincing marketing plan, based on realistic assumptions.

■ Conduct a strategic analysis of the venture, measuring internal and external factors, strengths and weaknesses, opportunities and threats.

■ Clearly identify the venture's competitive advantages by analysis and interviews with "strategic partners."

BUSINESS PLANNING OVERVIEW

The purpose of a business plan is to recognize and define a business opportunity, to describe how that opportunity will be seized by the management team, and to demonstrate that the business is feasible and worth the effort. One size does not fit all; the length of an effective business plan can vary widely based on the complexity of the opportunity, familiarity of the industry, and financing details, among other factors.

Specificity is what differentiates excellent from poor business plans. The more facts that you can provide, the better. Fill your business plan with certitude! Reduce conjecture! When developing models for emerging markets, base the model on well established data points and benchmarks. Cite your sources. Define your market segments with specificity, rather than presenting data at the industry level.[1]

The business plan is used in two primary ways:

1. Among the organizers of the venture, it provides a plan for early corporate development. This includes guiding the organization toward meeting its objectives, keeping the business and its principals headed in a predetermined direction, and explaining how the company will be run for the next three to five years.
2. Its second application is as a device for securing financing for the venture.

As a developmental tool, the plan simulates operating the company on paper. The aim is to validate an idea and challenge every aspect of the business. A well-conceived business plan can serve as a management tool to settle major policy issues, identify keys to success, establish goals and checkpoints, and consider long-term prospects.

A business plan precisely defines your business, identifies your goals and serves as your firm's résumé. It helps you allocate resources properly, handle unforeseen complications, and make the right decisions. Because it provides specific and organized information about your company and how you will repay borrowed money, a good business plan is a crucial part of any loan package. Additionally, it can tell your sales personnel, suppliers and others about your operations and goals.[2]

The discipline of writing a plan forces us to think through the steps we must take in getting the business started, and according to business consultant Eric Siegel, to flesh out ideas, to look for weak spots and vulnerabilities.

Many entrepreneurs insist that their business concept is so clear in their heads that the written plan can be produced after start-up; this attitude short-circuits one of the major benefits of producing the plan, that is, serving as a reality check. "A realistic business plan might save you from yourself by persuading you to abandon a bad idea while your mistakes are still on paper," says Roger Thompson in the journal *Nation's Business*.

I once had a job that required me to read and evaluate a constant stream of business plans. . . . The great majority of the plans projected spending $1 million to $3 million in start-up costs, with the business breaking even in the third year. . . . I would check the business plans' spreadsheets, mostly examining the expense side. That's because while projected revenues might or might not materialize, planned expenses surely will.[3]

If we react to a Business Plan with incredulity ("It is too good to be true" or "Some of the assumptions are nonrealistic")—then . . . the Business Plan is a failure. . . . We must respond with a modicum of awe and fascination ("That's right! I never thought of it" or "This way it makes sense"). The Business Plan is supposed to resonate within the mind of the reader and to elicit the reaction: "How very true!!!"[4]

The business plan is also a vital sales tool for approaching and convincing financial sources, be they investors or lenders. It is used to demonstrate to prospective stakeholders that the idea is promising, the market is accessible, the firm's management is capable, serious, and disciplined, and the return on investment is attractive.

Sources of financing need to be assured that the entrepreneurial team has carefully thought out the plan. They want to be convinced that the team has the skills and expertise needed to manage the company effectively, and that it is prepared to seize opportunities and solve the problems that arise. These goals are best accomplished with a business plan that is well prepared, professional in tone, and persuasive in conveying the company's potential.

John Bousquet, owner of JFB Desktop Publishing, says, "Use your business plan as if it were a brochure as well as a tool to coach the loan rep to sell your company internally. Believe it or not, bankers want to know about your market so include a strong analysis of your market as well as a sensible marketing plan."

For maximum effectiveness, the business plan should be directed specifically to the funding source and satisfy its particular concerns. For example, you would orient and write the plan differently for presentation to a lender than you would for an investor. The lender is primarily interested in collateral, and the ability of the venture to make debt payments. The investor would be more concerned about what risks are involved, the rate of return on the investment, and methods for liquidating the investment at a later stage.

According to James Arkebauer of Venture Associates, "It cannot be stressed too strongly that a good business plan is the cornerstone of successful financing. If you want investors' money, you've got to give them good reasons to buy in. The business plan is where you lay out the reasons. It doesn't have to be unduly lengthy or complicated, but it must be informative and relevant. It needs to maintain logic and order, and show the company as effectively positioned as a good investment."

GETTING STARTED

Before getting into the details of preparing a business plan, Jack Kaplan of the Columbia Business School suggests that we ask ourselves a series of warm-up questions:

- What is the type of our business? How will we be classified by others?
- What is the purpose of this plan?
- What is its target audience?
- How can I use the plan to advance the project?
- What market need am I filling? How is my approach better than existing products/ services?
- What is my timetable for getting my offering to the marketplace?

Consulting firm Venture Associates offers advice on writing the plan in the form of what they term the nine guiding principles:[5]

1. **Make it easy to read.**

   With all the competition for the interest of investors, your plan will have to be well formatted and easily understood. Your introductory statement summarizing your operation must capture readers' attention and motivate them to read the balance of your plan. Construct a glossary if you have to use technical terms.

2. **Be sure your approach is market driven (rather than product driven).**

   Investors are primarily interested in how the product or service will be received in the marketplace. Before they buy into your plan, they want to see your research demonstrating and substantiating how the customer will benefit and be motivated to purchase.

3. **Qualify the competition.**

   Qualify your product according to cost or time savings and revenue generation. Show projections for sales growth, how your product is superior to others, and how you intend to exploit the competitive advantage.

4. Present your distribution plan.

Be specific as to how the company will sell and distribute its product or service. Clearly describe the methods and what it will cost to get the product or service into the ultimate customer's hands.

5. Exploit your company's uniqueness.

Explain what will give your company a competitive edge in the marketplace—special attributes like a patent, trade secrets, or copyrights.

6. Emphasize management strength.

Show proof that the company is comprised of highly qualified people who can cover all the bases. Show how the management team, the directors, and the advisers possess the necessary credibility. Indicate the incentives that will keep them together.

7. Present attractive projections.

Paint a realistic picture—substantiated by assumptions—of where your company is going with the requested funding. Be detailed and keep it credible. Projections and forecasts validated by market data and expert opinions are impressive.

8. Zero in on possible funding sources.

Design versions of the plan to fit the idiosyncrasies of each financing source you plan to approach. A banker's interest lies in stability, security, cashflow coverage, and sound returns, whereas a venture capitalist is more interested in high leverage resulting in outrageous returns. Both want to know how the proceeds are going to be spent.

9. Close with a bang.

Drive home the point that you're offering a good deal. Specify the return rates. Be definite about how investors will get their money back and when. For lenders, show that their funds are adequately secured and that your cashflow more than covers their interest and principal payments.

After you have drafted your business plan, solicit feedback on it. Ask a cross section of people whose judgment you respect to review it. Make revisions where they add to its accuracy or clarity.

MINICASE 6.1   How Not to Write a Business Plan

A business plan can fail, even though the venture is viable, in three primary ways:

1. By failing to communicate the nature of the venture effectively—for example, by omitting important information, by not "selling" it strongly, or by not generating sufficient enthusiasm.

2. By failing to provide a management "blueprint"—for example, by vagueness in key implementation issues, such as management structure and responsibilities, focus on the key features and benefits of the product or service, marketing and sales promotion strategies, and analysis of existing and potential competition.

3. By failing to convince prospective lenders and investors to participate; stakeholders expect the plan to detail how much money is required, indicate the expected financial return on investment, propose specific deal terms, discuss management's qualifications to run the business, and show comprehensive *pro-forma* statements for profit and cash flow.

As we discuss details of writing the business plan, we will address how to build a successful plan that avoids these pitfalls. For now, let us examine more closely some keys to getting the plan funded.

1. Detail cash requirements and timing.

The plan must consider both short- and long-term needs, the amount of money required initially and at various stages, and how the funds will be used.

2. Describe benefits to investors.

There must be a realistic and attractive return for the investor, and specification of what the company is prepared to offer in return for the capital investment.

3. Outline reasonable assumptions.

A plan is only as good as its assumptions and the data backing them up. Sometimes, there is insufficient market analysis data in the plan to substantiate the assumptions on which projections were based. Many plans show unrealistic revenue growth, practically overnight.

4. Show management depth and commitment.

Many business plans fail because the firm does not portray a management team with sufficient depth to handle effectively the responsibilities identified. Specific operating experience is key to a plan's chance for success. Most investors recognize the vast differences between working for an organization and developing a successful entrepreneurial business; they are often looking for a successful track record at a previous, directly applicable venture. This makes venture capital extremely difficult to get for first-time entrepreneurs; we will discuss their options later.

5. Demonstrate know-how in the money-raising process.

Simply having access to venture capital mailing lists or computer databases is not sufficient; statistics indicate that less than 1 percent of unsolicited deals mailed to venture capital sources will ever get funded. Stock offerings are expensive; those of $1 million or more typically generate expenses amounting to about 8 to 12 percent of the amount raised. Deal structure is key; the entrepreneur should be familiar with available structures and terms, and which structure is most advantageous to both the company and investors.

Many times a proposed deal fails because management believes their company is worth much more than the investor believes it is worth. This discrepancy usually is the result of a poorly prepared business plan that is predicated upon unrealistic economic and operational assumptions. Investors are usually quite knowledgeable as to the variables associated with corporate valuations.

Many companies, unfortunately, seek assistance only when their firm is "near death." At this point, prospective investors often suspect poor judgment on the part of company management for not accurately projecting cash needs and for not seeking assistance in a timely manner. Very few negotiations are successful when the potential for staying in business is questionable.

Thomas A. Martin, of Financial Consultants Ltd., advises that "raising money is a difficult, time-consuming process that leads down many blind alleys before (maybe) achieving the projected goal. View raising money as making any other sale. Only in this case, management is selling its vision."

Study Questions

1. What are your qualifications for starting a venture? Do they meet the requirements outlined above? What is missing?

_____

_____

_____

2. If something is missing, what are some career choices that would fill the gap? How long might it take before you could present a convincing case to a prospective investor?

---

3. For a venture you are considering, or for the coffee shop, present a rough outline of financial requirements, the amount of funding required, and how much is needed at each stage of development of the venture. Could the venture be "bootstrapped," that is, started with personal funds until a convincing case for outside funding could be made?

The formats of business plans can be as varied as the businesses themselves. There are, however, components that should appear in all plans. These include the following:

- the "packaging" elements, which frame the business opportunity;
- the descriptive elements, such as history, the product, and market analysis; and
- the subplans, for marketing, strategy, logistics, and financial performance.

Let us discuss each of these in a little more detail, with an audience assumed to be a reader who might be a prospective investor or lender, a trusted professional advisor, or a friend whose business judgment we value.

ELEMENTS OF A BUSINESS PLAN

Excerpts from a plan for a fictitious company called Light-Guard Manufacturing have been adapted to illustrate the following discussion of business plan elements. The original plan appears on the Web site of the Canada/British Columbia Business Service Centre.[6]

"Packaging"

The Cover Sheet

The cover sheet is the "formal" introduction of your company to the reader. It should look appropriately professional for the venture, and include at least the following:

- The full formal name of the company; if you have a logo, use it.
- The ownership status: sole proprietorship, a Louisiana corporation, etc.
- Street address; mail address if different.
- Phone and fax numbers, e-mail and web site information.
- Principal contact name and title.
- The month and year of the plan.

Many business plans also include a copy number on the title page, to assist the entrepreneur in keeping track of copy distribution.

Closing Summary

The closing summary, or "wrap-up," is generally shorter than the executive summary, and more directed to what is being asked of the reader. It often highlights the major financial projections, and urges the reader's support, financial and/or otherwise.

Appendix

The appendix contains much of the detailed analysis and supporting documentation behind the recommendations and projections in the plan. This includes relevant marketing research, financial details and statements behind the financial proposal, and other items important to the plan, the level of detail of which would disrupt the plan's narrative. These essential pieces of evidence can include résumés, product brochures, customer listings, testimonials, and news articles. A glossary is sometimes included, particularly in more technical proposals.

Descriptive

In order to evaluate the business proposal reasonably, the reader needs some background on the proposed company and the industry in which it will compete. A company mission statement can be an effective starting point in conveying the business concept. Also of interest are company goals, such as commitment to long-term results, innovation, productivity, and social responsibility.

The way in which background information is presented can vary widely, but a thorough business plan should contain the following sections:

History

A brief introduction to the company history could begin by describing the product or service that will be offered (or is currently being offered), to whom it is sold, the current status of the industry, and where your new company fits in. This is your second chance, after the executive summary, to give the reader an overview to establish a basis for detailed understanding.

The body of the history section should include the evolution of the business idea, to the extent it is relevant, and a description of how, when, and by whom the company to implement the idea was started. The primary stakeholders and their roles should be discussed.

Any early achievements and acceptance setbacks should be frankly discussed, along with the lessons learned thereby. These experiences, and their impact on the business approach, should then be brought to current-day status. For example:

COMPANY HISTORY

Light-Guard Manufacturing Ltd. was established to develop and manufacture a specialty electronic light control product. The company was incorporated in the Province of British Columbia on June 1, 1997.

The idea for the product was conceived by Mr. Bright as a result of numerous inquiries received by Mr. Bright's present employer for a simple, automatic light control device. The employer is not involved in the lighting or light control marketplace and is not interested in developing a product or entering the marketplace because of other commitments and business priorities. Mr. Bright has received permission from his employer to pursue the development of the product as a private venture providing that the venture does not interfere with the employer's business.

Mr. Bright has contacted various prospective users of the product to determine product requirements and develop specifications. An engineering prototype of the product has been developed. The prototype was developed by Mr. Bright in his spare time with limited resources. The product to be offered to the public is still under development.

At present, the Company does not have any full time employees.

Product or Service

This section should display the thorough knowledge of your product or service necessary to success. After a simple, straightforward description, outline the need for the product or service in today's marketplace. Describe how it will make a difference, the benefits derived from using it (or what will make the customer buy it), and its advantages.

Explain any special training needed to sell or use it. Include all relevant regulations that may affect its sale or use. Describe any exclusivity agreements or technological uniqueness. Unless your plan is going only to specialists in your industry area, assume you are writing for the layperson, and spare them industry jargon.

THE PRODUCT

The new product, which is called "Light-Guard," will automatically turn lights on and off when the ambient light in a room reaches a predetermined level.

Increasing concerns about security, personal safety, energy conservation and the general trend towards automation has created a market for devices which reduce or eliminate the problems associated with manual control of lighting systems. Homes, offices, factories, hospitals, schools, public buildings and construction sites are only a few of the more obvious applications. Light-Guard will be particularly valuable in remote or unattended locations.

Light-Guard is an automatic electronic switch for controlling electric lights. The complete assembly is the same size and shape as a standard wall-type electric light switch and is designed to replace the wall switch using the same standard mounting screws and electrical wiring. No modifications to the mounting or wiring is required.

Light-Guard consists of an optical sensor which detects the amount of light in the room and an electronic circuit which operates a sensitive relay for turning the lights on and off.

The adjustment control is easily accessible on the face plate of Light-Guard. A manually operated switch is also available on the face plate of Light-Guard to disable the automatic control and enable Light-Guard to be used as a standard manual on/off light switch.

A unique feature in Light-Guard is the extremely sensitive and reliable light sensing circuit. The Light-Guard product is not patented. However, a detailed description of the product and design drawings have been witnessed and dated by a notary public and two independent electronic engineers.

Market Description and Analysis

The primary objective of this section is to convey your perception of the opportunity, and the relevance of the marketing research that convinced you that it is real and achievable. Of particular interest are the size of the market you will enter, trends in demand, and threats to the market. Describe also the significant factors affecting the market; these can be cultural, attitudinal, demographic, legal, and technological.

- Describe what *customers* form your market, where they can be found, why they might purchase your product or service rather than another. Document quality, warranty, service, and price significance. Pinpoint the buyer and user. Describe market coverage, whether local, regional, national, or international.

- *Industry* information should include the industry's size (such as total sales and profits), geographical dispersion, some history, and its current status. Discuss pertinent trends, past, present, and future, in the industry in which you will be competing. Quotes and statements from recent periodicals on the directions of the industry can be very useful.

  For the period of time covered by the plan, generally 3 to 5 years, a projection of where the industry will be, and what your role in it will be, can be of considerable interest. Offer available statistical data on sales and units. Use charts, graphs, and tables if they can make the presentation clearer and more impressive. Refer to trade associations if helpful.

- *Competition* should be discussed in terms of their offerings, market niches, and the extent of the threat to your proposed venture. Discuss the appropriateness of buying an existing business or acquiring a franchise.

  Stress opportunities related to price, quality, warranties, service, and distribution over the offerings of the competition. Include operational strengths and weaknesses. Identify your competitive advantage or unique strength, and the company's "value adding" process. Project potential market share over time, and trends in sales and profitability.

Check all the facts used, and note all your sources; these will be checked closely during an investor's due diligence process. If you are citing voluminous reports or statistical information, note that you have them available for further review.

MARKET DESCRIPTION

The primary markets which provide the greatest sales potential in a relatively short period of time are in Canada and the United States.

Consumer, commercial and industrial users are all prospective customers for the product. The major potential market in the consumer sector will be accessed through the large retailers of small appliances, lighting fixtures and electrical hardware such as:

- Major department stores
- Hardware store chains
- Retail lighting outlets
- Mail order houses

The primary customers in the commercial and industrial sector will be electrical engineering firms, electrical contractors, industrial plant and commercial building maintenance departments, security companies and public buildings. The target markets are easily accessible and identifiable.

Considerable interest in the product has already been expressed by the following:

- Happy Harry's Hardware Chain in the U.S.
- Wonderful Wally's emporium in Canada
- The Federal Government
- Hydro Generating Companies in Canada and the U.S.
- Solvent Sol's Electrical Distributors in the U.S.
- Several large engineering and architectural firms in Canada and the U.S.
- Two major department store chains in Canada

All of the above feel that there will be a demand for Light-Guard because of the practical value of the product, and because there is no other product currently available which provides the features and low price of Light-Guard.

They are primarily interested in a product which is fully automatic, highly reliable, can be adjusted for different light levels, is CSA approved in Canada and U/L approved in the United States and will have a retail price of less than $125 U.S. ($165 Can).

Letters of intent have been received from three large retailers in the U.S. for trial orders totaling 1,500 units. The purchases are subject to the product meeting all specifications. An industrial distributor in Canada has issued a purchase order for 1,000 units subject to successful demonstration of the prototype unit.

Approximately 200,000 products similar to Light-Guard were sold in 1995 and approximately 280,000 were sold in 1996. The market is expected to grow at an annual rate of 40% over the next 5 years.

The suggested retail price (end user price) of the Light-Guard product will be $128 CAD ($98 USD). Average wholesale price (from Light-Guard to distributors and retailers) is expected to be $70 CAD/$55 USD.

There are three known competitors in North America for products that are in part, similar to the proposed Light-Guard product. The three competitors are:

- Glow Worm Industries
- Light and Lively Enterprises Inc.
- Shadows Unlimited Inc.

Glow Worm Industries *(estimated market share of 20%)*
Glow Worm Industries is a small manufacturer located in the Mid West United States which sells primarily to the farming industry. The product is not easily adaptable to other applications. They do not have a distribution network and they sell directly to the end user. The reported selling price of the product is $220 U.S.

Light and Lively Enterprises Inc. *(30% share)*
Light and Lively is located in the South Western United States and manufactures a very simple, low cost device which is capable of controlling only external desk or table lamps, etc. The device is plugged into a standard wall outlet and the lamp to be controlled is then plugged into the device. The unit sells for $125 U.S. retail and is widely distributed throughout the United States and Canada.

Tests on the product indicate that the device will only sense an extreme change in light conditions (i.e., from very bright to very dark). Because of the limited applications and operation of the product, it is not considered to be a serious threat to the marketability of Light-Guard.

Shadows Unlimited Inc. *(40% share)*
Shadows Unlimited is located in Eastern Canada and has a product similar to Light-Guard but which sells for almost twice Light-Guard's projected retail selling price. The product is sold direct to the end user by Shadows Unlimited.

Marketing Plan

This is a critical section that should clearly specify the company's marketing goals, how they are to be achieved, and who will have the responsibility for achieving them. It builds upon the market description and analysis by focusing more specifically on how you will seize the described opportunity. Simply, you must detail how you are going to sell the product or service.

In this section, you need to clearly delineate your niche and your distinctive competence. Investors are particularly interested in measuring the extent to which you are "market-driven"; they would rather have you be focused on the potential of the product's market, sales, and profit than on its appearance or technology.

First, we must ask ourselves a basic question, the answer to which is not as simple as it seems. What business are we in? A related issue is what we are selling. Is it a product or service, or is it convenience, "peace of mind," or some other abstract principle? Is Tammany Supply selling tubs and toilets, or luxury kitchens and baths?

Next, we describe our target market. Who are our customers (age, income, etc.)? How many of them are there? Is the number growing? Where are our customers? How are they best reached? How will we advertise and promote ourselves? How will we get our product to them?

How much do they buy? From whom do they currently buy? What are their motivators? How well does our product meet their needs?

Next come questions about the industry in which we will compete. Are there any barriers to entry: patents, sources of supply, distribution channels, and so on? How strong is brand loyalty? Can a small independent company compete? How are prices set? Is the market seasonal? How important is the "experience curve"? What sales aids and training plans might give us an edge? Are there barriers to a major redirection or to exiting the industry?

Finally, we must address the competitive situation. Will we price our product as price leader, value leader, or prestige product? Is there any opportunity for a unique form of service or support? What market share can we reasonably expect? How long will it take us to get there? The better and more accurate our source of these answers, the more compelling our proposal will be.

The marketing plan should include comments and statements from respected sources about buying patterns and trends; these can add strength to our statements.

ENTREPRENEURIAL RESOURCE | EntrepreNet's Electronic Library

EntrepreNet's Electronic Library suggests how to get the marketing plan to "jump out" at the reader:[7]

No business should underestimate the cost of marketing a new product. It usually takes far more time, effort, and money than anticipated. An early stage company with cash constraints must create sales revenue quickly. Having an obvious and meaningful customer benefit, and being able to effectively communicate it, is essential to generating such sales.

EntrepreNet has chosen to take the essence of these observations and call it the *Declarative Imperative.* The Declarative Imperative states that the cost of selling increases dramatically with the length of a company's marketing message. An early stage company must be able to sell its product (or service) to a customer with one declarative sentence.

Marketing communications for an early stage business fall into three general categories: philosophy, education, and sales. The philosopher says, "Let me convince you why our approach to your business is correct, regardless of how you currently operate." The educator, on the other hand, proposes to the potential customer, "Let me explain how my product or service works," often leaving it up to the customer to decide whether it has any applicability in his/her company. The salesman, though, says, "Buy my product or service to solve your problem." Each approach may be appropriate under a given set of circumstances, but only the salesman is attempting to generate revenues.

What are some of the questions raised by the *Declarative Imperative* for a start-up company?

- Is the **basic** benefit to a customer simple and clear? While many subsidiary benefits may exist, is there an obvious one that cuts across all targeted customers?
- Can the benefit be **quantified** in a meaningful and effective way, such as increased sales, reduced cost of sales, higher production output, and/or reduced operating costs? Can a salesperson say, for example, "You are spending $10,000 more per month than you need to and by purchasing our product for $40,000 you can save that $10,000 each and every month. May I take your order, please?"
- Can you identify a **segment** of your anticipated customers who will immediately react to your proposed benefits more strongly than others? That is, is there a set of customers you do not have to educate before getting their order?

The marketing plan for Light-Guard represents a company that is still in the process of defining itself, and needs to be developed further.

THE MARKETING PLAN

The sales program for the first year will concentrate on developing the Canadian market. The U.S. sales program will commence within six months after the product is available on the Canadian market. The sales organization will be divided into two groups, consumer sales and commercial/industrial sales.

The consumer sales group will concentrate on developing a dealer (retailer) network that will sell the product to the consumer. The initial sales efforts will concentrate on the national department store chains, national lighting outlets, hardware store chains and a major international mail order house.

In general, each of the above retailers uses a central purchasing department for all outlets in Canada and the United States. The purchasing decisions are generally made by merchandising managers who are responsible for small electrical appliances and other similar hard goods.

Initially, the consumer sales group will require two full time sales people to develop the Canadian consumer market. A secretary and a sales order clerk will provide sales support for both the consumer sales group and the commercial/industrial sales group.

The commercial/industrial sales group will also require two full time sales people to concentrate initially on developing a wholesale distributor network with a least 6 distributors in Canada and 10 to 12 distributors in the U.S. The distributors will have access to the major electrical contractors, engineering firms and electrical suppliers in their respective areas.

All sales to Provincial and Federal government departments in Canada will be handled by Light-Guard Manufacturing Ltd. U.S. government sales will be handled by the U.S. distributors.

A simple but effective advertising campaign will be implemented to support the sales efforts. Consumer advertising will consist of monthly advertisements in publications such as *T.V. Guide, Reader's Digest* and *People* magazine. Half page advertisements will be placed in two monthly trade publications with a large circulation to the electrical contracting and plant maintenance markets in Canada and the U.S.

The following sales forecast, assuming a wholesaler price of $70 Canadian, is based on responses from companies surveyed. Additional sales can be anticipated with increased market penetration and product recognition.

	Unit Sales	Total Sales ($CAD)
Year 1	7,000	$490,000
Year 2	17,000	1,190,000
Year 3	42,000	2,940,000

Note: Year 1 will commence approximately 5 months after financing has been arranged, and Year 3 sales will represent approximately 30% of the estimated total market (year 2002).

Geographic distribution of sales is expected to be as follows:

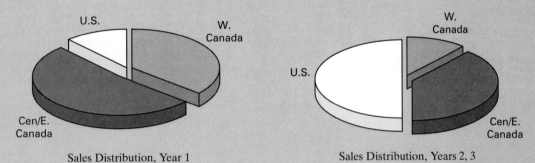

Sales Distribution, Year 1   Sales Distribution, Years 2, 3

The above estimate of sales are considered to be extremely conservative in view of the wide range of applications, the unique operating features and the low selling price of the product.

Entrepreneurs must learn to question continually the assumptions on which their projections are based. The decisions that are most likely to come back and haunt them, perhaps put them out of business, are typically not the consequence of bad judgment or faulty reasoning, but the consequence of applying perfectly sound judgment to wrong assumptions.

REALITY CHECK   **What Assumptions Are Guiding the Marketing Plan?**

The Entrepreneur Network Web site (www.tenonline.org) suggests that there are several common marketing assumptions, that prospective entrepreneurs generally accept, that can disrupt a good marketing plan:[8]

• *Everyone will love my product/service as much as I do.*

They will not! They will not see any of the advantages and benefits you see until you make them stop and recognize and think about them. That is called selling, and requires a great deal of time and energy.

- *A good product/service will sell itself, . . . or . . . If I build it, they will come and buy it.*

    Not necessarily! Get out and talk to prospective customers about the product, not just friends and neighbors. Talk to direct customers, distributors, retailers, purchasing agents, etc., about how your product compares to what is already available in the marketplace.

- *In this business, I must purchase (build, own, have rent, show, etc.).*

    Not if you cannot afford them! Such acquisitions could seriously reduce your margin for errors, decimate your life savings, expose you to impossible debt, or put you into business with investors you neither know nor understand. In these situations, you must think hard about whether they really are "affordable." Look for "better ways"—ways to do what you want with what you CAN afford. In the process, you might discover that the new ways you find—albeit through necessity—result in better value—including quality, service and/or price—to your customers.

- *My competitors have _____ , therefore I must also.*

    Your customers are looking for the best value, from either you or your competitors. If you simply copy your competitors, where is your edge, or added value? Going in, your competitors have all the advantages. They are better established. They have more capital, more resources, more contacts, more knowledge. You find a competitive edge by looking for things that they are doing—preferably things that cost them considerable capital or operational resources—that you can "invent" ways of doing as well or better, but for less.

- *My customers expect me to have _____ .*

    Do your customers expect you to own a factory, to have an expensive office, to entertain them lavishly? Do not believe it! Excellence in delivery—in quality, service, and price—will overcome these "handicaps" every time.

- *My business plan is so good, it just cannot fail.*

    Danger! Great business plans fail every day. Things never happen the way they are planned. Sales will not grow as quickly as you project, costs will be significantly higher, time to reach goals and milestones will be longer than estimated. Your success—or failure—will largely be determined by how well you see and handle unexpected events.

- *It is important that I not make mistakes.*

    Wrong! It is important that you not persist in mistakes, that you recognize your mistakes early and correct them (i.e., try a different approach) before they get out of hand and become costly mistakes. If you are not making mistakes, you are probably missing some opportunities, which can be just as detrimental to your business as any operational loss.

These are just a few examples of assumptions that can derail otherwise viable businesses. Every decision we make is based on assumptions, most of which we are not even aware of until we stop and think them through. The way to minimize bad business decisions is to minimize bad business assumptions. And the best way to minimize bad assumptions is to stay constantly aware of how susceptible we all are to them.

Strategic Plan

Small businesses are not scale models of big businesses; they are often characterized by resource poverty and dependence on a fairly localized market. Their greater vulnerability to the consequences of a lack of focus stresses the importance of their strategic plan.

The strategic plan defines the company's competitive edge, that collection of factors which sets the business apart from its competitors and promotes its chances for success. It requires a clear evaluation of the competitive business climate and an intimate knowledge of the market for the entrepreneur's product.

The strategic plan borrows from other sections of the business plan those items that help to establish the venture's uniqueness, and some overlap will be observed. At start-up, the marketing plan is generally the strategic road map for the venture, and a separate strategic plan is sometimes omitted. For an ongoing business, particularly one considering a major expansion or change in direction, the strategic plan is crucial.

STRATEGY

The Light-Guard Advantage

The cost of Light-Guard will be substantially lower than the Shadows Unlimited product because of Light-Guard's superior design and use of more advanced and lower cost technology.

The balance of the market is shared by 4 or 5 small U.S. manufacturers and 2 imports. None of the products are considered to be reliable and are sold through mail order catalogues only.

Light-Guard combines low cost, high reliability and adaptability to a wide range of applications.

Light-Guard will be CSA approved for sale in Canada and U/L approved for sale in the U.S.

Light-Guard will also be sold through an effective distributor and dealer network and will be adaptable to a wide range of industrial, commercial and consumer needs.

A complete strategic plan contains the following elements:

The Mission Statement

The foundation for the strategic plan is a clear mission statement for the venture that identifies our corporate philosophy. Examples would be our commitment to employee fulfillment, quality management, partnership with customers and suppliers, and good corporate citizenship.

A primary goal is often to maximize long-term stakeholder wealth. Secondary goals might include targets for market share, innovation, productivity, manager performance and development, employee performance and job satisfaction, and social responsibility.

Management expert Russell Ackoff suggests that most corporate mission statements are worthless. "They consist largely of pious platitudes such as: 'We will hold ourselves to the highest standards of professionalism and ethical behavior.' They often formulate necessities as objectives; for example, 'to achieve sufficient profit.' A mission statement should not commit a firm to what it must do to survive but to what it chooses to do in order to thrive."

A mission statement should contain a formulation of the firm's objectives that enables progress toward them to be measured. The statement should also establish the individuality, if not the uniqueness of the firm.

A mission statement should define the business that the company wants to be in, not necessarily the one it is in. However diverse its current business, it should try to find a unifying concept that enlarges its view of itself and brings it into focus. For example, a company that produces beverages, snacks, and baked goods, and operates a variety of dining, recreational, and entertainment facilities identified its business as "increasing the satisfaction people derive from use of their discretionary time." This suggested completely new directions for its diversification and growth.

The statement should be relevant to all the firm's stakeholders. These include its employees, customers, and suppliers, and sometimes the general public and shareholders. The mission should state how the company intends to serve each of them. For example, one company committed itself "to providing all its employees with adequate and fair compensation, safe working conditions, stable employment, challenging work, opportunities for personal development, and a satisfying quality of work life."

COMPANY MISSION

We will strive to supply quality electronic products to our distribution network. We will maintain and raise our level of capability in every aspect of our business by investing in personnel training and equipment. We will retain flexibility of mind, policy, and capability in order to respond quickly and effectively to changing market opportunities. Our success is based upon excellence through teamwork among all personnel and associated companies.

Internal Factors

The internal factors component of the strategic plan relates to how we apply our resources to gaining a competitive edge. These resources include the following:

- **Human Resources:** Are our people motivated, imaginative, qualified, and dedicated? Do we possess all the skills we need? If not, can we develop these skills, or should we outsource or develop strategic partnerships to provide them?
- **Physical Resources:** Are we strategically located? Are we using equipment and technology to best advantage? Are we effectively distributing our products?
- **Financial Resources:** Do we have sufficient funding to run the business effectively, and take advantage of emerging opportunities?

The next case in our TSI series offers a slightly different perspective of the strategic planning process. The company had achieved a successful start-up, but now finds itself in a difficult period caused by external factors. A significant strategic redirection is called for.

CASE STUDY 6.1
Tammany Supply, Inc. (C)

INTRODUCTION

Tammany Supply, Inc. (TSI), a plumbing supply distributor in Covington, Lousiana, got off to a running start in mid-1978 (see Case Study 5.2). TSI's timing was fortuitous, opening just as its market area, western St. Tammany Parish, was becoming the New Orleans suburb of choice for upscale professionals. TSI's marketing approach, unconventional by supply house standards, contributed to this success; they openly courted retail sales, even advertising on television.

By the time other supply houses began to look covetously at the market, TSI was firmly established. Their preemptive strike, opening before the opportunity was obvious, had created a barrier to others' entry. TSI exceeded $1 million in sales in its first full year, 1979, $2 million in 1983, and $3 million the very next year.

Pretax profits during this period approached $100,000 per year (see "Sales and Profits, 1980–84" graph).

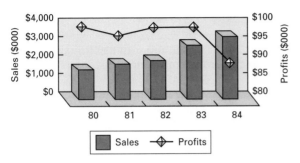

Sales and Profits
Tammany Supply, Inc., 1980–84

THE "CRASH"

A more serious barrier to entry arose in 1985. The collapse of world oil prices took a devastating toll on the Louisiana economy, and the high-end suburb of the state's largest metropolitan area was hit particularly hard. While TSI showed only a slight sales decrease and a small profit in 1985, the bottom fell out the next year. Sales fell almost 40 percent in 1986, and even lower in 1987. When most of TSI's bad-debt losses were written off in 1987, the operating loss for the year exceeded $100,000 (see "Sales and Profits, 1984–87" graph).

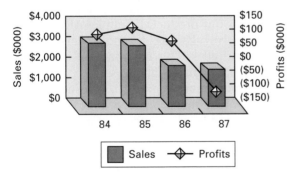

Sales and Profits
Tammany Supply, Inc., 1984–87

It was obvious that changes in the external environment had caused a need for reevaluating TSI's strategy, and the free-fall of the company's fortunes made this need seem immediate.

WHAT DO WE DO NOW?

The options available to TSI were limited by the size of their market, the condition of the local economy, and their resource position. Inventory had shot up in 1984, in response to the higher level of business, and the increased sales raised accounts receivable accordingly. By 1985, the slowdown was becoming apparent, and TSI was beginning to get its inventory down, while stepping up collections to improve its cash position (see "Major Assets by Year, 1980–97" graph).

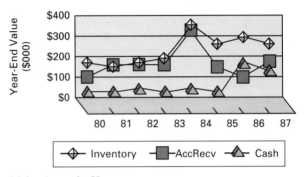

Major Assets by Year
Tammany Supply, Inc., 1980–87

Cash was sufficient at the end of 1987, $70,000 or so above usual levels, to support some diversification. This could take the form of additional inventory items, or the start-up of some new activity. Could TSI succeed in a related business when so many others dependent on homebuilding in the area were failing? Were their chances better in a field unrelated to construction?

TSI's core business had shrunk by 40 percent. Expenses could be cut some, but to cut them enough to matter would have left the company considerably less than a full-service supply house, and much more vulnerable to competition. John was also reluctant to cut TSI's excellent work force, even though they were working well below capacity.

TSI's options were few, and decidedly unattractive. They could return their building to the bank and negotiate a lower monthly payment as a renter. They could downsize their payroll to a level appropriate to sales volume. Or, they could try to apply the vacant space and underutilized human resources to generate some added sales volume and profits; the challenge lay in deciding how.

STUDY QUESTIONS

1. Why is John so reluctant to scale the business down to a level appropriate to sales? What would the longer-term consequences be?

2. How would the competition view such a move? What would it do to the chances for recovery as the economy improves?

3. What information would help in evaluating possible new product lines or related ven-

tures? What new offerings would fit well with traditional plumbing supply lines?

4. Is it better to sell more things to existing customers, or to bring in new customers?

5. What options exist to leverage available cash, or generate more? Would it be better to preserve the cash to ride out the difficult period? Is this any time for adventurism, or should John scale back and concentrate on holding on to what is left of his core business?

External/Competitive Environment

Once we have set internal objectives, we must examine the external and competitive environments in which we will be trying to achieve them.

The external environment consists of those factors that are largely outside our control, but which affect the market for our product. Examples of these factors include general economic conditions, regulations, technological developments, and consumer demographics and attitudes. This environment is very dynamic, but some attempt must be made at projecting its changes.

Analysis of the competitive environment must begin with consideration of whether there are any barriers to the entry of a new competitor into the market. How strong is consumer loyalty to existing brands? How important are economies of scale? Can a small independent firm compete?

Are capital requirements prohibitive? Is there some proprietary technology that puts prospective entrants in a serious competitive disadvantage? Is access to raw materials or to distribution channels limited in some way? Are new entrants limited by permit restrictions or regulations? Will current competitors attempt to punish new entrants, such as through a price war, heavy advertising, or exercising their clout with key suppliers?

The competitive structure of the industry is another important consideration. Are there a few dominant firms, or is the industry fragmented? Do buyers have a wide choice of vendors? How are prices set? What factors create cost advantages or disadvantages? Is there some geographic niche we can serve? Are there less expensive or superior substitutes to our product in some segments of the market? How important is a firm's position on the learning and experience curves?

Is demand rising, even, or falling? Are there exit barriers, such as long-term contractual commitments or large initial investments, that raise the risk of entry?

Relative strengths of our strategic partners must also be considered. What is the bargaining power of suppliers? How wide is our choice of suppliers? Is it costly for us to switch? Can our suppliers compete with us for the same customers? How important is our industry to our suppliers?

SWOT (Strengths/Weaknesses/Opportunities/Threats) Analysis

1. *Competitive Advantage.* The major strength of a company is that which most clearly distinguishes it from the competition, referred to as its competitive advantage, or "edge." It can take many forms, but it must be identified and built upon. This can be in a primary aspect of the business (manufacture, sales, service), or a secondary one (support, personnel, purchasing, etc.). It is the critical factor in the company's value-adding process. Areas in which we can seek a competitive advantage include the following:

- **Logistical.** The new business can secure a particularly desirable location, and enter the market with the latest facilities and equipment.
- **Skilled People.** A new business offers the opportunity to hire well-qualified and technologically advanced personnel, and those with records of success relevant to the opportunity.
- **Management Attitudes.** Founders and managers of a new business are generally highly focused on the opportunity, and are motivated and enthusiastic.

The following are areas in which new businesses often find themselves at a disadvantage:

- **Financial Strength.** Economies of scale require large amounts of capital. For these types of markets, small producers have a tough time competing due to the large capital requirements.
- **Sources of Supply.** Supplier relationships and sources of raw material can play a major role in minimizing costs associated with production and the delivery of products to market.
- **Brands.** If existing firms have developed a group of loyal supporters, it may be difficult for new and unfamiliar competitors to invade their market.
- **Patents.** The competition may possess a patent that may force you to use substitute processes that are often more costly and time-consuming.

Strategies for minimizing the impact of competitive disadvantages should be formulated, and then presented in the plan.

A sample business plan, written by students as a course requirement, appears at the end of this chapter. It offers a detailed strategic plan that illustrates many of the principles discussed here.

2. *Strengths and Weaknesses.* To identify your firm's strengths and weaknesses, try to analyze these factors from the perspective of outside sources. An effective approach is to ask open-ended questions of various types of sources. For an existing business, its employees, customers, and suppliers generally can offer the most valuable insights into the firm's position in the market.

Questions for employees:

- What do you think is the primary reason for the company's success?
- What does the company do best? What allows it to do this so well?

- What does it do poorly? Can you give a recent example?
- What should the company discontinue doing and why?
- What should the company consider adding and why?
- What are the characteristics of a typical customer?
- What are the primary reasons for a customer buying from the company?

Questions for customers:

- How long have you been a client or customer of the company?
- How did you hear of them? What criteria led you to select them?
- Do they perform all of your work in this area?
- What do you like best about them? What benefit does this offer you?
- What do you like least about them? What could they do to improve?
- Compared to other firms, what are their advantages? Disadvantages?
- Are there any other services you would like them to provide?
- Would you recommend them to others? How would you describe them?

Supplier questions vary depending on the nature of the relationship to the company, but generally can be drawn from both of the previous sets of questions. The primary goal of your supplier relations should be to achieve strategic partnerships, where each firm seeks a style of cooperation that benefits both parties; the supplier then functions almost as your employee.

While the venture's weaknesses need not be emphasized, they should be recognized and identified. A plan to overcome them, or at least minimize their impact, is far more credible than denying that they exist.

3. *Opportunities and Threats.* Certainly, the opportunity addressed initially is central to the business plan, but a discussion of peripheral and/or future opportunities demonstrates a deeper understanding of the full range of possibilities of the venture. These can include a broader geographic area, wider product line, and new applications for current products.

Threats to the future success of the business must be recognized. These can be internal, such as a concept that can be copied easily or limitations of working capital. Threats can also be external, such as an economic downturn, shifting demographics, or technological developments. Competitive factors can also come into play, such as entry of a major company in a related business.

ENTREPRENEURIAL RESOURCE | Management Simulations

Management simulation programs create an economic environment in which managers or entrepreneurs can test the results of their business decisions without real-life consequences. Participants develop strategies for some time period as input to the simulation, and the program projects how the market might have responded.

Computer-based models of companies are often developed to indicate how a company might fare using each of various strategies available to them. The predictive power of the model is limited by the skill of its developers, and the basic difficulties relating to predicting the future in any context.

Frequently, simulations are used as a teaching device, where students direct a hypothetical company through a series of marketing and strategic issues. One particularly effective example is the *Threshold* series by Anderson, Beveridge, Scott, and Hofmeister.

As with most training simulations, *Threshold* uses a highly simplified company in order to allow the focus of the participants to remain on decision making and problem solving. The following is from the *Threshold Competitor* manual:[9]

> In the *Threshold* simulation, you will operate a small manufacturing firm that produces two plastic molded products—Product 1 and Product 2. The manufacturing process consists of forming plastic raw materials (sheets of plastic) into the finished consumer product. You will sell these products through retail markets to the general public. The products are not substitutes for one another, nor are they complementary. This means that sales of one product do not affect sales of the other product.
>
> Given the inherent durability of your products, the likelihood of immediate repeat purchases by a customer is small. This means if a customer has just purchased one of your products in Quarter 1, that customer is not likely to purchase another one in Quarter 2. Consequently, you should assume that sales for a particular quarter will come from new customers that you have attracted to your product based on that quarter's marketing efforts and product characteristics. You should not assume that customers will buy your product because of past experiences with that product. In addition, your company is too new to the market to expect brand satisfaction with one of your products to boost the sales of your other product. In short, each quarter's sales have to be earned that quarter. Brand loyalty is not part of your sales environment.

Strategic options open to participants include product mix within total capacity of 11,100 units combined, use of overtime, advertising budget, investment in improving product quality, and borrowing operating or expansion funds. The *Threshold* simulation includes an economic indicator, and additional market research data can be purchased.

The instructor or simulation administrator processes each set of decisions, reporting results to each participant (often a team of participants). Strategies are then formed for subsequent quarters.

Logistical Plan

Location/Facilities

This section of the plan is primarily oriented toward facilities, production capability, and equipment. We should describe all present capabilities as to equipment and facilities, as well as further projections for offices, branches, production, and distribution.

How many employees do we need at start-up? How much space and equipment do we need to compete effectively? What other facilities are important?

Should we buy or lease property and equipment? Which makes exit easier?

Is business location a significant factor? If so, what are our location criteria? Location criteria can be applied at three levels: the city or metropolitan area, the neighborhood or section of town, and a specific site. Is the city or our chosen section growing? Is it prospering, or is it going "downhill"? Is the area perceived as safe? Is the demographic profile (age, income, etc.) favorable to what we are offering?

Specific sites within acceptable areas require a more detailed level of analysis. How close are our competitors? How well are neighboring businesses doing? Is access easy? Parking available? Will there be zoning problems or neighborhood resistance? It often helps to include current floor plans when available, and to project future space needs.

Legal Structure

The most common business structures are proprietorships, partnerships, and corporations.

A proprietorship is simply a one-owner business. It is the most prevalent form (about 70 percent of all businesses) because it is the simplest and least expensive to start.

A partnership is basically a proprietorship for multiple owners. Most are general partnerships, where each partner is held liable for the acts of the other partners. A limited partnership allows for general and limited partners; limited partners' liability is limited to their contributed capital.

The decision to enter a partnership should be based on whether or not you can go it alone. The main reasons people feel they cannot are lack of money, skills, connections, and confidence. Are there other ways to address these needs?

If you choose to go into business with a partner, be sure to prepare a formal, written partnership agreement. This should address the contribution each will make to the partnership, financial and personal; how business profits and losses will be apportioned; the salaries and financial rights of each partner; and provisions for changes in ownership, such as a sale, succession, or desire to bring in a new partner.

The corporation is a legal entity, separate from its owners. It is a more secure and better defined form for prospective lenders/investors. Incorporation is perceived as limiting the owner's liability, but personal guarantees are generally required whenever there is liability exposure. The traditional form in the United States is called the C-Corporation.

Where the C-Corporation files a tax return as a corporate entity, an S-Corporation "passes through" its proceeds to its owners. The S-Corporation is frequently preferable as a start-up form, since the losses expected in the early stages of the business may be applied to the owner's personal tax return.

A relatively new form gaining in popularity is the LLC, or Limited Liability Corporation. For some businesses, it can offer the pass-through tax benefits of the S-Corporation with the limited liability of the C-Corporation. Enlist the legal and tax advice of the professionals as to which form suits your venture best.

Ownership Structure and Capitalization

Once the legal structure is decided upon, issues of distribution of ownership and distribution of risks and benefits may be addressed. The primary decision to be made is whether the venture will be financed by the entrepreneur or whether there is a need for other stakeholders, and whether these stakeholders will be investors or lenders or some combination thereof.

The entrepreneur must keep the long term in view. Shares of ownership may not seem very valuable at startup, but the entrepreneur could seriously regret having sold them so cheaply when the company begins to prosper. On the other hand, borrowing for a new venture can be extremely difficult. The criteria for making decisions about capitalization are discussed at length in the financial section.

Human Resources

Many business plans are evaluated largely on the qualifications and commitment of the management team. The human resource plan must assess realistically the skills required for success of the venture, initially and over the long run, and match the skills and interests of the team to these requirements. Gaps must be filled with additional employees, learning activities, and/or consultants.

Once tasks are assigned, an effective responsibility structure must be designed. This structure would include the management of the organization, formal and informal advisors, and a board of directors. Methods of staying in touch with the market, such as association memberships and networking systems, can also be part of the human resource plan.

The Financial Plan

The financial plan is an integral part of a complex process of financing an entrepreneurial venture, and we will discuss it in that fuller context in the following chapter.

LOGISTICS

The Company is presently operating out of the residence of one of the principals. The two principals, each of whom currently owns 50% of the Company (a Canadian corporation), are:

Mr. I. M. Bright, President and original developer of the product.

Mr. N. O. Howe, Secretary of the Company, responsible for production.

Any questions relating to the business plan should be directed to Mr. Bright.

In production, approximately 4,000 square feet of space will be required to store inventory, assemble and test the product. Suitable manufacturing space has been identified in Richmond. The owners of the property are prepared to enter into a 3 year lease agreement or longer if required.

The engineering prototype satisfactorily demonstrates the technical feasibility and basic operation of the product. There are no major or critical risks that are anticipated to impede the successful completion of the engineering development.

Special engineering test equipment will be required to conduct performance and reliability tests. Each unit will undergo 24 hours of continuous testing before shipping to a customer. The test equipment will consist of special light-sensing and measuring equipment and controlled light sources.

Three months from the time that financing has been arranged will be required to set up manufacturing and start production of the first 1,000 pieces. The first 1,000 production units will be complete within two months after the start of production.

$310,000 is required to complete the development of the product, to set up manufacturing and to establish a sales and marketing program. The $310,000 will be supplemented by revenue generated from sales of the product to cover the total financial requirements for the first year of operation. The business will be self-sustaining by the end of the first year of operations.

Light-Guard Manufacturing Ltd. is prepared to offer common (voting) shares in return for the investment. Light-Guard Manufacturing Ltd. is also prepared to consider other forms of financing such as debentures, preferred shares or other arrangements.

Mr. Bright is responsible for technical development. He is a graduate from the British Columbia Institute of Technology. Mr. Bright has 7 years industrial experience progressing from a technician to the supervisor of an engineering test laboratory with a local manufacturer of electronic equipment. Any questions relating to the business plan are to be directed to Mr. Bright.

Mr. Howe will be responsible for production and project management. He also graduated from the British Columbia Institute of Technology in Operations Management and has over 10 years industrial experience in electrical components and electronics manufacturing. He is currently employed as the production manager with the same electronics firm as Mr. Bright.

The sales and marketing functions will be the responsibility of an individual who is currently employed as a sales manager for a home entertainment distribution company. The sales manager has over 15 years sales and marketing experience in the home entertainment industry.

All three individuals are prepared to resign their present positions and make a full time commitment to Light-Guard when financing has been arranged.

A technician will be required to assist Mr. Bright with the engineering development. A total of 6 assembly personnel, plus an assembly line supervisor, will be required to assemble the product. Two test technicians will be required to inspect and test the product before shipping.

Initially, the accounting and financial control functions will be handled on a part-time basis by a senior member of a firm of chartered accountants.

Detailed résumés of the management team members are available to serious investors.

Summary

We can evaluate our business plan according to the following checklist:

1. General.

   Is it clear what business the company is in? Is the concept well thought out? Is it expressed effectively? Is the overall presentation concise and businesslike?

   Is the plan attractive and well-written? Is it interesting? Does the plan "sell"? Does it generate enthusiasm?

2. Marketing Plan.

   How good is the market research? How applicable is it to this specific business?

   How well do the principals understand the industry? Is the target market clearly identified? Is it the right market? Is it big enough? Is it growing? Is the marketing approach credible and convincing?

3. Strategic Issues.

   Is the business sufficiently differentiated? Is its competitive advantage clear and convincing? Is product positioning and pricing appropriate to the competitive situation?

   Are company strengths sufficient for success? Are any company weaknesses fatal? Are all promising opportunities recognized? Are all significant threats adequately considered?

   Are the human resources indicated sufficient to the task? Are they used well? Is the scope of operations appropriate to the opportunities? Are the keys to success clearly identified?

4. Overall.

   Is the plan convincing? Are the principals realistic about where the industry is headed and the competitive situation, and reasonable in their projections? Is company management capable of implementing the plan? Do they recognize any shortcomings, and have a plan to address them?

   Is the presentation clear and concise? Does it stress benefits to the prospect? Is it attractive and interesting? Does it end with a call to action?

Review Questions

1. What is the major purpose of a business plan? Is a business plan needed where the entrepreneur can finance the venture without assistance?

_____

_____

_____

2. What are the primary components of the business plan? Is there a standard format? An appropriate length? A specific audience for whom it is written?

_____

_____

_____

3. What are the major objectives of the marketing plan?

_____

_____

_____

4. What are the logistical issues that should be resolved in the plan?

_____

_____

_____

5. What is the purpose of the strategic plan?

_____

_____

_____

6. How well does the Light-Guard plan meet our objectives? How would you strengthen it?

_____

_____

_____

The following case study continues our consideration of the development of Tammany Supply, Inc. Following this case study is a sample business plan.

CASE STUDY 6.2
Tammany Supply, Inc. (D)

INTRODUCTION

From its 1978 start-up through 1985, Tammany Supply, Inc. (TSI), of Covington, Lousiana, was the dominant plumbing supply wholesaler in western St. Tammany Parish. St. Tammany, an upscale suburb of New Orleans, was one of the country's fastest growing counties during this period, and TSI's growth rate reflected it.

Sales evened off in 1985, then fell precipitously in 1986 as the collapse of world oil prices took the energy out of the Louisiana economy. Sales fell even further in 1987, as TSI suffered its first money-losing year (see Case Study 6.1).

New residential construction, which had been a mainstay for TSI, fell off dramatically, as homes were left vacant all over the parish by people leaving Louisiana to find work. TSI had to perform a reevaluation of their strategy, and do it fast, to cope with a 40 percent decrease in their core business.

DIVERSIFICATION

As the "crash" damages to TSI were being assessed in late 1989, its president, John Vinturella, began to write the company's first formal business plan. The 1990–1992 plan serves to illustrate that planning is not just for start-ups, but is useful at every stage in the development of a business. The following excerpt from the 1991 update to that plan describes the recovery strategy:

The decreased demand was addressed on three fronts: the impact on sales volume was softened by diversifying product lines, cash was preserved by a gradual selling off of inventory, and expenses were cut.

Diversification of product lines was intended to increase retail sales, particularly in remodeling and add-on items. The company began emphasizing spas and whirlpools, and became a master distributor for Toro sprinkler systems. In 1987 TSI opened the Outdoor Living Center (OLC), to retail outdoor and patio furniture and accessories. In 1988 the company opened a Singer Kitchens and Baths franchise, selling cabinets and appliances. In 1989 the company broadened its water treatment and air-conditioning supply offerings.

Equally vital were the inventory reduction and cost-cutting campaigns. Low turnover items were returned to the manufacturer or offered to other suppliers and the public at break-even pricing or less. Staff was reduced by attrition, one truck was retired, insurance was tightened, and some functions previously contracted out were brought back in.

Inventory had been reduced by about 25 percent, generating about $90,000 cash. Expenses were cut by about 30 percent, largely coming out of personnel and related costs. The company now had some working capital and an organization appropriate in scale to the reduced level of business. By the 1991 update, a preliminary report on results could be made:

The last three years have seen the end of "free-fall," as business stabilized but did not really improve. Sales volume is recovering, but margins have remained weak; 1988 was a moderately good year, 1989 a moderately bad one, and 1990 was essentially break-even.

Some mid-course correction was called for:

At the end of 1990, by mutual agreement, TSI returned control of the SKB store to the franchiser. SKB continues to operate the store, effectively shutting TSI out of the cabinet business.

Despite our high hopes for the kitchen business, it did not create as good a fit with our overall operation as we had hoped, and the attractive margins were eaten up by heavy personnel demands.

The result of this decision is a slight downsizing of our operation. . . . In 1990, SKB sales represented almost 15% of TSI sales.

Some good news could be found:

On the positive side, we feel that we can make up this volume in our mainstream business. We see a definite increase in construction activity, and our two local competitors left the area in October 1990.

The local competitors referred to were Park Supply, a Picayune, Mississippi, company that opened a Covington branch in 1986, and Plumbing Specialty of New Orleans, which entered the market in 1988. All was not quiet on the competitive

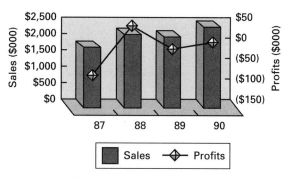

Sales and Profits
Tammany Supply, Inc., 1987–90

front, however; Southern Pipe, a regional chain based in Meridian, Mississippi, announced in early 1991 that they would open a western St. Tammany branch by the end of the year.

PERFORMANCE

Since TSI could hardly survive another year like 1987, the following three years were projected to be the recovery period. It was a spotty recovery at best. Sales drifted upward, exceeding $2 million again by 1990. Of the three, only 1988 was profitable, and would not have been but for a large income tax refund reflecting the huge loss of the previous year (see "Sales and Profits, 1987–90" graph).

Still, some cause for optimism could be found:

> We hope that the worst is behind us. All reasonably questionable debts are written off and expenses are tightly controlled. State and area economic outlook have improved, and the local recovery seems to have some strength.

Projections for 1991–1992, developed with the assistance of the TSI accountant, Dennis K. Frentz, Sr., show expectations of profitability on the order of $30,000 per year.

STUDY QUESTIONS

1. Was 1987 too late for TSI to write its first business plan? Would a formal written strategic plan in 1985 have helped guide the company through the difficult period? Could it have helped soften the impact? What was the purpose of the 1990 plan?

2. Evaluate the strategic plan. Does the assessment of external forces seem reasonable? Are internal capabilities reasonably assessed? Does the strategy selection follow logically from the assessments?

3. Are the goals expressed too modest, reasonable, or too ambitious? Are they relevant to the problems facing TSI? Are the tools necessary to their accomplishment identified?

4. Is management in control and on target? Are they collecting the right information, and evaluating it properly, as a guide to future actions?

5. How successful has the diversification strategy been? Should it be abandoned, or simply refined? Do the reasons for dropping SKB make sense? How is SKB significantly different from the other forms of diversification?

6. Why did two competitors move in after the crash? Why do you think they could not make it? Why were the earlier entries small independents, while the regional chain waited until an apparent recovery was under way? What effect do you expect the 1991 entry of a competitor with "deep pockets" will have on TSI's recovery?

7. Are you confident about TSI's prospects for the remaining two years of this planning period? What would you do differently?

CASE STUDY 6.3

The "New" DistribNet[10]

Jay Beavy was sure he wanted his next venture to be based on the Internet, but was having trouble developing a solid concept. He had made one abortive attempt at forming a Web site design service company (see Case Study 2.1). He then considered forming a company to build Internet catalogs for electronic commerce, but found this to be too far outside his expertise.

At a party, a friend of Jay's mentioned that his son, Ben Eason, was dabbling in Web site design and doing quite well. Ben's efforts were on a small scale as he completed college but, with a couple of fellow students assisting him, Ben was building a significant clientele of small to medium

size businesses new to the Web. Jay asked Ben's father, Bob, if he thought Ben might want seed money to take the venture larger upon his graduation, and Bob suggested that Jay propose the idea to Ben.

Ben was excited about the possibility, and had written a brief business plan for such a venture as a school project. The next step would be for Jay to study the plan before proposing a partnership arrangement.

Ben modified the plan to call the company "DistribNet, Inc." since Jay already owned that domain name on the Internet. The plan he presented follows:

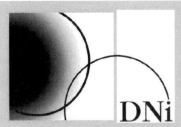

DistribNet, Inc (**www.distribnet.com**)

TABLE OF CONTENTS

EXECUTIVE SUMMARY

DNi is a new business venture created to provide specialized on-line services for small to medium size companies. Its initial focus will be on companies in the Minneapolis–St. Paul area, but markets out-of-state will be evaluated during the second year of operations.

The objective of DNi is to provide its clients with superior on-line services to those provided by competitors, at a highly competitive price. This approach is designed to attract clients that wish to take advantage of this new marketing medium without going broke doing it.

DNi will be successful in meeting these objectives, based on the following factors:

- the strong business and computing orientation of its principals,
- the rapid growth of the Internet, particularly as a means of commerce,
- the services that we provide, and the resulting benefits to our clients.

We have determined a price of $1,500 for a basic site, generally well below prices of our competitors. Additional services will be offered at modest cost.

Our clients for 1998 will be identified by researching directories of companies that fit our definition of the target market. During the first year of operations, we need to sell 104 Web Sites to break-even, but we project a small operating loss. This number, however, is conservative, since we have assumed that first year sales will consist solely of 100 basic sites at $1,500.

Beginning with the second year, we expect operating profits to continue to increase each subsequent year. Our growth will be measured against the rate of industry growth. Although we expect our growth to exceed that of the industry, we have chosen to base our conservative projections on the industry growth rate.

COMPANY DESCRIPTION AND LOCATION

DNi will be located in the growing metropolitan area of the Twin Cities of Minnesota. It is important to note, however, that a company such as DNi does not depend on geographic location in order to achieve success. The initial focus will be towards local companies, but with the possibility of expanding to selected markets across the United States.

STRATEGIC FOCUS AND PLAN

Mission and Vision

The mission and vision of DNi is to provide our customers with individualized service, expert knowledge of all aspects of Internet marketing and Web Site capabilities, and to ensure that our employees are in command of the current technologies and innovative approaches necessary to develop the best quality Web Sites available.

Goals

DNi will be striving to achieve the following goals:

Non-financial goals:

1. Develop a reputation as the high quality, full service Web Site design company.
2. Continually attract new customers, while still focusing on satisfying current customers' needs.
3. Provide new technologies and innovations to our customers quickly and efficiently.

Financial goals:

1. Break even or better in our first year.
2. Provide quality services at competitive prices.
3. Continuously lower costs of operations without sacrificing effectiveness.

Core Competency and Competitive Advantage

The core competencies of DNi are our professionalism, and extensive Web programming knowledge.

These skills will translate to a competitive advantage over other Web Site developing companies by allowing us to stay on the cutting edge of information and new technology, while providing our customers with services that gain them maximum marketing effectiveness for their Web Site. Our competitive advantage, then, will allow us to provide high quality Web Sites with superior design and better service than that of competitors.

SITUATION ANALYSIS

The following SWOT analysis will identify the internal strengths and weaknesses our company has, and the external opportunities and threats with which we are confronted.

SWOT Analysis

Our *strength* is our team of technically experienced and creative computer programmers and operators. Our team is also experienced in business management, and is able to understand the needs of our customers. We have very little overhead and low operating costs. *Opportunities* are created by the acceptance and phenomenal growth of the World Wide Web as a tool for business, commerce, and entertainment. The growing access of the general population to personal computers with Internet access, and the growing dependence of large and small companies on computers for their everyday operations, are additional positive indicators for our success.

Initially, our *weaknesses* are the size of the company, and our newness in the marketplace. While rapid growth is a goal, our limited financial resources may restrict our growth. Our external *threats* include the problem of being in a market with very easy entry. As the number of Web Sites increases, so does the number of companies willing to help others create them. Also, companies of any size are able to author their own Web Sites if they have personnel with the capability and the time to develop them.

Industry Analysis

The Internet and the World Wide Web will most certainly change the way companies do business, and the way customers shop. Those that do not embrace the Internet will quickly fall behind. More and more companies seek to promote their products and services on-line, and as new technologies continue to develop, the reasons for not taking advantage of this medium decrease.

Like most other technologies, on-line marketing must be understood by the employees of a company, and this requires some experience with the technology. If a company with no experience on the Internet suddenly decides to use this medium, it is a safe bet that most of its competitors already take advantage of it, and the company is at a competitive disadvantage.

The infrastructure for a new economy is currently being built by the Internet. The number of Web Sites on the Internet has been estimated to double every 53 days (see Chuck Martin's *The Digital Estate,* McGraw-Hill, 1996).

Sustaining this growth are:

1. The increasing number of people with access to a PC.
2. The increasing number of people with access to the Internet.
3. The increasing amount of investment in Internet- and Intranet-servers.

As the Internet becomes a utility, and hundreds of millions of people and companies get connected, DNi believes that there will be little choice for companies but to publish as much on the Internet as possible. This will include everything from applications to services.

Competitor Analysis

The competitors in the field of Web Site authoring are many, and their numbers are increasing every day. A quick search on the World Wide Web for companies who will help you place a static advertisement in the homes of millions of spellbound Internet surfers yields the following results:

- There are many who will set up a site with your company's name on it, and add a little information about you. But there are very few who will take the time to consult with you about your type of business, what information about your customers is important to you, and what information about you is most important for your customers to see.
- Many of our competitors are out for the quick sale, moving quickly to the next. What makes us different is our commitment to our clients. Our goal is to tailor our services based on a complete understanding of their business needs; after the construction of their site is complete, we continue to support them by maintaining and updating the content and design of their site frequently. Many other companies are able to offer maintenance and continual improvement, but a scan of the field shows that there are few that are willing to go the extra steps.
- We have also chosen to price our services competitively, as we believe that this lower price will enable us to "lock in" customers who currently do not have the budget required to buy the services offered by our competitors.

Company Analysis

The "new" DNi began in January of 1997, as the current principals expanded on an earlier plan, while building on and merging with an existing Web domain. DNi's major asset is its expertise in one of the most significant new marketing tools to come along since the advent of television.

The company's presence on the Web will be the company brochure, showing prospective customers exactly what our services can do for them and how they will benefit from our help. We will supplement this with advertising in the local media, and through referrals by our satisfied customers.

Customer Analysis

Our target market is small to medium-sized businesses with a need for inexpensive advertising and marketing tools that will reach the highest number of customers possible. Any business with a product or a service to sell would be able to make use of our services; this is not a very exclusive club.

Those most likely to purchase our service are the smaller businesses seeking inexpensive advertising, an efficient way to take orders, and a reliable way to collect and analyze data about the visitors to their site. In general, these businesses will have computers in use in their workplace, do a good portion of their everyday tasks with their computer's help, and will be familiar with and/or have access to the Internet.

A study by Hoffman, Novak, and Chatterjee, entitled "Commercial Scenarios for the Web: Opportunities and Challenges" (www.ideacentral.com/wmi/hoffman1.htm), estimated that 62% of businesses with annual sales between $10,000 and $100,000 use computers for at least part of their business applications. Of those businesses, 55% have Internet access. Businesses with annual sales between $100,000 and $500,000 have a rate of 96% of computer usage, with 85% of those having Internet access.

With all this computer usage and Internet familiarity, most small to medium sized businesses have already realized the benefits of the Internet. However, the same study also estimated that only 8% of all businesses with annual sales less than $500,000 have their own Web Sites.

Obviously, the market is wide open for companies such as DNi. While our initial focus will be on customers in the Minneapolis–St. Paul area, this is an online market, where location matters little.

MARKET/PRODUCT FOCUS

Marketing and Product Objectives

DNi's marketing intent is to take advantage of the increasing number of individuals and companies going on-line, which is creating an increased demand for Internet service providers and Web Site developers. The product objectives of DNi are to continually provide high quality, error free Web Site developing, in addition to staying up-to-date with new technologies that will increase the marketing potential and effectiveness of our customers.

Target Markets

DNi will initially target small to medium sized businesses in the Twin City area who do not currently have Internet access and Web Sites. We will identify these companies through business directories.

The market could then expand to larger companies based in the Twin Cities, and companies throughout the United States who will have access to DNi through our Web Site. One of the great advantages of being on-line is that our "local" market is a global one.

Points of Difference

DNi has four main points of difference that set it apart from competitors:

Staff. A professional consulting staff that understands all aspects of business and the full marketing capabilities of the Internet and Web Sites.

New Technologies. DNi strives to provide customers with cutting edge technology, such as tracking Web Site visitors, that will give them a competitive advantage in their line of business.

Consulting Services. DNi provides customers with more than just a Web Site. Consulting with customers regarding their Web Site on an ongoing basis will enable them to utilize the full potential of their on-line presence.

Full Internet Service. DNi can equip their customers with Internet access, an electronic mail program, and site capabilities that include on-line product ordering.

Positioning

DNi will position their Internet service package as a very effective, low cost way to market a company's products. Internet marketing also allows a company to easily update pricing and product information. Other services provided by DNi, such as on-line product ordering and electronic mail capabilities, will increase companies' operational effectiveness.

Product Strategy

In addition to our design expertise, we can also offer the hosting of client sites on the DNi server. The primary function of the Web Sites we develop for our clients will be to market products and collect information. The typical DNi site might contain up to 20 Web "pages," and data collection and interactivity capabilities. Other services offered our clients will include registration of the site with all major search "engines," and site maintenance and consulting services after the development process.

Product Quality

The differentiating factor in the webs we design is the ability of the Web Site to collect information from those who visit it. The information that will be collected includes:

Product marketing information. This includes a site visitor access profile regarding the various products or services that our client is offering. This information will enable our client to adjust their marketing strategies, change their product line, etc., in an informed and customer-oriented manner.

Demographics. This includes information on visitor name, geographic area, previous visits to our site, previous purchases from the site, etc. Like any marketing organization, we want to know our customers as well as possible so that we may continuously refine our marketing strategy.

Product Packaging

"Packaging" in this business refers to the design of Web pages. Our designs will reflect simplicity with a high level of functionality. One of the big concerns of web design is the accessibility of the page to visitors, that is time required to load at the visitor's computer. Currently, most people access the Internet by dial-up connections (see Georgia Tech Research Corp. "GVU's 4th WWW User Survey," 1995). The standard phone line is a rather slow channel for information flow, and Web site design must acknowledge this limitation.

Price Strategy

The typical DNi site will be priced at $1,500. This is a very competitive price, lower than that of competitors who offer similar characteristics in webs. Research done by ActivMedia Inc. shows that a typical site's development costs by a company with 500 employees is in the range of $10,000 to $100,000 (see *Web Marketing Insider*, "Reports and Surveys," 1996).

NetMarketing sent out bids for three prototypical sites to 21 web developers and ad agencies. Each participant was given a site description and asked to submit a bid for a small site (about 20 pages), a medium-sized site (about 100 pages) and a large advanced site (custom programming, database front-end, secure transaction capability, etc.). NetMarketing's findings indicate that prices for web development vary greatly. For example, bids for the large site ranged from $15,000 to $2.8 million.

We have chosen to price our product at the lower end of the price continuum in our industry, even though our product is relatively high in quality, so that we can more easily penetrate the market. Since there is so much competition present in this fast-growing industry, our strategy is to lead the market in both cost and quality.

Promotion Strategy

The primary goal of our promotion strategy is to bring about name recognition and brand awareness. We hope to make "DNi web" connote a highly interactive data collection and marketing tool. Promotion will be done through on-line, print, and referral methods, and sales presentations to prospective customers.

On-line. We will promote our products by advertising in frequently visited sites on the Web, registering our Web Site with search engines, and participating in on-line forums for Web development questions. Also, we will provide a daily tip in Web development at our site for beginning, intermediate and advanced Web developers; daily tips elicit frequent visits and also associate our name with expertise in Web development.

Print. We will have ads in small business journals and other popular business and Web development magazines to promote our name in our targeted market.

Referrals. Our clients will find it easy to refer our services to acquaintances. Through our close and on-going relationship with our clients, we will develop many promising leads.

Sales Presentations. We will identify potential clients that will benefit from our services, and offer to present them full explanations of the advantage of a DNi site.

Place (Distribution) Strategy

Distribution of the product will take place entirely on-line; there is no need to have a traditional place of distribution. For face-to-face consulting, our offices will be in the Minneapolis area. We will also consult via "cyber-conferencing," and personal visits to remote client locations, depending on their needs and preferences.

ORGANIZATION

DNi will begin with four principals, each with business expertise and extensive computer training. They will also serve as the board of directors, and work full-time in the business.

The principals are Ben Eason, Amanda Shull, Chad Allen, and Cari Lee. Mr. Eason will serve as president of the corporation; the Board will elect the corporate secretary.

FINANCIAL DATA AND PROJECTIONS

Clearly, on-line marketing has benefited greatly from the explosive growth of the Internet and Web. The number of users of the Net/Web is expected to reach a high of 153 million people in the year 2000 (see *Web Marketing Insider,* 1996).

Since DNi is a new venture, it has based its projections on extensive research of the general market. Although attempts to predict future growth should be considered carefully, DNi is confident of future demand for its services.

Two financing scenarios are offered: a self-financed startup, and one utilizing venture capital.

Scenario 1

The first assumes that the venture will be financed through the limited resources of the principals and any family money that they can borrow. The expense structure under this scenario is as follows:

Expenses	*Annual Fixed Costs*	
Equipment will be rented to allow continuous upgrades as new technology becomes available.	Rent of Office	$6,000
	Rent of Office Furniture	$3,600
Note that there are no variable costs, since we are	Rent of PC/Server Eqpt.	$6,400
selling the services of full-time employees.	Wages for 4 employees	$140,000
Break-even sales = $156,000 cost/$1,500 per site = 104	*Total Fixed Costs*	*$156,000*

While it would be possible to lower expenses at startup by using contract labor rather than full-time employees, we feel that any unused site design capacity can be productively utilized in the marketing campaign. Similarly, while we could begin by working at home, it is our sense that an office presence enhances our credibility with the target market.

With this strategy, we have developed the following implementation plan. We would like to complete the pre-opening activities in the remainder of 1997 to allow for a full year of revenues in 1998.

Task	*Pre-Open*	*1998*	*1999*
Identify area Web sites design prospects for 1998	X		
Sign rent/lease contracts for office, furniture, PC's and Servers	X		
Finalize design tools and Web software to be used	X	X	X
Sharpen design skills in chosen tools	X	X	X
Develop methods of payment, billing and accounting guidelines	X		
Identify potential firms out-of-state		X	X

The following five-year projection is based on the above expense structure and implementation schedule. Sales estimates are in the number of basic sites sold, since it is difficult to characterize an average Web site design cost. Additional design services on an hourly or contract basis are expected, but are not included. Annual growth in sales is felt to be extremely conservative.

Revenues/ Profit (Scenario 1)	Year 1 1998	Year 2 1999	Year 3 2000	Year 4 2001	Year 5 2002
Web Sites Sold	100	110	116	122	126
Net Sales	$150,000	$165,000	$174,000	$183,000	$189,000
Total Expenses	$156,000	$156,000	$156,000	$156,000	$156,000
Operating Profit	–$6,000	$9,000	$18,000	$27,000	$33,000

Note that the loss in Year 1 is minimal, and is more than exceeded by profits in Year 2. Projected sales are well within the capacity of the principals to fulfill; the profitability of work beyond this capacity will be balanced against the cost of contract labor.

Scenario 2

The preferred approach is to pursue a rapid-growth strategy. Due to the limited resources of the principals, this strategy requires outside investment.

The realities of starting such a venture "from scratch" cause us to project first-year performance at no more than under Scenario 1. Growth in succeeding years will be measured against the industry growth rate; projections are left to the reader

Revenues/ Profit (Scenario 2)	Year 1 1998	Year 2 1999	Year 3 2000	Year 4 2001	Year 5 2002
Basic Web Sites Sold	100				
Net Sales (Basic)	$150,000				
Other Services	$0				
Total Revenues	$150,000				
Total Expenses	$156,000				
Operating Profit	–$6,000				

STUDY QUESTIONS 1: THE VENTURE

1. Fill in the blanks in Scenario 2. What growth rate in sales might we reasonably expect?

   _____

   _____

   _____

2. What kind of "markup" might we get on the use of contract labor? At what level of utilization might we convert the contract arrangement to full-time employment?

   _____

   _____

   _____

3. What is your feeling about their chances of success under Scenario 1? Justify your assessment of their chances.

   _____

   _____

4. How much should they ask of Jay? What might Jay ask in return? Would you invest in them?

   _____

   _____

   _____

5. Write a summary paragraph to the business plan that attempts to secure Jay's participation.

   _____

   _____

   _____

STUDY QUESTIONS 2: THE PLAN

1. Does the plan flow well, or is it "choppy"? Is it repetitive on some themes? Is it easy to read?

   _____

   _____

   _____

   _____

2. Does the plan generate enthusiasm? Suggest changes in plan organization and format that would improve it along these lines.

   _____

   _____

   _____

3. Is the concept of the company and its place in the industry clear? What areas could use a clearer or more complete description? Are the company's competitive advantages clear and convincing?

   _____

   _____

   _____

Notes

1. Jenny C. Servo. "Developing Effective Business Plans for Advanced Technology Firms" (www.dawnbreaker.com/article1b.html).

2. www.sba.gov/starting/faqs/quet3.html

3. William S. Rukeyser. "How to Write a Business Plan," *CNNfn* (www.cnnfn.com) (5/31/96).

4. Sam Vaknin. "How to Write a Business Plan" (www.focus-asia.com/home/samvak) (2/13/97).

5. Venture Associates (www.venturea. com/ business.htm).

6. Canada/British Columbia Business Service Centre (www.sb.gov.bc.ca/smallbus/workshop/download/samplebp.html) Sample business plan (1/6/98).

7. EntrepreNet's Electronic Library (www.enterprise.org/enet/library/declimp.html). (4/11/98).

8. The Entrepreneur Network (www.tenonline.org/art/sm/1.html), from the "Seven Principles of Marketing" series (1994) by John Agno.

9. Philip A. Anderson, et al. *Threshold Competitor.* Upper Saddle River, N.J.: Prentice Hall, 1998, p 11.

10. www.distribnet.com.

CHAPTER

Financing the Venture

7

Chapter Objectives

After completing this chapter, you should be able to

■ Prepare credible, meaningful forecasts of sales and expenses that can serve as the basis of a convincing financial plan.

■ Develop *pro-forma* financial statements that provide quantitative targets for progress measurement during implementation.

■ Examine the impact of variations in values of key variables on the profitability of a venture.

■ Construct a cash-flow statement to determine the capital requirements and their timing in bringing the venture to self-sufficiency.

■ Devise a financing strategy that optimizes use of the various methods for financing a venture.

■ "Sell" your project to prospective stakeholders and your "support structure" of family, banker, accountant, and so forth.

FINANCIAL PLANNING OVERVIEW

Financial planning of the sort used in a business plan is essential for all companies, not just start-ups. The process of putting together financial forecasts enables entrepreneurs and managers to spot both potential shortfalls and opportunity areas much sooner than they might otherwise be noticed. Still, the reluctance of many entrepreneurs to prepare business plans is often based on their discomfort with making financial forecasts.

When hopeful entrepreneurs do prepare plans, bankers and investors complain that the financial plans they receive are often sloppy and incomplete. "A lot of the plans that come across my desk are pretty pathetic," says Michael Carter, managing director of Carter & Co., an investment-banking firm in Southport, Connecticut.

Why is this process viewed as so difficult? Because plans are like term papers: You're never sure what information is supposed to be in them, how it's supposed to be arranged, and whether you have caught all the mistakes. These fears have spawned an industry, business plan assistance.

ENTREPRENEURIAL RESOURCE   Need Help with That Business Plan?

Nancy Russell is a business-development officer at the Irvine, California, branch of the Money Store, a leading Small Business Administration lender with offices in every state. In meeting with entrepreneurs seeking loans, Russell notes one universal trait: "They all roll their eyes when I tell them they have to do a business plan."

Help Is on the Way

1. *Get someone else to write it.*

To avoid the headache of writing a business plan, some small-company CEOs farm out the task to accountants or consultants who specialize in plans. Many are listed on the Internet. Brett Silvers, chairman and president of First National Bank of New England, says the plans prepared by accountants are the best he encounters: complete and professional looking.

That's what Laurel Hendrickson hoped for when she hired the local office of a national consulting firm two years ago to help her prepare a plan for Global Business Solutions, her $10 million computer consulting and software business in Costa Mesa, California. The cost: a hefty $80,000. "It ended up being a very poor investment," she says. "We got busy, and the consultants ended up doing the plan by themselves, without input from us. So it didn't focus on the things we felt were important. Plus, we never learned how to do a plan ourselves." Global's plan is now collecting dust on a shelf in Hendrickson's office.

Others are not convinced of the wisdom of using consultants. Michael Carter of Carter & Co. says that "the plans they create may have all the right pieces, but they don't sell the company well." When an outsider writes the plan, the entrepreneur can sometimes answer questions from prospective investors in a way that does not align with what they read in the business plan.

2. *Can't the computer do this?*

Ads for business plan software promise that, for $50 to $100, their products will help you create professional, "winning" plans. But do they?

They can help you organize your work, forcing you to think logically about many of the issues confronting new business efforts. Most offer tips and suggestions regarding what to think about when preparing a plan, and then help you assemble the package into a credible whole. Some even provide business tips and a list of resources you can consult for more information.

These ads are obviously convincing to some prospective entrepreneurs. Two leading business plan software vendors, Jian Tools for Sales, in Mountain View, California, and Palo Alto Software, in Eugene, Oregon, both report 50 percent sales growth over the past three years. According to PC Data, a Reston, Virginia, company that tracks software sales, $12 million worth of business-plan software was sold through retail channels in 1995.

3. *Use a template* (see "Attachment: Business Plan Template," at the end of this chapter).

ESTIMATING AND FORECASTING

The information necessary for the financial plan section of the business plan depends on the company's stage of development and the objectives of the plan. An existing company will have historical data available, and more complete financial statements will be expected than for a start-up. For any company seeking financing, the plan should describe in general terms the type and amount of funding being requested.

The company's financial statements are the core of the business plan's financial information section. They present the company's past results, where applicable, and its forecasts for the future. For new companies seeking capital, we must forecast sales along with information on cost of goods sold, selling and administrative expenses, and cash flows.

The accounting firm Deloitte & Touche LLP suggests the following parameters for financial plan forecasts:[1]

- The typical business-plan forecast should cover three to five years.
- Cashflow and income statements should be shown on a monthly basis for the first two years; thereafter, they can be shown on a quarterly basis. The prospective balance sheets should be prepared on at least a quarterly basis for the first two years and annually thereafter.
- A forecast should represent your best estimate of future operations. To enable the investor or lender to evaluate the reliability of that estimate, you must provide the assumptions used in preparing the forecast. To the extent possible, your assumptions should be supported by facts, market surveys, or detailed analyses, and reflect conditions in your industry.

The sales forecast "scales" the business. It determines the amount of people, space, and equipment the venture will require, which can then be related to financial requirements. Often, separate statements are produced for optimistic, expected, and pessimistic (OEP) projections.

Questions that can help lead us toward meaningful sales projections include: How big is the market? Is it growing? What share can we reasonably expect? How long will it take us to get there?

The sales forecast should conform to our earlier description of the market, the marketing strategy, and our anticipated position in the market, as described in the marketing section of the business plan. For example, our market share projection should be consistent with our estimate of the total market and our competitive advantage over others.

We can estimate how many units of each of our products we expect to sell, and at what price, extending these figures to yield projected sales dollars. We may project future sales over the planning period as a percentage increase in dollar volume each month. Comparative information adds credibility and perspective; government and trade association publications can be productive sources.

Success certainly requires that sales be made at a profit, and this profit is generally expressed in terms of "margin." The margin percentage, often called gross margin, is that fraction of our sales dollars that exceeds the cost of the goods sold. For example, if our product sells for $100, and we pay $80 for it, then each sale yields $20 margin, or 20 percent of sales.

Ideally, we should analyze the material, labor, and any other elements that go into making the product to determine our cost of goods sold. Where this is impractical, industry norms for gross margin can be adapted to our concept to yield margin dollars. With margin dollars we pay operating expenses; whatever then remains is profit, often called net margin.

The break-even point is that sales level at which margin dollars just equal operating expenses. A critical issue in the early financial analysis is whether the market potential of the product supports the break-even sales level.

Where does this sales level fall within our OEP spectrum? Should we proceed if break-even requires our most optimistic sales projection? Should we reexamine our numbers? Which can be changed or improved (sales, margins, expenses)? Would selling at a smaller margin percentage increase sales sufficiently to increase total margin dollars? Can expenses be cut?

MINICASE 7.1   Forecasting for Light-Guard Manufacturing

In the previous chapter, we established in our marketing plan that the Light-Guard product (LG1) would sell for $70. Based on information gathered in the building of the prototype, company president I. M. Bright has developed an estimate of unit production costs, as follows:

Materials	$15.00
Subcontractor circuit board assembly	$10.00
Assembly, inspection, testing, and packaging for shipping	<u>$10.00</u>
Total Product Cost (per unit)	$35.00
Net selling price by Light-Guard Manufacturing	$70.00
Cost of Goods Sold (Product Cost) per unit	<u>$35.00</u>
Gross profit per unit	$35.00
Margin	50%

Further, Mr. Bright has estimated that operating expenses for the plant in the first year, exclusive of production expenses, will be $213,000. This includes marketing, administrative, and engineering expenses.

How many units will Light-Guard have to sell to cover operating expenses? After the cost of producing the unit, the company grosses $35 on each LG1 it sells. The number of unit sales required to cover nonproduction expenses is then $213,000/$35 per unit, or about 6,100 units. The break-even point is then at annual sales of 6,100 units. Projected sales for year 1 were 7,000 units.

Study Questions

1. Do you think that expected sales exceeding the break-even point by only about 15 percent offers sufficient margin for error? What would you consider a comfortable percentage?

_____

_____

_____

2. How is the competition likely to respond to Light-Guard's entry into the market? How might their response affect the break-even analysis?

_____

_____

_____

The reliability of any forecast is dependent on how accurate the underlying assumptions turn out to be. We should identify the most critical assumptions used, and then determine what the impact would be if those assumptions were changed. Investors, in particular, may want to see the effect of variations in the forecast on the profitability of the venture.

Sensitivity of financial performance to changes in sales assumptions are particularly critical. If we achieve profitability quickly when we project an annual growth rate of 50 percent, what would the results be with a growth rate of 30 percent? The slower rise in sales extends the time required to reach profitability, and could possibly lead to severe cash-flow problems.

The expense section of the statement can be divided into functional categories such as personnel, administrative, sales expense, and operations. Within these categories, it is helpful to develop estimates as sums of items that can be priced relatively easily. For example, summing estimates of such things as rent, vehicle expense, utilities, and supplies will lead to a better estimate than picking a figure for overall operating costs.

Personnel expense consists of salaries (often split into "Officers" and "Others") and related costs, such as payroll taxes and benefits. These costs are sometimes allocated based on personnel functions, that is, salary and benefits for salespersons are charged to sales expense, and so on. Other sales expenses include advertising and promotion, and sales commissions.

Initially, marketing expense estimates should be based on the activities necessary to meeting the goals of the marketing plan. This plan should include a personnel forecast and the related costs, sales commission arrangements, trade show costs, promotional campaigns, and overall advertising costs. From this analysis we can estimate marketing expense as a percentage of sales, and apply this factor to the sales projection to calculate marketing expense in subsequent years.

General and administrative expenses, such as salaries for administrative and support personnel, rent, and supplies, generally can be estimated from personnel and floor-space requirements, and market rates for these items.

CASE STUDY 7.1 *Evaluating Business Plan Programs*

Business plan programs generally take one of two approaches. Some use generic templates to organize plan content; others are interactive applications that take the planner through interviews and/or samples to customize the plan.

TEMPLATE APPROACH

The first provides templates for popular word processing and spreadsheet programs. Most include word processing documents that are preformatted with sample text, or with instructions that indicate where you should place your own text and totals, a kind of modified fill-in-the-blanks approach.

Critics suggest that such programs are simply a collection of "boilerplate" text, charts, and spreadsheets. When you install Jian's market-leading BizPlan Builder, for example, you are simply storing six or seven of their word-processor and spreadsheet documents files. There is no executable software at all.

But having templates to organize all your data can be a valuable assist. One entrepreneur that used the Jian package praised it over the "from scratch" method: "I had done plans in the past by hand, but it was tedious and I was never sure that I had covered everything." Another suggests that "the program doesn't write the plan for you, but it disciplines you and helps you organize and distill your thoughts."

INTERACTIVE APPLICATIONS

The interactive group guides you through building a custom plan with an interview, or helps you develop text and numbers by following examples. The interactive products generally use a split screen for the text or financial sections of your plan, offering explanations or samples in the screen's top half and a custom word processor document or spreadsheet in the lower half. The programs then consolidate text, graphics, and attractive charts into a printable plan, with a wide range of content and format quality.

Although developers such as Palo Alto Software like to refer to their product as "content-rich software," none of the packages offers anything close to artificial intelligence or expert-system technology. Palo Alto's Business Plan Pro does "interview" the user before it sets up a template, to determine the type of business (service, retail, distribution, manufacturing, or a mix), the age of the business (start-up or an ongoing operation), and the form sales take (cash or credit). Depending on the user's answers, the software brings up different screens for inputting text or numbers.

As one satisfied user of interactive software puts it: "Most small-business people don't have an MBA and don't know how to calculate things like debt ratios or net-income projections. But the software walks you through that, and having those numbers really impresses lenders."

CAUTION

The marketing hype for business-plan software runs ahead of what the products actually deliver. No amount of automation can turn a lousy idea into a winning business. Nor can any of the available software relieve you of having to think hard about how you intend to execute your idea.

Business-plan software may generate a glossier plan than most entrepreneurs would be able to create on their own, but by definition it is going to produce a pretty generic business plan. Can a much-like-the-others plan effectively sell a business and its management? Timothy Dineen, founder of Leprechaun Capital, an investment-advisory firm in Lilburn, Georgia, believes that investors can easily spot "canned" plans. "The most important thing a venture capitalist is looking for is quality of management. You can sabotage your credibility with some of those packages," he says.

Many business-plan packages seem to treat planning as a hoop entrepreneurs have to jump through to get money, as though being successful at raising capital were the key to being successful in business. Business Plan Pro addresses plan implementation. There's a table for tracking date and budget milestones, and the software allows you to keep three versions of the numbers: the plan, the actual, and the difference between the two. Tim Berry, program author and Palo Alto's CEO, says, "It's important that plans stay alive and not end up in a drawer."

Philip Albinus, software editor for the magazine *Home Office Computing,* conducted evaluations of several business-planning software packages in 1996 (we have added their Web addresses). Below are three of those reviews:[2]

PLAN WRITE 4.0 FOR WINDOWS
(www.brs-inc.com): RATED *EXCELLENT*

Plan Write is the best product for guiding you through the stormy waters of creating a business plan. Even before you start the interactive interview process, Plan Write can step you through a basic break-even analysis. The program asks you for the unit cost, average unit price, number of units you will sell, and operating expenses, then displays a break-even chart with explanatory text customized to your situation.

When dealing with financial information, Plan Write stands apart from the rest. You enter values one-by-one on some screens, viewing an explanation for each entry at the top. The program's "Text" screen offers an explanation of each topic (called a Rationale) and an example at the top of the screen, either of which you can copy completely with a single mouse click to the bottom half of the screen, where you compose your text. As you progress, you'll soon see a summary spreadsheet that consolidates all the previous information.

For screens that let you enter data for an entire year, you left-click the mouse button on the row header (such as Royalties) to read an explanation of what should be included in this category. Your financial data is instantly reflected in the good cross-section of charts. Double-click a bar in a bar chart and Plan Write takes you back to the financial screen where the data was originally entered; click on the Next button and you're back to your chart.

The program includes an excellent outline view for jumping between topics, and you can even use it to insert new text topics, spreadsheets, or charts anywhere you like. If you're stumped for ideas, click on the Internet button for access to more than 100 Web sites containing tips for using the program, improving your business plan, and locating investors.

BUSINESS PLAN PRO 1.2 FOR WINDOWS
(www.pasware.com): RATED *GOOD*

Business Plan Pro offers excellent interactive guidance and sophisticated tools for creating detailed business plans. The program opens a split screen for developing the text of your plan. It provides instructions or examples in the top half of the screen allowing you to toggle between the program's instructions and your plan. In the lower panel, you simply enter your own text. You can copy and paste from the well-worded sample text to your own business plan.

Business Plan Pro uses its own integrated word processor and spreadsheet, though the spreadsheet offers few timesavers. Where Business Plan Pro really shines is in the quality of the finished business plan. The text, tables, and charts are automatically integrated and professionally formatted.

BIZPLANBUILDER 5.0 FOR WINDOWS
(www.jianusa.com): RATED *FAIR*

BizPlanBuilder includes separate word processing templates for each component of your business plan. We started by filling in the Vision/Mission template, discussing where our company is going. In the Company Overview template, we entered basic information concerning company structure, management, and alliances. Other templates include Product/Service strategy, Market Analysis, Marketing Plan, and Financial Plan. Sample nondisclosure and cover letters are included as is a list of 20 key business-plan questions.

Fill in the templates after reading the appropriate section in the Reference Guide, a user manual that offers an overview and points to consider for each template. We found it to be up-to-date, because it includes a brief description of limited liability companies (LLC).

Financial Plan spreadsheet templates offer one- and five-year balance sheets, cash-flow and income statements, as well as break-even analyses, budgets, and gross-profit analyses. There is also a personal financial statement and a working capital worksheet. Unfortunately, the word processing templates take little advantage of a word processor's power; if you want professional-looking results, prepare to do a lot of reformatting before you're finished.

STUDY QUESTIONS

Visit the three Web sites and view improvements since the 1996 reviews, and any available sample plans and case studies. You may be able to download a demo copy, and try entering information on your business idea.

Would you change the ratings above based on new information provided at the site?

_____

_____

_____

Evaluate the package that you think is best for your needs. What features are most useful? What features or resources would you not use? How much of the final plan would reflect the help offered by the software?

_____

_____

_____

PRO-FORMA FINANCIAL STATEMENTS

"Pro forma" is defined as an adjective meaning "provided in advance to prescribe form or describe items." In the business plan, we present our expected financial performance, *pro forma,* within the structure of standard financial statements as would be used to report actual performance. These statements usually include an income statement, showing the profitability of the venture, a cash-flow statement, highlighting cash needs and availability, and a balance sheet, showing assets and liabilities.

In building a spreadsheet *pro-forma* income statement, we are building a model of the business. It should be constructed using variables for key factors, rather than constant values. For example, we should express margin and expenses as a percentage of sales, sales increases with time as a percentage growth, and so on. Then we can experiment with a range of reasonable alternatives for these "basis variables," such as estimated sales and profit margins.

CASE STUDY *Light-Guard Manufacturing, Ltd.* 7.2

INTRODUCTION

When I. M. Bright first got the idea for forming Light-Guard Manufacturing, his first concern was whether the "numbers work," that is, whether it could become a commercially viable venture. Earlier, we saw his sales and margin projections, and they indicated that the company could

quickly become a factor in the growing electronic controls market.

Next, Bright turned to how large an investment would be required to get the company to be self-sustaining. He apportioned his first year's sales and expense estimates by calendar quarter:

1999: Quarter	1st	2nd	3rd	4th	TOTAL
INCOME					
SALES	$0	$49,000	$171,500	$269,500	$490,000
CGS (50%)	0	24,500	85,750	134,750	245,000
GROSS MARGIN	$0	$24,500	$85,750	$134,750	$245,000
EXPENSES					TOTAL
Sales Expense	$7,000	$40,000	$25,000	$34,000	$106,000
Admin/Overhead	11,000	21,000	16,000	24,000	72,000
Engineering	13,000	10,000	6,000	6,000	35,000
TOTAL EXPENSES	$31,000	$71,000	$47,000	$64,000	$213,000
PROFIT/LOSS	($31,000)	($46,500)	$38,750	$70,750	$32,000

Bright assumed that there would be no sales in the first quarter, as the company geared up production and began to call on customers. He then distributed his first year sales estimate over the remaining three quarters as 10 percent, 35 percent and 55 percent of the annual figure. Expenses were distributed using his best judgment of when they would occur. With these estimates, the company showed profits beginning in its third quarter, and a cumulative profit by the end of the year. He knew he had a winner on his hands.

While the income statement measures the performance of the company from an accounting standpoint, the cash-flow statement focuses on the more tangible issue of whether our cash balance allows us to meet our obligations. To estimate the investment required to get the company started and ride out the months of losses, he then developed a cash-flow statement. In his first pass, he assumed that the initial cash balance of the company would be $0:

CASH FLOW					TOTAL
Beginning	$0	($80,000)	($245,000)	($304,000)	
+Cash Received	$0	$24,500	$122,500	$245,000	$392,000
−Expenses	($31,000)	($71,000)	($47,000)	($64,000)	($213,000)
−Production Costs	$0	($24,500)	($85,750)	($134,750)	($245,000)
−Equipment/Inventory	($49,000)	($94,000)	($48,750)	($42,250)	($234,000)
=Cash Out	($80,000)	($245,000)	($304,000)	($300,000)	

The cash-flow statement shows that our deficit grows as large as $304,000 in the third quarter before beginning a gradual turnaround. Bright ran these statements on his spreadsheet program for two additional years to confirm that this was the low point. Let us now replace the $0 starting cash balance with the $310,000 we hope to raise from investors, to eliminate the negative ending balances:

CASH FLOW					TOTAL
Beginning	$310,000	$230,000	$65,000	$6,000	
+Cash Received	$0	$24,500	$122,500	$245,000	$392,000
−Expenses	($31,000)	($71,000)	($47,000)	($64,000)	($213,000)
−Production Costs	$0	($24,500)	($85,750)	($134,750)	($245,000)
−Equipment/Inventory	($49,000)	($94,000)	($48,750)	($42,250)	($234,000)
=Cash Out	$230,000	$65,000	$6,000	$10,000	

Note in the first quarter that our cash requirements include the $31,000 in expenses shown in the income statement and $49,000 for equipment and some start-up inventory. The latter figure did not show up in the income statement because it has no impact on profitability; it is simply converting one asset, cash, for others, equipment and inventory.

Note too that cash received is not the same as sales. Most sales are made on credit, and payment often falls into another accounting period.

From an estimating standpoint, our problem is solved! From a practical standpoint, we now have to find investors and convince them that these estimates are valid and that they will get an attractive return on their investments.

Whereas the income and cash-flow statements show performance over some time period (here, the quarter), the balance sheet shows another perspective. It is a "snapshot" at a point in time, generally year-end, that balances assets and liabilities. The excess of assets over liabilities is the net worth of the company (often termed "owners' equity"), an indication of its financial strength.

Note how the balance sheet relates to the other statements:

- Cash at the end of the year equals last-quarter ending cash from the cash-flow statement.
- Accounts receivable equals sales less cash received.
- Equipment/Inventory, combined in cash flow, are split between current and long-term in the balance sheet.
- The net worth of the company is equal to the initial investment plus profits earned.

BALANCE SHEET, as of December 31, 1999

Current Assets

	Cash	$10,000
	Accounts Receivable	$98,000
	Inventory	$120,000
Long-Term Assets		
	Equipment	$114,000
TOTAL Assets		$342,000
	Liabilities	$0
	Net Worth	$342,000
TOTAL Liabilities and Net Worth		$342,000

STUDY QUESTIONS

1. As a prospective investor, are you convinced of the company's viability? What else would you want to know?

   _____

   _____

2. Do you feel that the $310,000 asked for will be enough? With such large cash flows, is a $6,000 cushion enough? How much would you recommend? What are the consequences of falling short?

   _____

   _____

3. What estimates do you think are weakest? Are sales estimates too optimistic? Can a 50 percent margin hold in the marketplace? Are the cash requirements properly distributed over time?

   _____

   _____

The estimation of cash required by Light-Guard was simplified by the fact that we were raising it by selling "equity," that is, partial ownership of the company. Had Bright been trying to maintain complete ownership, and borrowing to avoid a shortfall, administrative expenses would have included interest on the amount borrowed.

Estimation of interest paid on a loan would then be "iterative." That is, the amount to be borrowed would be estimated, yielding a number for interest expense; this interest figure becomes part of the profit/loss picture, which determines how much must be borrowed.

Seldom are more than two or three passes required to converge to a final estimate. Spreadsheet programs make the process simple, often providing a method of calculating the amount directly.

Exercise 7.1   Developing the Financial Plan
Develop a sales forecast for the venture you are considering, or for the coffee shop. Describe the basis for this forecast. Identify the expense areas, and take a first pass at estimating these values. (We will have an opportunity to refine these estimates later.)

A critical aspect of the *pro-forma* statements is internal consistency. The cash-flow statement, income statement, and balance sheet must be based on the same assumptions. For example, sales forecasts will appear on the income statement. Cash receipts, as shown on the cash-flow statement, must be a function of those sales forecasts and your estimate of the collection period. Outstanding accounts receivable, as shown on the balance sheet, is then the amount of charge sales, less cash receipts against these accounts, and less an amount or percentage assumed as an allowance for bad debts.

Purchases must include the level of inventory needed to support your estimated sales volume. The timing of your inventory purchases will be a major factor in forecasting your cash needs.

Cash received includes all forms of payment, such as cash, checks, and credit card sales. Payments on charge sales trail the sales by an amount of time generally referred to as the collection period, for example, 40 days between sale and payment. Industry statistics may provide a good indication of the collection period to expect, and a percentage allowance for bad debts.

Many business owners prefer to maintain enough cash (including cash investments) to cover three months' disbursements, in order to allow some cushion for unexpected problems and costs. If you raise capital by selling stock, your investors will expect you to invest any idle funds in low-risk, quickly redeemable investments, such as money-market funds or certificates of deposit.

Just as we must have additional cash to cover collection periods, we get a small cash cushion from payment periods for the goods that we buy. Initially, however, we should pay promptly to establish a good credit history. Therefore, we should assume that our payment period will generally be shorter than the industry average during the early years.

Cash flow is a particularly difficult issue for start-up businesses. Expenses are often higher than expected, as the entrepreneur begins to acquire the tools necessary to do business. Deposits must be made on rental space and utilities. Many of these disbursements must be made before any cash is collected. In the start-up months, expenses generally exceed collections; initial marketing efforts may take several months before yielding results.

In the balance sheet, assets are classified as "current" or "long-term." Current assets include cash and "liquid" investments such as certificates of deposit and items relatively readily converted to cash, such as inventory and accounts receivable.

For companies already in business, current asset values presented in financial statements are often discounted to reflect some fraction of the inventory being obsolete, and some amount of accounts receivable being uncollectible. This is not generally applicable to start-up ventures, which start with fresh inventory and new accounts.

Other assets are primarily "fixed," that is, they have some relatively long service life over which their value is amortized. These include property and improvements, vehicles, and equipment. These assets are generally depreciated aggressively, taking maximum advantage of tax law, and this frequently causes fixed asset values to be understated relative to the market value of such assets.

Liabilities are generally classified as "current" and "long-term." Current liabilities consist of items due in the relatively short term, such as accruals of sales and payroll taxes, and "accounts payable," or invoices for goods received. Long-term liabilities are generally "notes payable" with fixed repayment terms.

The difference between assets and liabilities, as though the company were being liquidated, is the net worth of the business, or "owners' equity." Equity is generally shown on the liability side of the balance sheet, since it is conceptually a debt to the owner.

The balance sheet, generally produced at year-end, must be consistent with the income statement with the same ending date. Accumulated profits shown on the income statement become a gain in equity on the balance sheet. Similarly, purchases become assets, note payments decrease loan balances, and depreciation reduces asset values.

Exercise 7.2 Refining the Financial Plan

Refine the expense estimates of Exercise 7.1. Cite sources of expense information. Construct a cash-flow statement coordinated to the income and expense data. Use a starting cash figure of zero to see how overdrawn we would get without start-up funds.

THE FUNDRAISING PROCESS

How Financial Experts Evaluate Forecasts

Potential investors closely examine a plan's forecasts and assumptions for reasonableness. Items of particular interest are margins, asset management, and company valuation.

Margins

Investors evaluate your gross margin, and key expenses such as marketing and administrative as a percentage of sales. They then compare these percentages with those of other companies in your industry. A gross margin of 50 percent of sales, forecast in an industry where other companies are realizing only 30 percent, can raise a red flag. When prospective investors question your assumptions, be prepared to defend them with supporting data.

Asset Management

Your forecasted balance sheets should demonstrate that you understand how to manage cash, receivables, and inventory. Such evidence is extremely important to potential investors and bankers alike. Again, comparison to industry norms is often used.

Company Valuation

Investors will often estimate a company's value by looking at forecasted earnings (profits) at the end of a certain period (usually three to five years), and multiplying those earnings by a factor that is relevant to your industry. In growth industries, such as computing or telecommunications, investors might use an earnings multiple of 15 or 25. In consumer-oriented business, a multiple of 5 to 10 might be used.

For example, Light-Guard forecast annual sales of $3 million at the end of three years, with a profit of just over $1 million. Multiplying the forecasted profit by 10 yields an estimated value of $10 million. This is the value one could assume for your company if it went public or were offered for sale.

Investors use this figure to indicate whether your company will be large enough someday to make their investment worthwhile, and to determine whether their percentage of ownership in the company would be commensurate with the amount of their investment.

Determining Capital Requirements

The amount of capital required to start a business may be considered to be made up of two components: the amount needed before the first sale is made, and the amount needed to cover operating losses from opening day until profitability is reached.

Half of business startups achieve their first sale after having invested less than $25,000, based on data from the National Federation of Independent Businesses (NFIB) through the early 1990s, adjusted for inflation to 1996 dollars. The Wells Fargo/NFIB report on Business Starts and Stops for 1996[3] shows further that most startups are rather modest ventures; two-thirds were home-based businesses and nearly half were begun on a less than full-time basis.

Additional significant assets could be needed after opening for business, but before profitability is reached. To the extent that we can delay their acquisition without harming our business prospects, we can lessen our capital requirements. Often we can lease equipment, sometimes with credit toward later purchase, until our longer-term needs become clearer.

Pre-start-up outlays and equipment needs are fairly tangible and easy to conceptualize, but the other component of our capital requirement, the accumulated operating loss (AOL), is more difficult to estimate. In the process of reaching profitability, we will probably have to endure a period of operating losses. The total of these losses is often termed AOL, and the need to finance this amount adds to our capital requirement.

The earlier Light-Guard case demonstrated one way to estimate AOL, that is, by running our company model with a zero starting cash amount. Starting with no cash, we notice that period-ending cash figures decreased for three calendar quarters to its largest negative balance ($304,000) before the company reached profitability and began to turn the balance back upward. This most negative value is our best estimate of AOL, and our starting cash must be this amount plus some contingency cushion.

We now have estimates for how much we must invest before opening, and how much working capital we need to ensure that we can sustain the business until sales margins begin to exceed expenses. As we assess our capital requirement, it is important that we not cut it too close.

Some conservatism must be applied to the model, and some contingencies must be allowed for. We want to provide enough capital to make the business a long-term success; potentially profitable businesses often close because they lack adequate operating capital in the start-up period. On the other hand, providing for too large a cushion could make the investment less attractive.

Exercise 7.3 How Much Do We Need to Raise?
Establish the amount of start-up funds needed for your project. Suggest a mix of personal funds, loans, and money from outside investors to meet this need. Construct a balance sheet, coordinated to the previous statements, to describe the financial position at start-up.

In order to be able to calibrate performance against expectations, we must document the assumptions made in arriving at our estimates, and establish milestones and benchmarks for our financial performance. It is much harder to be objective about how we are doing once into the venture, and possibly faced with the question of whether it is worth continuing. Where investors or lenders are involved, part of their financial commitment to the venture may be contingent on reaching these milestones.

The most significant milestones are generally the amount of time to reach profitability and the amount of time before accumulated profits exceed the accumulated operating losses associated with start-up. Light-Guard, for example, projected its first profitable period as the third year, and by the fourth year had covered all previous losses. How do you think their investors would react if, at the end of their first year, losses significantly exceeded projections?

Once capital requirements are established, we must consider whether we can fund the start-up ourselves. Otherwise, we now enter the fundraising stage.

Sources of Funds

While the discussion of capital requirements may have seemed pessimistic, with its mention of exit costs and whether it is worth the effort to continue, pessimism is what will generally greet the entrepreneur at fundraising. A prospective stakeholder, that is, an investor or a lender, generally applies a significant skepticism factor to projections for new ventures.

It is the entrepreneur's dream under consideration, about which he or she has great difficulty being objective. Stakeholders have often seen ventures fail, but never have they seen an entrepreneur who allowed for that possibility in advance.

Stakeholders generally expect a substantial financial commitment to the venture by the entrepreneur. Their sense is that it should not be easy for the entrepreneur to give the venture a half-hearted try, leaving the consequences of failure to the stakeholders.

The entrepreneur's financial commitment is often a combination of personal funds and investments and loans from "friendly" sources, that is, family and friends, as shown in Figure 7.1.

Stakeholders are often hard to find at start-up, but sources of assistance are available. A good starting point is the U.S. Small Business Administration (SBA). Their Small Business Investment Company (SBIC) program allows private investment partnerships, or SBICs, to leverage their own capital using SBA guarantees. SBA guarantees of bank loans to small businesses totaled about $9 billion in 1995. The SBA's Microloan program was created in 1992 for borrowers who need $25,000 or less.

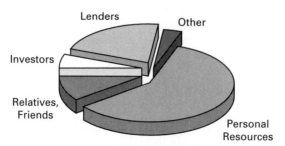

FIGURE 7.1 Sources of Start-up Capital

ENTREPRENEURIAL RESOURCE

MESBICs

Working capital, used to cover the day-to-day expenses of the business, is the most common type of financing, and often the hardest to obtain. Rudy Lombard, president of Lombard Tire Sales, Inc., borrowed money to start his business, but within a year he was having trouble meeting daily expenses. Because his existing start-up loan wasn't paid off, he found banks unwilling to lend him any more capital.

Lombard sought help from the local Minority Enterprise Small Business Investment Company (MESBIC). "They got me a short revolving line of credit at the bank at a competitive interest rate," says Lombard. "That's how I developed my credibility with the bank, and since then I've been getting lines of credit utilizing receivables and inventory as collateral."

Soon, Lombard paid off the $100,000 he borrowed from MESBIC. Last year MESBIC invested $1 million in his tire company, in exchange for preferred stock. At the end of five years, MESBIC will sell the stock back to Lombard at book value. "They're on my board of directors, so they're very helpful in guiding me in my business. If it's not successful, then they don't make any money," says Lombard.

Serafin Mariel, president and CEO of New York National Bank, recommends that a borrower start with the local economic development agency or minority enterprise lender. "Community-based programs usually lend at a very good rate, in some cases less than banks," Mariel says.

Many community banks and minority enterprise lenders work in conjunction with Small Business Development Centers, which are funded by state and federal governments. The centers provide only technical assistance, but this includes preparation of paperwork to get a loan.

Centers exist in all 50 states and may be accessed through each state's commerce department or department of small business. These centers can introduce patrons to local capital programs for minority businesses, including the SBA's Minority Pre-qualified Program.

"The Minority Pre-qualified Program is open to any business that has 51 percent minority ownership, and we will lend up to $250,000," says Lorenzo Flores, assistant district director of economic development at the Los Angeles SBA office. "We look for good credit; a couple of 'dings' are OK, but nothing major. The person must be of good character."

Microloans

Banks are seldom interested in making small start-up loans, especially to anyone without a business track record or collateral, or with a weak credit history. Under these circumstances, a Small Business Administration microloan may be your best bet.

Michael Day wanted to do more than just get by financially, working for someone else in a hardware store. With a wife and family to support in an area plagued by the fluctuations of a tourist economy and a declining oil industry, Day figured that a take-out food store could succeed, especially with his recipe for Buffalo-style chicken wings. But no bank was interested in the expense and risk of making him the modest $12,000 loan he needed.

A local banker then told Day about the Small Business Administration's microloan program. And now, since getting his loan, Day is the proud owner of Zingers Buffalo-Style Take Out. "I didn't have a lot of collateral. And banks aren't in the business of prospective investments," Day says. "It was a surprise, the fact that that kind of money was available." He now makes very affordable monthly payments of $260 on a five-year, $12,000 loan at a fixed rate of 11 percent.

The SBA describes its microloan program as "designed to encourage economic self-determination among the many thousands of individuals now standing on the sidelines of the economic playing field." Borrowers must present a realistic business plan that shows they can repay the loan while supporting themselves and their enterprises. A perfect credit history or even personal equity in the planned business is not necessary.

Microloans of as little as a few hundred dollars are available; these are often used to start up small services businesses such as lawn and cleaning contractors. Loans up to $25,000 are made through the program, although the SBA tries to keep its average loan size to about $7,500. Those who seek to borrow more than $15,000 must show they cannot get credit elsewhere on comparable terms. To find a microloan provider near you, contact your SBA district office or call the SBA Answer Desk at 800-8-ASK-SBA.

FUNDRAISING STRATEGIES

How much money is required to start a business? Depending on the type and scope of the business, you must purchase licenses, pay for permits, engage professional services (e.g., legal, accounting, insurance, etc.), secure a location and make the necessary deposits, tailor location to your needs, buy furniture, fixtures, and equipment, and so forth.

You may require initial retail inventory, repair parts, and accessories, and office supplies such as business cards, letterhead, envelopes, and staples. Once you start operating, you must replenish inventory and pay day-to-day expenses including rent and salaries.

How do we raise the money required to get a new business off the ground? The basic decision to be made in raising the required money (or "capital") beyond our current resources is how much will be borrowed, and how much will be raised by selling equity, that is, shares of ownership in the venture.

To the entrepreneur, the advantage of using "equity financing" is that *the investor is sharing the risks of the venture;* this lowers expenses, since there is no debt service to be paid. The investor also shares the rewards, however, and the entrepreneur must be careful not to sell the equity too cheaply. "Debt financing," on the other hand, *adds to our fixed costs, but makes no claim beyond the amount of the debt,* no matter how great our success. Unfortunately, lender requirements for substantial loans are generally very difficult for start-ups to meet.

Debt Financing

Bank loans approved for day-to-day business operations (generally called "working capital") have characteristics that make them different from those approved for equipment purchases (long-term capital or capital assets). "Term" refers to the time for which money (a secured loan) is required and the period over which the loan repayment is scheduled. A bank loan officer can often assist you in finding a workable combination of these different types of capital.

Long-Term Loans

A loan is considered long term when the scheduled repayment of the loan and the estimated useful life of the assets purchased (e.g., building, land, machinery, computers, equipment, shelving) is expected to exceed one year.

Long-term loans are normally secured, first by the new assets purchased (generally up to 60% of their cost) and then by other unencumbered physical assets of the business (for the remaining 40%). Lenders also frequently require personal guarantees from the principals. The personal guarantee commits you, if the company is unable to repay the loan, to do so personally. Once the business is sufficiently established to carry debt on its own security, you should ask the lender to transact future loans without requiring your personal guarantee.

Debt lenders (creditors) make loans to businesses that exhibit strong management ability and steady growth potential. A written business plan, including a cash-flow statement demonstrating the ability of the business to repay the loan principal and interest over the term of the repayment schedule, is mandatory. The lender will expect you to have appropriate insurance to protect the assets.

Most people approach the subject of borrowing money with some trepidation. You should never view borrowing money from a commercial loan institution as begging for money. In fact, you will be "renting" money from people who, in turn, are soliciting your business. Banks, credit unions, finance companies, and others need your business to make their money work for them.

Your challenge, working with a loan officer, is to find that financial institution's product that best fits your circumstances. A loan officer's job is to rent money at profitable rates of interest with a minimum of risk; their goal is to recommend an astute investment, predicated on tested principles of lending.

Short-Term Loans

Short-term loans, generally those offered for less than one year, are often called "operating term loans." These can be used to finance the day-to-day operations of a business, including wages of employees and purchases of inventory and supplies, until sufficient revenues are accumulated to operate on a current basis. Short-term loans are very helpful in start-up situations and for seasonal businesses. Loans with a short, fixed term (sometimes called "bridge financing") can also be used to finance a company's accounts receivable while awaiting collections.

Inventories, other unencumbered assets, personal guarantees, and cosigners can be used to secure operations loans. Lenders normally charge a higher base rate of interest for operating loans, reflecting this relatively weaker security position.

Revolving Lines of Credit

A line of credit is a long-term commitment by a commercial lender to honor the day-to-day checks of a business up to a maximum figure agreed to in consultation with the business. The business then deposits sales revenues on a regular basis into the account to "buy down" the outstanding loan balance whenever there are funds available to do so.

This up-and-down fluctuating nature of the loan amount (account balance) is why it has come to be called a "revolving line of credit." There is no scheduled repayment of principal because there is no set principal amount of the loan.

Revolving lines of credit are popular credit vehicles for many businesses and manufacturers that require differing amounts of cash each month to meet their operating commitments. They want to pay only interest justified by the actual usage of borrowed cash, and they want to pay nothing at all when revenues are entirely sufficient to pay the month's expenses.

7.1

Expert Opinion: Commercial Banks and the Start-up Venture

Conventional bank loans are traditionally not used by start-up businesses. Banks do not *exclude* start-ups, but they look for collateral, solid credit, substantial capital and a business track record. "Most of the time, businesses start up with a few people and an idea. They borrow from family and friends, or they use personal credit cards to fund the growth," said Grant Pavolka (Seattle), Seafirst Bank's senior vice president for community business.

But there are lenders that target businesses that banks consider high-risk. The SBA works with the Private Industry Councils in many areas to provide loans, from $500 to $25,000, for small borrowers. Those loans are often for start-up businesses that are not quite able to get traditional bank loans.

In the northwestern U.S., the Cascadia Revolving Fund is a nonprofit group that makes business loans to women-owned, minority-owned and environmentally friendly businesses in Washington and Oregon. The fund tries to fill in part of the gap between start-up businesses and those stable enough for bank loans, said Dave Kleiber, associate director. "People come to us with nothing," he said. Good credit and collateral are important to Cascadia, but even more important are the person's knowledge of the market, determination and character.

Kleiber said he likes to spend a lot of time getting to know potential borrowers before lending, and Cascadia staff help fine-tune business plans. "You rely on your gut," Kleiber said. "Does this business make sense? Is this the person to do it? Some people out there tell a good story, and they want to do this badly, but they just can't." Thus far, Cascadia's gut reaction has proved fairly successful. Since 1987, the group has lent $3 million to more than 100 borrowers. Ninety percent have stayed in business, and the fund has only a 1 percent loan-loss ratio.

Source: *Seattle Times*, "Helping entrepreneurs make that step" by Leyla Kokmen, April 23, 1996 (www.seattletimes.com/extra/browse.html/biz_042396.html)

Trade Creditors

Suppliers generally offer terms of 30 days from delivery of goods for resale before payment is due; occasionally, vendors will offer 60-day payment terms. With newer, unproven operations, COD (cash on delivery) is often required.

Many suppliers offer a 2 percent discount to purchasers who pay in 10 days, or by the tenth of the following month (termed "2% 10th *prox*"). Foregoing a 2 percent discount generally only delays payment 20 days, and does not represent good cash management. Service charges (e.g., 1.5% per month interest) are generally imposed on account balances unpaid after 30 days.

A company with a substantial amount of accounts receivable can convert some to cash by a process called "factoring." Factoring companies buy accounts receivable at a discount, and assume the risk of collection. The discount is based on the age of the receivable; typical is 10 percent of the amount owed that is less than 30 days old, and 90 percent of the amount over 90 days old.

Commercial finance companies often advance funds against purchased goods (sometimes called "floor planning") receiving payment plus some interest charge as these goods are sold. Often we can negotiate full or partial advance payment from customers to help finance the costs related to taking on their business. In some project-oriented industries it is customary to receive partial payments at defined stages of project progress, prior to the completion of the project.

Consider requiring a deposit for all work. Deposits collected for work that involves special orders for goods or services will serve to prove that the customer was committed to the order and will prevent the business having to absorb costs resulting from nonpayment.

Equity Financing

Equity required for a new venture begins with funds from personal money of the entrepreneur (such as savings, inheritance, or personal loans from financial institutions, friends, relatives, and business associates). When 25 to 50 percent of the funds required by the business come from the entrepreneur's money, this shows a prospective lender or investor that the entrepreneur is prepared to assume a significant share of the risk of the venture.

The most accessible sources of personal money are savings, inheritances, and mortgage extensions on a personal residence. The next most common source is money borrowed from family and friends. Unfortunately, many cherished friendships and family relationships have been strained or even destroyed by using such arrangements.

If you borrow money from family members and/or friends, consider structuring the loan on a straight business basis. You may also want to provide some personal security or personal guarantee outside of the business itself. Often these persons are assuming a high risk, as a favor to you, with little real basis for the investment.

Funds required in excess of the entrepreneur's resources and ability to borrow must generally be raised from objective parties, in exchange for stock in (that is, partial ownership of) the venture. Such investments are normally unsecured, that is, they have no registered claim on any of the assets of the business. This approach leaves the business assets, such as equipment and inventory, available for use as collateral for loans.

Equity owners have accepted the risks and rewards that go with the business. The rewards are direct participation in the profits of that business as well as any appreciation in the perceived value of the shares. The risks represent the possibility that the share value could drop to zero.

MINICASE 7.2   Grandma Pfeiffer's Cakes-in-a-Jar

Before Richard Sears would invest in Grandma Pfeiffer's Cakes-in-a-Jar, which is just what its name implies, he told the founder that he would be the one in charge. "What I offer isn't money; it's my expertise," Sears says. "The only way I can leverage my expertise is to be here every day, in the thick of it, in control."

Linda Pfeiffer, the founder of Grandma Pfeiffer's Products, Inc., admits that giving way to Sears was difficult. But, she also admits, she had little choice. While she may have been in charge of the company on paper, in reality it was spinning out of control.

Her product, cakes baked in jars with a shelf life of almost two years, grew from zero to $250,000 in sales in two years, but costs were spiraling much faster than revenues. "I had no partners to share my frustrations with, and I was running the business on a credit card," she remembers. "I'd been sleeping on the warehouse floor, and my marriage was crumbling."

Pfeiffer and Sears first met in February 1988 when Pfeiffer signed up for an entrepreneurship course taught by Sears. What started as a student-teacher relationship quickly moved beyond hypothetical casebook exercises. After class Pfeiffer grilled her professor. Should she take a contract from one of the country's largest food companies? What if she couldn't meet its demands? How should she manage a new-product introduction?

Six months later Sears offered to invest up to $150,000: $15,000 in equity and $75,000 in debt initially, with a verbal agreement to kick in more after the first year. With that investment, Sears owned 80 percent of the company and installed himself as president. Sears did a lot of legwork before investing. For example, he spent three months at trade shows selling Pfeiffer's cakes at the company's booth, gauging customer demand for himself before taking a stake in the company.

While Pfeiffer conjures up new twists on old cake recipes, alternate sales approaches, and creative marketing tactics, Sears talks of cost of goods sold, product specifications, and financing agreements. Sears feels it's his job to yank Pfeiffer "out of the engine room and teach her how to navigate." When food giants such as Hershey's came knocking on the door with offers of large contracts, Sears urged Pfeiffer to consider them, despite her mixed feelings about selling the company.

In two to three years Sears intends to be out of his management role at the company and expects at least a 20 percent return on his investment if all goes well. Each year, assuming Pfeiffer meets her sales projections, she earns back a percentage of the company. "This is patient money," Sears says. "You've got to be more patient than with your own company. It's hard," he continues. "I can't tell her about all the problems, or I risk squelching her fire, her excitement, and that's all that keeps this company going. This is her company; without her fire it fizzles."

Study Questions

1. Do you agree with Linda Pfeiffer's decision to yield control of her company to Sears? Why? Were there other alternatives that she should have considered? Which?

_____

_____

_____

2. How could Sears justify 80 percent ownership for only a $15,000 investment? Was Pfeiffer receiving enough credit for her "sweat equity"?

_____

_____

_____

Public Offerings

How do we identify prospective investors? We could sell stock to the public. The initial public offering (IPO) has traditionally not been an option for start-ups, however, unless they have a "breakthrough" product with high growth potential. The high costs involved make about $2 million the minimum feasible IPO; more often they are in the $8 million to $15 million range. Fortunately, alternative methods for limited public offerings, more suitable for smaller and start-up businesses, are beginning to become available.

ENTREPRENEURIAL RESOURCE   Direct Public Offerings

Adapted from "When Mom & Pop Go Public," by Stephanie Gruner:[4]

For most of this century, companies have tapped interstate public markets through stock brokerage firms (acting as "underwriters"), and complied with the stringent disclosure requirements of the U.S. Securities and Exchange Commission. Then, in 1989, the SEC approved a simpler way for small businesses to make a public offering, best known as a *small corporate offering registration* (SCOR). Enterprising company owners can now use SCORs to sell stock directly to investors rather than through Wall Street brokers.

Today, 45 states allow companies to use an implementation of SCOR called *direct public offerings* (DPOs) to raise up to $1 million in a 12-month period without filing with the SEC. The much simpler state filing procedures make these offerings considerably less expensive than offerings under SEC regulations. Last year 31 percent of all companies trying to raise public equity capital in the United States for the first time used DPOs. As the SEC continues to ease restrictions and the Internet becomes a more appealing venue for selling stock directly, that number promises to increase.

Although they're attractive to capital-hungry entrepreneurs, direct public offerings don't represent easy money. As Barry Guthary, chairman of the Small Business Committee of the North American Securities Administrators Association, puts it, "There's no simple way to get money from the public." According to the *SCOR Report,* a newsletter published by Tom Stewart-Gordon, there were 253 DPO registrations filed in 1995. However, in Stewart-Gordon's experience, about 60 percent of DPOs fail.

The reasons for the high failure rates are simple. "A SCOR is typically the last resort for a lot of people," explains Bill Beatty of the Washington State Securities Division. "It's a good tool, but it doesn't turn a company that wouldn't be a good candidate for the public markets into one."

While bypassing the need to pay a stockbroker's fees and commissions, the firm making a direct offering often feels the loss of the broker's access to regular investors. Without a ready market for their offering, those entrepreneurs that raise the necessary funding in this way generally sell to affinity groups, such as customers, employees, suppliers, distributors, friends, and next of kin.

"If you don't have a strong affinity group, you'd better have a good marketing concept," advises Lisa Sireno, assistant director of the Missouri Innovation Center. Many DPOs fail even with a loyal following and a strong marketing plan. Still, it is possible for ordinary small companies to raise money through this new method—but there are plenty of hurdles.

For starters, there's the nagging problem that most of the general public has no idea what a DPO or a SCOR is. "Investors are naturally cautious because they're dealing with both a company and a type of offering they've never heard of," explains Stewart-Gordon. Even if you have a ready-made pool of potential investors, selling stock directly is difficult.

In addition to new methods for raising public funds, new media are also broadening opportunities, as shown by the following press release from the Wit Capital Web site.[5]

ENTREPRENEURIAL RESOURCE   Internet Public Offerings

MICROBREWER RAISES $1.6 MILLION IN UNPRECEDENTED INTERNET OFFERING

NEW YORK, NEW YORK (February 26, 1996)   Spring Street Brewing Company has completed the world's first digital public stock offering, and the three year old microbrewer has more than its place in on-line history to celebrate: the craft brewer of Wit and Amber Wit raised nearly $1.6 million in the innovative stock sale without having to share any of the proceeds with Wall Street underwriters. At the same time, the New York based brewer has added more than 3,500 craft beer enthusiasts to its shareholder list.

The initial public offer was made through an official circular linked by Spring Street to its World Wide Web site. Anyone with a personal computer and a modem could peruse the offer, and with a click of the mouse download the circular into their home or office. Subscriptions, executed through a subscription agreement attached to each circular, could be e-mailed directly to the company.

Thousands of technologically savvy investors apparently liked Spring Street's offer. The company sold 844,581 shares of common stock. The share price was $1.85.

The offering was qualified with the Securities and Exchange Commission under Regulation A of the Securities Act of 1933. It was also registered in 22 states.

Secondary trading in Spring Street's common stock is set to begin March 1st through the microbrewer's newest digital innovation: a Web based bulletin board mechanism, called Wit-Trade, that will enable buyers and sellers to trade shares without having to use brokers or pay commissions.

(Note: Secondary trading *refers to investors buying from other investors, rather than from a company stock offering.)*

The Venture Capital Market

Venture capital firms look for generally larger deals and impressive returns. Many venture capital firms fund projects only in specific industries; some work only from referrals from within their network.

It is estimated that investments made by venture partnerships in private companies were on the order of $8 billion in 1996. Carol Steinberg in the May 1995 issue of "*Success Selling,*" puts the venture capital funding option in perspective: "Each year a venture capitalist fields 400 to 500 deals, seriously reviews 40 or 50, and funds only 4 or 5."

Despite the odds, there are many sources for venture capital, and you as the entrepreneur should be willing to solicit several firms. A venture capitalist will generally require a review of your business plan before talking with you. Send your plan in advance of any conversation, and follow up on the stated date and time mentioned in your cover letter.

You are asking prospective investors to take a relatively unsecured position in the company, and they should be presented with a detailed financial plan that includes all the data necessary to make an informed decision. Sophisticated investors will rigorously evaluate the abilities of the management team, the financial strength of the company and its principals, and the commercial viability of the enterprise, while considering risk factors portrayed in the financial projections.

In seeking active investors for a project, look first within the industry. Investors prefer involvement in a business they know, and you will also have less explaining or selling of the concept to do.

Other possible advantages of teaming with such an investor is the possibility of "synergies," such as their involving your company in their projects, and providing valuable contacts in the industry. In exchange, accept the fact that such a partner will often expect to be involved in the decision-making process of the venture, or at least kept updated.

You may also seek passive investors, who will have little or no involvement in the project. These could be companies with excessive retained earnings, companies who wish to diversify, or venture capital corporations formed for tax advantage reasons.

Less visible as a source of start-up capital are individual investors, known as "angels," who typically invest $20,000 to $100,000 in private companies. Angels are thought to represent a pool of risk capital in excess of $30 billion each year.

What do we have to offer prospective investors? For most, their primary interest is in a high return on their investment, through dividends and appreciation. Other considerations might be opportunities for tax benefits, and for director and consulting income. Of generally lesser interest are noncash rewards, such as privileged information, access to new products, and "psychic income."

7.2   *Expert Opinion: My Life as an Angel*

It's taken me 25 years and a lot of bad deals to get it right. In the process, however, I developed a few rules of angel investing. They may not be right for everyone, but at least they've allowed me to find what I've been looking for all these years.

Rule 1: *Invest in people who want your help, not your money*

If I'm going to invest in a new venture, I want to play a role in its success. I like my opinions to be heard. That means investing in someone who wants to listen. The problem is, people always come across as good listeners when they're asking you for money. So I prefer to give my financial support to those who ask for help rather than money.

Rule 2: *When possible, go it alone*

I don't do large-scale, limited-partnership investing anymore. I have my own ideas about how to build a business, and they sometimes differ from other people's ideas. I don't mind trying to work out those differences with the person running the business, but I have no interest in getting into debates with other investors. Granted, I have to stay away from deals that require more capital than I can come up with on my own, but that's a trade-off I'm willing to make.

Rule 3: *Take a majority stake until your investment has been repaid*

Most people build their investment strategies around achieving a certain rate of return on their capital. My number one goal is preservation of capital. Not that I don't want to make money, but I focus first on getting my investment back. I insist on owning a majority stake in any new venture I finance. As soon as I've been paid an amount equal to my initial investment, we'll issue new stock, and my stake will shrink to 25%.

Rule 4: *Retain the right to force a payout*

Nobody invests in a new venture just to avoid losing money. If the business is successful, I expect to make a lot of money, more than I would from a bank or bonds or publicly traded stocks. My goal, after getting my principal back, is to earn 33% of my initial investment annually as long as the business is in operation. I don't want to bankrupt the company or leave it undercapitalized. Nor do I want to deprive the person running the business of the opportunity to make money as well. So I'm prudent about what I take out.

Source: Norm Brodsky, "My Life as an Angel," *Inc.* July 1997, vol. 19, no. 10, p. 42(6).

There is little appeal to most investors in being a long-term minority owner in a closely held business, so some way of "cashing out" should be offered. This could be a provision for company buyback of their partial ownership, or a plan for a future public offering.

MINICASE 7.3 Light-Guard Tries the Venture Capital Market

Mr. I. M. Bright has determined that all he needs to make Light-Guard Manufacturing a successful company is some start-up capital. He has developed a three-year sales forecast that indicates a profit in the first year, increasing to a before-tax profit in the third year of over $1 million. His cash-flow statement indicates that $310,000 will get him through the losses that will occur at start-up.

Bright's activities to date in building and testing prototypes and doing test marketing have drained his personal capital. A discussion with his banker convinced him that the venture is not a good candidate for a commercial loan. The banker suggested that he contact Chestnut Street Capital (CSC), a venture capital firm specializing in manufacturing.

Bright called CSC for an appointment, and was told that he would have to submit his business plan, along with a summary financial proposal in a specific format for which he would be sent guidelines. His business plan was in good order, and his first requirement for the summary proposal was that he extend his projected income statement from three to five years:

	Year 1	Year 2	Year 3	Year 4	Year 5
Sales (Revenue)	$490,000	$1,190,000	$2,940,000	$3,500,000	$4,000,000
Cost of Sales	−245,000	−595,000	−1,470,000	−1,750,000	−2,000,000
Gross Profit	245,000	595,000	1,470,000	1,750,000	2,000,000
Sales Expense	−106,000	−177,000	−248,500	−350,000	−400,000
Admin/Overhead	−72,000	−110,000	−130,000	−175,000	−200,000
Engineering Expenses	−35,000	−24,000	−80,000	−87,500	−100,000
Pretax Profit (Loss)	$32,000	$284,000	$1,011,500	$1,137,500	$1,300,000

The additional requirement, estimating what percentage of the business he was offering, was a bit more complex. After consulting his finance textbook from graduate school, he recalled the market approach to valuing a business as the *earnings of the business* multiplied by a typical *price to earnings (P/E) ratio* for similar companies.

The after-tax profits of a business are often referred to as its **earnings.** A company's **price to earnings ratio** (generally written "P/E ratio") can be used as a measure of the value of a business. In the Light-Guard example, we earlier referred to their earnings as $1 million per year, and a suggested sale price equivalent to 10 years' earnings, or $10 million. This represents a P/E of 10. A sale price can often be put in better perspective by comparing the P/E for the transaction to norms for other companies in its industry

---

P/E ratios are often used to evaluate the stock of a publicly traded company on a per share basis, that is, the market price of a share divided by the earnings per share. It is often referred to as the number of times you are buying current earnings in paying market price

Among public companies, the ratio at which a stock is trading indicates the stock market's expectation of company performance. A low P/E, relative to companies in similar fields, is an indication that buyers anticipate a poor profit performance from that company in the future. A high P/E indicates that either a better performance is expected in the future, or that the stock is being valued more for its assets than its earning potential.

✓ **Checkpoint:** *What P/E Ratio Norms Are Relevant to Light-Guard?*
Let us begin our estimation of the appropriate ratio to use in evaluating the company by looking at averages for the past three years in some key industries:

P/E ratios for selected industries (from various published and on-line sources, mid-1998)

INDUSTRY	P/E 1995	P/E 1996	P/E 1997
Miscellaneous Services	21	21	17
Retail merchandise	22	22	17
Electronics/Electric	19	16	14
AVERAGE OF ALL INDUSTRIES	18	17	14
Manufacturing/Distribution	17	15	13
Consumer Products	27	25	21

Note that in the most recent year, the averages for all stocks, and for manufacturing stocks, are between 13 and 14. Since ours is a startup venture, and earnings are projections, we will examine P/E ratios somewhat less than those for established companies. In particular we will evaluate the company for P/E ratios of 8, 10, and 12 for comparison purposes.   ✓ ✓

The next step in this process is to determine what the company will be worth at the end of the planning horizon of *n* years, referred to as the *future valuation.*

We have projected fifth-year pretax profits (*n* = 5 years in this case) of $1.3 million. Assuming a tax rate of 34 percent, fifth-year earnings (profits after taxes) will be 66 percent of $1.3 million, or $858,000. The future valuation is the product of this earnings figure and the P/E ratio.

This future valuation will then be used to establish the present value of the investment. *Present value* is the value in today's dollars assigned to an amount of money in the future, based on some estimated rate of return over the long term. This is expressed as the following formula:

$$\text{Present Value} = \text{Future Valuation} / (1 + r)^n$$
where ^{n} indicates the *n*th power

In this equation, *r* is the expected rate of return to the venture capital firm. Bright understood that venture capital firms generally expected a return on the order of 50 percent. From the present value, we can then calculate the share of the company that the venture capital firm should receive for their investment:

$$\text{Investor's Share (\%)} = \text{Investment} / \text{Present Value}$$

Bright ran cases for P/E ratios of 8, 10, and 12 for comparison:

P/E	nth-year Earnings	Years	Return	Present Value	Investment	Share
8	$858,000	5	50%	$903,901	$310,000	34%
10	$858,000	5	50%	$1,129,877	$310,000	27%
12	$858,000	5	50%	$1,355,852	$310,000	23%

Study Questions

1. Based on the results of Bright's analysis, what percentage of the company would you offer CSC for a $310,000 investment? Are they likely to accept minority ownership when Bright is not putting up any money? What demands might they make?

_____

_____

_____

2. Is CSC likely to accept these calculations, based as they are on Bright's projections? What other cases might they suggest need to be run?

_____

_____

_____

3. In Bright's position, what is the maximum percentage you would give CSC? What are your alternatives if it is not enough for them to make the deal?

_____

_____

_____

THE FUNDRAISING "TOOLKIT"

The Written Presentation

With our financial plan prepared, and our fundraising strategy determined, we have all the components of the business plan and can begin to craft the final product. Some "first impressions" criteria for a good business plan are that it be attractive and interesting, well organized and carefully edited, and easy to understand.

Readers of our business plan must be led through our analysis in a way that leads them to accept our conclusions. Our primary objective is to convey that there is an opportunity, that we are equipped to seize it, and that "the numbers work." It is helpful to be concise and focused, and to avoid vague and/or unsubstantiated claims.

Potential problems must be anticipated and addressed, leading to a convincing likelihood of success. Projections must be rigorously realistic and objective, and based on reasonable assumptions.

The primary reasons that business plans fail to convince prospective investors are: success depends on too many or too shaky contingencies, an inadequate return to justify the risks, and the absence of a "graceful way out," that is, a credible exit strategy, for stakeholders. Other deal killers can include carelessness in preparation (what does this convey?), insufficient belief in the project by its principals, and a lack of comfort with and confidence in the company principals on the part of prospective stakeholders.

M. John Storey, principal of Storey Communications, suggests that we "keep the plan incredibly simple. Talk in pictures. Back up your images with a phone-book-size financial package, but only at the end. Never allow a reader to say 'Too complicated, not for me,' on the first page." He also cautions that we "leave out the mumbo-jumbo," keeping the focus on "who's going to buy what product, and at what price?" He urges the use of summaries to help plant the key facts in a prospective investor's mind: profit, potential, costs, key customers.

Katie Muldoon, president of Muldoon & Baer, suggests that the plan, which she views as a prospectus, should reflect your personality and ambitions: "Investors bet on people, and the prospectus is an opportunity to sell your qualities. Make sure the writing reflects your drive and professionalism." She adds, "It's like any other selling job. You've got to know your audience, write to your audience."

The key to writing to your audience lies in knowing how they will evaluate the plan. Financial specialist David Stegall says that there are seven questions we should ask ourselves about a business plan before seeking financing.[6]

1. Can you successfully operate the company?

   Does your résumé show sufficient experience in company operations? Make sure that if you do not possess all the skills to run your company, that you have hired the talent to do so.

2. Does your Pro Forma demonstrate the ability to repay the loan?

   "Pro Forma" refers to the financial statements projecting how your company will perform. Many investors and lenders also like to see certain financial ratios that we will discuss later as we develop our financial plan.

3. Have you conducted a complete market analysis?

   It is important to show that your product or service will actually be in demand in the quantities that your Pro Forma states. Show the market research that supports your sales projections.

4. Is your plan easy to follow?

   You should index and tab your plan, and create a table of contents so the lender can easily refer to various sections. Also, check to ensure that the flow of information in the table of contents is logical and realistic.

5. Did you write an executive summary and put it at the beginning of the plan?

   This is your company's cover letter. It will be the first thing the lender reads. It needs to spark enough enthusiasm to keep the reader's interest.

6. Is the plan grammatically correct?

   If you are not sure, hire someone to help you. Nothing will kill your chances faster than if you have spelling errors and typos.

7. Have you convinced the reader that your product/service will work or is needed?

   Is a working model appropriate? Is a meaningful test marketing campaign feasible?

The written presentation is generally only the door opener. When seeking financial stakeholders, we want the opportunity to present the highlights of our proposition in person. For the size financial commitment that the entrepreneur is generally looking for, the prospective stakeholder must be sold face-to-face.

The Oral Presentation

A request for an oral presentation of your proposal could be met with resistance; that resistance could imply disinterest, or may simply be testing your commitment to the project. A. David Silver of ADS Financial Services suggests that "lenders and investors are more interested in tenacious entrepreneurs than in relaxed or casual" ones. He cautions, though, that you "balance your persistence, so that you don't appear 'pushy'."

Oral presentations are generally characterized by a very short time allowance, and a somewhat skeptical audience. Venture capital network meetings often schedule several presentations, frequently allowing only one to five minutes to each entrepreneur. Here, the emphasis must be on the uniqueness of the proposal, its high probability of success, and the high returns that will be produced. M. John Storey says that you should explain the business opportunity in 25 words or less, and leave them with a "tell me more" curiosity.

Private meetings with venture capital prospects are often scheduled for 15 to 30 minutes. Do your homework on the venture capitalist. Know the previous deals they have funded and the current structure of their portfolio.

Make your case quickly, even when the time allowed provides for a more comfortable pace; do not lose audience attention with too long a buildup. A good approach is to complete the presentation in two-thirds of the time allowed, with the remainder for questions and discussion; be sure to have some supplemental information ready if this creates a lull. Stress the benefits that the prospect will enjoy if they invest.

Start-up plans need to detail start-up use of proceeds and then generalize on the additional stages. Judiciously present a timetable indicating how much money will be needed, when it will be needed, and how it will be used. Most companies require multiple stages of financing, including both debt and equity. Show the proposed capital structure, including who is going to own what part or percentage of the company at what stage.

The oral presentation must answer many of the same questions as the written; it can be more difficult due to time constraints, or easier because we can appeal to more senses. Computer presentation packages can be used to generate attractive, professional visual aids. Do not use copies of spreadsheets or printed pages as visuals; design slides that convey your major points concisely and without complication.

Use the visuals as an outline of your talk so that you do not have to refer to notes. Be sure to adapt your presentation to the medium, and to your audience. Be positive and enthusiastic about your company and product/service.

A presentation must be balanced between information elements and relational ones, those that relate to your audience. Rehearse your presentation until you are very comfortable with it. Present it to a knowledgeable and objective friend for feedback. Time it to make sure you do not overstay your welcome.

Corporate trainer and speaker Lani Arredondo suggests the AMMA rule for presentations: They should be attention-getting, meaningful, memorable, and activating. She stresses that the purpose of a presentation is to persuade. She cautions that perception is more powerful than fact; people are inundated with data, more than they can absorb, and they forget quickly.

Ideally, the presentation should lead the prospect directly to asking how they can participate. Know your minimum deal and walk away if necessary. Remember this is a long-term relationship. Negotiate a deal you can live with.

ENTREPRENEURIAL RESOURCE **Communications Consultants**

Public relations consulting firm Persuasive Concepts represents a new specialty in their industry—providing presentation advising and coaching for individuals who must present to the financial community.

Alvin D. Gottlieb is president of Persuasive Concepts, headquartered in Wyncote, Pennsylvania. The company is also on-line to offer interactive editing of presentations materials, development of visual aids, and coaching on delivery techniques. Lynne Lowe Jacobus is vice president of Persuasive Concepts and is president of Jacobus & Associates, an executive communications coaching and training firm, also located in Wyncote. In their article "Presenting Your Company to Investors," Jacobus and Gottlieb provide sound advice in plan presentation.[7]

Imagine having to ask for five million dollars in just fifteen minutes. That's what most entrepreneurs face when seeking capital for their company.

Obtaining financing can be an arduous process. Whether you're an entrepreneur seeking start-up capital, an existing business looking for second stage funding or an investment banker raising money, you will find competition is so keen that every appointment must be maximized. The 15 minutes before the decision makers is your financial window of opportunity.

Not long ago we worked with a young entrepreneurial company seeking financing. One of the principals was a talented lawyer who had to convince his "techie" business partners that the presentation mattered. He quoted the famous 19th century industrialist and co-founder of U.S. Steel Henry Schwab who said, "I will pay a man more for his ability to communicate than for any other quality he may possess."

If that was true 100 years ago, it is even more significant in today's information age. The proliferation of computers, e-mail, fax machines, and modems has created a false sense of security for the millions of business people who are uncomfortable speaking in front of groups. They believe they can hide behind the printed word—let the information speak for itself. Data alone will not persuade. Face-to-face oral communication is inescapable in the quest for venture capital—and it must be the money seekers themselves who present.

After months of diligently preparing a detailed business plan, the presentation is often considered an afterthought. Enlightened entrepreneurs seek professional advice to create a credible and professional presentation that will engender confidence and enthusiasm from prospective investors. They learn to avoid the three pitfalls that often stand in the way of success.

PITFALL 1: READING NOT SPEAKING

The most prevalent mistake we see is the presentation that is essentially a business plan read aloud. A business plan is meant to be read, a presentation is meant to be heard. Consequently, the presentation must be developed in a different manner. Of course, the material is the same—the data never changes. But, people listen in sound bites. Good oral style is more personal, more concise, uses less jargon and technical language, more qualifying terms and personal pronouns, and, since the human attention span is just 35 seconds, lots of repetition and restatement. Take this excerpt from a typical business plan:

"From inception, Company A's management, staff, and consultants have kept well abreast of developing technology, markets, and market trends through publications, customer relationships and industry contacts. This network provides insight into technological advances that are most likely to result in opportunities for Company A."

No one speaks like that. To make this work in a presentation you would say, "Right from the beginning, we followed developing technology and market trends through publications and industry contact. We have taken advantage of every opportunity." Notice the more concise and personal tone.

PITFALL 2: NOT FOCUSING ON THE PROCESS

What is the purpose of your presentation . . . to create enough interest to get a second meeting, to further explain your product or services, to deal with objections or to close the deal? Rarely will entrepreneurs get financiers to agree to capitalize their business on the first presentation. Understanding the need to persuade in steps (to build interest) is critical to the process. All too often the need for instant gratification sabotages desired results. If you don't know what you hope to get out of the meeting, chances are your listeners won't know either.

Once you have clarity of purpose you must decide how you will organize the information so it is convincing and to the point. You must not exceed the time allotted so preparation is paramount. Most financial presentations follow a typical pattern of development discussing the product or service, targeted market, sales and marketing plan, management team, financial arrangements and exit strategy (pay back plan). There are, however, other organizational structures that may work such as a chronological or a question and answer format. The presentation should be developed in a manner that maximizes the presenter's style.

A good technique for staying focused is to use visual aids—usually overhead transparencies or slides. Overheads are easily produced and the frames allow you to write notes for yourself. You can also refer back to transparencies with little difficulty, while slide carousels do not provide such flexibility. Make sure visuals are carefully designed and produced—a picture can be worth a thousand words or it can be confusing, hard to read or simply unnecessary.

PITFALL 3: LACK OF ATTENTION TO THE NEEDS AND DESIRES OF THE POTENTIAL INVESTORS

It has been said, "All audiences listen to the same radio station WIFM or What's In It For Me." As much as you believe you need to explain every detail of your business product or service, chances are your listeners are more concerned with your management, your projections, the validation of your projections and your exit strategies.

Often we engage in debriefing sessions and question investors as to why they decided to back a certain business. One told me, "I haven't a clue as to how the technology works, but I'm convinced the opportunity is sound based on the experience of their management team, the team's projections and operational strategies, and after all, I'm in the business of making money."

One of the most successful Initial Public Offerings of the last few years was Boston Chicken. Imagine if their principals spent the majority of their presentation time discussing the way they raise chickens, the seasoning secrets, the roasting methodology, etc. Do you think that would have been a successful strategy for obtaining financing?

Why then do entrepreneurial manufacturers feel the need to explain the intricacies of their process and product? It usually bores or confuses the investor who then only half listens to the information that hits his "hot buttons." It is better to capsulize the technical information. Give them only what they absolutely must know to understand the opportunity.

Focus on what interests them, not you. Keep your technical charts as backup. If additional technical details become required you will find out in the question and answer period following your presentation or in the next session.

Preparing a professional presentation should be viewed as a management act. Work on the content and delivery as diligently as you worked on the development of your entrepreneurial idea. Work on it over time. Make midcourse corrections.

Practice it aloud to trusted colleagues and coaches. Give it the attention it deserves especially if you are anxious about face-to-face communication. Fear leads to procrastination. Procrastination results in the "wing-it" approach and that rarely succeeds. One poor presentation exacerbates the fear you will be feeling on any future presentations.

If the entrepreneur appears tentative or shows a lack of confidence in the presentation and question and answer session, potential lenders might question his or her credibility. Remember, perception is reality. You must do everything you can to create a reality that will persuade the financing source to say yes . . . and that means preparing, practicing, and delivering a professional presentation. The time and resources you put into your "15 minute window of opportunity" just might be the best investment you ever make!

Summary

The finance plan for a venture will be evaluated according to the following criteria:

Is start-up capitalization adequate? Is it used well? Are all start-up costs recognized? Are sales and sales growth expectations realistic?

Are sales projections credible? Are they achievable? Are expense estimates reasonable? Complete? Are margin goals realistic? Convincing? Is there a solid basis for estimates (industry norms, experience), or do they appear to be guesswork? Is the progression of income/expense estimates credible?

Are income, cash flow, and balance statements consistent? Is cash well managed? Is the cash management strategy clear? Does the total package (text, statements, assumptions, etc.) present a clear and complete picture of the financial position?

For a public offering:
Would the opportunity offered excite prospective investors, making them want to share in its future? Does your company have natural affinity groups from which to seek investors?

Might customers or suppliers be interested in investing? Do members of affinity groups have discretionary cash to risk for long-term gain? Would your company's natural affinity groups recognize your company's name and view it favorably?

For existing companies:
Does the company have a history of consistently profitable operations under the present management? Is the company's present management recognized in the industry as honest, socially responsible, and competent?

Review Questions

1. What is the basis of the financial plan? How can we forecast sales? How can we test projections for reasonability?

   _____

   _____

   _____

2. How do we determine the capital requirements of a venture? What are typical start-up investments?

   _____

   _____

   _____

3. What are the primary sources of funds for start-up businesses? What percentage, on average, comes from personal resources?

_____

_____

_____

4. What are the two primary types of venture financing? What are the relative merits of each?

_____

_____

_____

5. What are our options for equity financing? How are our chances?

_____

_____

_____

6. How are our chances for commercial loans? How can we reduce our borrowing requirements?

_____

_____

_____

7. Does the form and quality of the business plan affect our chance of convincing prospective stakeholders? Aren't most investors and lenders too sophisticated to be swayed by form? How do they use the plan to evaluate us?

_____

_____

_____

8. Is an oral presentation to prospects necessary? How desirable is it? What are the keys to an effective oral presentation?

_____

_____

_____

CASE STUDY 7.3
Tammany Supply, Inc. (E)

INTRODUCTION

The oil price collapse of the mid-1980s took a heavy toll on the Louisiana economy. In western St. Tammany Parish, an upscale suburb of New Orleans that had been experiencing explosive growth, new residential construction fell dramatically. Sales for Tammany Supply, Inc. (TSI), a Covington plumbing wholesaler serving that market, fell 40 percent from 1984 to 1987.

With the assistance of a broader product line, including the opening of a patio furniture store, a modest recovery in TSI's fortunes occurred from 1988 to 1990 (see Case Study 6.2). The company returned to modest profitability over the next couple of years, with sales climbing back near the level of the mid-1980s.

THE RECOVERY ACCELERATES

A building boom began in mid-1992. TSI sales for 1992 increased 20 percent over 1991. By the spring of 1993 homebuilding was so lively that the company decided to sell its patio furniture store to an employee. By shedding this operation, the company had undone much of the diversification it had undertaken in the late 1980s, and returned to its roots. TSI was now as heavily dependent on new residential construction in western St. Tammany as it had ever been.

But that was not a bad place to be. TSI sales in 1993 increased another 30 percent over 1992 sales, exceeding $3.5 million for the first time. Profits were likewise the highest in company history. In 1994, sales rose another 24 percent, exceeding $4 million, and profits decreased only slightly (see "Sales and Profits, 1990–94" graph). By the end of 1994, the company was functioning smoothly, and its cash balance was back in the $100,000 range for the first time in many years.

CLOUDS ON THE HORIZON

At the same time, local builders were beginning to catch up with the demand, indicating a leveling off of building activity, but at a comfortable plateau.

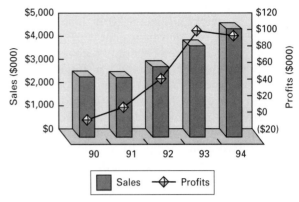

Sales and Profits
Tammany Supply, Inc., 1990–94

The boom was running its course, but there certainly did not seem to be a crash in sight.

There were ways, however, in which this situation felt different from the prosperity of the early 1980s. TSI's early success was accelerated by the high-end nature of the St. Tammany housing industry; their clientele bought luxury goods, with their attendant luxurious profit margins. In the 1990s, most of the housing being built was middle-range and below, margins were skimpy, and TSI had to move a lot more material to make as much profit.

The competitive situation also felt different. The regional plumbing supply chain that had opened a branch in the market in 1991 seemed to be there to stay, despite its inability to take a significant share of business from TSI. As the market downscaled a bit, TSI was becoming more vulnerable to the low-price, low-service sales approach of the larger companies. The resultant discomfort was intensified by the announcement of a Home Depot being built just two miles south of TSI. Home Depot is North America's largest house improvement retailer with fiscal 1997 sales of $24 billion.

RELATED DEVELOPMENTS

From 1986 to 1988, TSI president John Vinturella had worked on a personal-investment diversification program to supplement the one he directed at TSI. He seeded the start-up of a microbrewery, and then sold his stake to seed a cajun-food manufacturer. He bought a computer consulting firm and merged it with the software company used by TSI. He and his brothers opened a quick-oil-change franchise in New Orleans. John felt that he was now positioned to prosper when the area economy recovered.

While the area economy had found bottom in 1987, it merely bounced along that bottom for the next few years. John overestimated the pace of recovery, and experienced another "crash," this time in his personal finances, beginning in 1990. Investments from 10 years earlier had started to become drains on cash. The recent investments were taking longer to reach profitability than projected. Vacancies in the TSI building were causing tremendous strains in making mortgage payments. An orderly shutdown of these ventures was begun, climaxing in 1992 when John returned his building to the bank.

Because of his personal financial reverses, TSI had become John's only significant asset and his only reliable source of income. The thought of cashing out entered his mind; with a book value of almost $750,000 and annual profits approaching $100,000, the company could conceivably sell for $1 million. On the other hand, the company offered a solid base for an expansion program that could take it to another level in size and profitability.

EXAMINING THE OPTIONS

John projected financial performance for the next three years with TSI pursuing its current, rather conservative path (see "Sales and Profits, 1994 Actual, 1995–97 Projected" graph). He expected sales growth of about 10 percent annually, with profits reaching a plateau of just over $100,000 per year.

The major constraint on growth was that TSI's market area was beginning to be saturated. The company had tried expanding its product line in the western St. Tammany market with little success. For any real growth, TSI would have to think more regionally. An eastern St. Tammany location would be a natural next step, and could serve as a base for selling to the Mississippi Gulf Coast.

The business center of eastern St. Tammany is the city of Slidell, about 25 miles from Covington

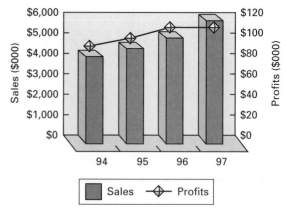

Sales and Profits
1994 Actual, 1995–97 Projected

via Interstate 12. TSI had competed over the years with the two supply houses located in Slidell for business in that area, though somewhat unsuccessfully. Thoughts of opening a TSI branch there had been entertained, but the thought of taking on the well-established competition was daunting.

While considering the Slidell branch option, another opportunity presented itself. TSI decided to consider supplying utility products, consisting primarily of pipe and fittings for the water and sewer systems supporting municipalities and private developments. A utility supply firm serving the area was closing down and selling off its inventory. One of their salesmen, Dave Foster, approached TSI about a job, and offered the promise of capturing much of the business of his former employer.

STRATEGIC ANALYSIS

The utility business had serious advantages over other new product lines that TSI had acquired. The primary difference, and the reason it had to be seriously considered, was that it built on TSI's current products, while opening the company up to a much wider geographic market. The downside was that it represented considerable additional inventory for TSI, since the size of these materials was well above that being stocked for its residential customers.

As John saw his choices, he knew that the challenge would be in generating the resources to be a competitive force in Slidell, and/or in the regional utilities business. One of the Slidell plumbing supply businesses had been rumored to be for sale, and John guessed that TSI could buy it for approximately $700,000. Dave suggested that it would take about $300,000 to enter the utility business with any credibility.

John had little concern about staffing either of these efforts. The TSI senior staff was very strong, and expansion would offer new opportunities that would be energizing, especially a branch manager position in Slidell. Dave would be a good hire in any case, as he was an experienced salesman with a commercial customer orientation, whereas TSI was focused on residential development.

DECISION TIME

John knew that his personal financial difficulties made borrowing difficult, except possibly for asset-based loans on TSI's inventory and accounts receivable. He could possibly raise $300,000 this way, but adding the loan payments to the working capital demands of a new venture could cause considerable strain on the entire operation.

He had considered going to the equity market once before, to try to save his outside ventures. Perhaps it was now time to consider selling a piece of TSI. It now had sufficient net worth that he could raise a significant amount of capital while retaining a controlling interest.

It was time to freshen up the business plan, and generate some numbers.

STUDY QUESTIONS

1. Is now a good time to approach venture capitalists and/or attempt a small stock offering? Will prospective buyers see the same danger signs for the current business that John sees? Are the expansion plans really opportunities, or merely designed to stave off stagnation?

   _____

   _____

   _____

2. Are the danger signs real or imagined? Is John overreacting, seeing shades of the earlier downturn? Would a few years at this comfortable sales volume and profit level adversely affect the company and its employees?

   _____

   _____

3. Has the market matured to the point where TSI has lost the competitive advantage of being the small, independent, locally owned firm? What do you see happening to TSI's market value if John waits a year or two to approach the equity market?

   _____

   _____

4. Assuming that the business might appraise for $1 million, how much might John realize if he were to sell it? What kind of income might that provide for life if wisely invested? What would the investment options be?

   _____

   _____

5. How much might TSI be able to raise on the equity market? What is the most that could be raised while allowing John to keep a controlling interest? Would you recommend trying a public issue, approaching venture capitalists, or looking for private investors?

   _____

   _____

6. What criteria would you apply, as a prospective investor, to TSI's financial proposal? Would you pay $1 a share if John were issued shares at $0.25? What "discount" should John get? What percentage return on your investment would make it attractive?

   _____

   _____

7. After years of operating independently, will it be a difficult transition for John to have some answerability to stockholders? Given John's experience and results to date, how active are the stockholders likely to be in the business?

_____

_____

_____

8. If TSI were to raise enough capital to open a Slidell branch *and* to enter the utilities business, should they try to do both? At the same time, or how far apart? Should they sell a smaller amount of stock to do one expansion now to see how that goes, and then reapproach the equity market later?

_____

_____

_____

Business Plan Template

Many books and articles on the subject of writing a good business plan are available. The Internet can be an excellent source for business plan templates that can be tailored to your specific venture. We have seen excerpts from the Light-Guard example, which can be seen in its entirety at www.sb.gov.bc.ca. Another excellent template can be found at The Money Hunter site (www.moneyhunter.com).

The following represents the author's best attempt at a consensus on a flexible basic structure for a business plan.

TITLE PAGE

Use an icon, like the light bulb in the Light-Guard example, or a picture of your product where applicable. Be sure to include the following information:

[Your Company Name]
[Month and Year issued]
[Name/Title/Address/City, State ZIP of contact person]
[Phone/e-mail/company home page URL]
Business Plan Copy Number [x]
Disclaimers: *This document is confidential. It is not for redistribution.*
(as needed) *This is a business plan. It does not imply an offering of securities.*

Here's a sample table of contents, as suggested by the Money Hunter:

TABLE OF CONTENTS

EXECUTIVE SUMMARY

If the executive summary does not grab the reader's interest, the business plan will never sell investors. Many write the summary last, but I have seen recommendations that the summary be written first and used as a template for the plan as a whole.

Since one of its primary functions is to capture the investor's attention, the summary should be no longer than two pages.

Mission

Our company's mission is to [describe your ultimate goal, or insert your mission statement].

Company

[The company] was founded in [date] and [describe what your business does, such as baby products manufacturer, distributor of pencils, provider of medical services]. It is a [legal form of your company, such as LLC, S-Corporation, C-Corporation, partnership, proprietorship]. Our principal offices are located at [address].

Business

We make [describe product or service that you make or provide]. Our company is at the [seed, start-up, growth] stage of business, having just [developed our first product, hired our first salesman, booked our first national order].

In the most recent [quarter, year], our company achieved sales of [x], and showed a [profit, loss, break-even]. With the financing contemplated herein, our company expects to achieve [x] in sales and [x] in pretax profits in 19[xx] and achieve [x] in sales and [x] in pretax profits in 19[xx + 1].

We can achieve this because the funds will allow us to [describe what you will do with the funds, such as (a) conduct a marketing campaign, (b) build or expand facilities to meet increased demand, (c) add retail locations or other means of distribution, or (d) increase research and development for new products or to improve existing ones].

Product or Service

Describe your product or service in layperson's terms.

[The company] produces the following products: [list products here briefly, in order of highest sales or significance in product line]. *or* [The company] delivers the following services: [list services here briefly, in order of highest sales or significance in product line].

Presently, our [product or service] is in the [introductory, growth, maturity] stage. We plan to follow this [product or service] with extensions to our line, which include [x, y, and z].

Critical factors in the production of our product [or delivery of our service] are [x and y]. Our [product or service] is unique because [x, y, or z], [and/or] we have an advantage in the marketplace because of our [patent, speed to market, brand name].

The Market

We define our market as [manufacture and sale of writing and drawing instruments, low-fat cheese, oral care products]. This market was approximately [$x] at [wholesale or retail] last [quarter, year], according to [cite resource], and is expected to grow to [$x] by the year [19xx], according to [cite resource].
Who are your customers? Where are they, and how do you reach them? Are they buying your product/service from someone else? How will you educate customers to buy from you? Why will they care?

Competition

We compete directly with [name competition]. *or* We have no direct competition, but there are alternatives to our product [or service] in the marketplace. Our product [or service] is unique because of [x], [and/or] we have a competitive advantage because of our [speed to market, established brand name, low-cost producer status].

Risk/Opportunity

The greatest risks we have in our business today are [market risk, pricing risk, product risk, management risk]. We feel we can overcome these risks because of [x].

The opportunities before us are significant; we have the opportunity to [dominate a niche in the marketplace, become a major force in the industry] if we can [x].

Management Team

Our team has the following members to achieve our plan. [v] men and women who have a combined [w] years of experience: [x] years in marketing, [y] years in product development, and [z] years in [other disciplines].

Capital Requirements

We seek [$] of additional [equity, subdebt, or senior financing] that will enable us to [describe why you need the funds, and why the opportunity is exciting]. We can provide an exit for this [loan, investment] within [x] years by [a dividend of excess profits, recapitalizations, sale of company, or public offering].

Financial Plan

At this point the investors must have a clear idea of where your business stands today. Do not bore them or make the necessary information hard to find. You must provide a snapshot, however sparse, of your financial position.

Sales Summary

	[Last Year]	[This Year]	[Next Year]	[Year Two]	*Balance Sheet Summary*
Sales:					Assets:
Gross Profit:					Liabilities:
Pretax:					Book Value:

In [x] years we will provide an exit, which we expect to be in the form of [sale to a competitor, initial public offering, distribution of profits] or perhaps [z]. We expect to be able to achieve this in [b months/years].

MISSION

Our goal is to become [describe your ultimate goal, or insert your mission statement; example: the leading manufacturer and marketer of branded in-line skate replacement wheels or the first name in low-fat cheese].

We aspire to carry a reputation in the marketplace for developing and delivering [time-saving, better-way products sold at a fair price for uses in the (x) market]. We can achieve this by [cutting-edge product development, close understanding of market trends and needs, innovative and profitable merchandising and packaging].

To accomplish our goal, [company name] needs [capital, management talent, larger, more efficient facilities]. In pursuit of our goal, we resolve to treat stakeholders, customers, and the community with [description of the reputation your company seeks]. These groups see our company as providing [describe benefits of being associated with your company].

COMPANY OVERVIEW

[The company] was founded in [date] and is a [manufacturer, distributor, marketer, service provider] of [describe your product or service]. The legal name of the business is [x; include d/b/a (for doing business as) in the legal name]. Our company is at the [seed, start-up, growth] stage of business, having just [developed our first product, hired our first salesman, booked our first national order].

Our principal offices are located at [list primary address as well as any other facilities]. We have approximately [x] square feet of office space and [x] square feet of [factory or warehouse]. Our current capacity is [x] units per month. If we exceed [x] units per month, we will need additional space. We expect this facility to be adequate for the company's needs for [two years, a year, a week] after funding.

[The company] operates in the [e.g., toxic waste, weapons and armaments, genetic engineering, explosives] industry, *or* [The company] uses controlled substances in [the manufacturing process or delivery of service], and falls under the jurisdiction of the [name government agency]. [The company] has all necessary permits to operate, and has an up-to-date record of inspections. These permits include [list briefly]. These agencies regulate our business in the following manner: [document and account for uses and disposal of all toxic materials or document and background check all employees with access to the launch codes for our missiles].

Legal Business Description

[The company] is a [legal form of your company, such as LLC, S-Corporation, C-Corporation, partnership, proprietorship].

Strategic Alliances

The leverage from relationships can be appealing to investors. Explain how you work with others to improve your performance.

[The company] has developed important and profitable strategic alliances with the following larger, more established business: [describe each company, its position in the marketplace, the details of the alliance, and what risks are involved in the alliance]. For example, we have developed marketing agreements with [x], the [market leader in gummed erasers, e.g.], which will enable us to sell, alongside them, our [e.g., extra messy children's pencils].

The side-by-side positioning at retail, as well as the ability to share wholesale sales leads with their established customer base, can help us penetrate the market more quickly. The risk in the relationship is that they may [e.g., decide to sell pencils themselves] and cut us out of the process.

Another type of strategic relationship that benefits the company is our development joint venture with [x]. We would never be able to fund the research of the new [e.g., low-fat Swiss cheese that melts smoothly], but with access to their prior research in [e.g., smooth melting cheddar] we cut our development time in half. By using some of their [equipment, people] who are not being utilized fully, we were able to avoid the expense of [major capital expenditures, additions to the payroll]. We have agreed to pay a royalty of [x] to this development partner for their role in this product's ultimate success.

We have a strategic relationship with a number of suppliers. In exchange for a blanket commitment to purchase [e.g., more than 80 percent of our supply of a specific raw material from them], they have agreed to [e.g., not make it available to the market at large for six months, or to give us a preferential price].

[The company] also has strategic Original Equipment Manufacturer relationships with a number of customers. This allows us to sell a large and steady volume of [e.g., in-line skate wheels] to [e.g., boot manufacturers, who use them to sell complete skate sets]. This gets many units of our product into the marketplace; however, it provides little or no brand awareness for us.

PRODUCT

Current Product

Explain how your product works or how the service is used. What burning marketplace needs are addressed by your product? What value do you add to the product?

[The company] produces the following products: [list products here, in order of highest sales or significance in product line. Be sure to refer readers to product pictures, diagrams, patents, and other descriptive material]. *or* [The company] delivers the following services: [list services here briefly, in order of highest sales or significance in product line. Be sure to refer readers to brochures and material describing your service].

Presently, our [product or service] is in the [introductory, growth, maturity] stage. We first developed our [product or service] in 19[xx] and have made [x] improvements and redesigns since then. [Provide a history of product developments, introductions, and improvements leading up to the present day. Table form may be appropriate.]

Point out the unique features or proprietary aspects of your product. Investors must see something unique, proprietary, or protected about your product or service.

Our products are unique because of [secret ingredient, our patented process, our proprietary manufacturing process]. Others in the market are able to provide somewhat similar products [or services], but we are able to differentiate ourselves in the market because of [x].
Tell about the unique value-added characteristics your product line or process provides to customers and how these characteristics translate into a competitive advantage for your company.

We have [applied, been granted, licensed] a patent for [x], an abstract of which can be found in appendix [x]. We have integrated this into our process, which others will not be able to duplicate. Our lead product, [x], addresses [list customer needs] and delivers [list benefits] to customers.

Research and Development

Our research and development is headed by [name of person or contractor], whose major objective is to use market input to [develop products that solve problems or provide superior benefits to customers]. Last [period], our R&D yielded the following products and innovations: [list products or innovations]. [The company] has spent [% of revenues, or absolute $] in the past year in R&D, and plans to spend [% or $] in the next [period].

Our R&D occasionally yields innovation without input from customers or the marketplace. Our product selection criteria in this case are as follows: [relatively low investment requirements, positive return on investment, fit with present strategy, feasibility of development and production, relatively low risk, time to see intended results, buyer in common]. Our R&D will require additional resources in the future. These will include [people, capital expenditures] to [speed up development process, test results more efficiently].
Discuss new and follow-on products.

Responding to market needs, we plan to follow [product or service] with extensions to our line, which include [x, y, and z]. Our target introduction dates for these products are [x, y, and z], which correspond with [a major trade show, industry event]. In addition, we plan to introduce the following new products in the upcoming season: [x, y, and z].

Production and Delivery

Our [product, service] is [manufactured in-house, assembled in-house from components from various vendors, (service) provided by our staff, or subcontracted to field consultants]. [Raw materials, subassemblies, components] used in our products are readily available from a variety of manufacturers who can meet our quality standards.

Critical factors in the production of our product [or delivery of our service] are [x and y]. *Enumerate and explain capital equipment, material, and labor requirements. Are these items readily available? Do you have multiple supply sources? List inventory requirements, quality and technical specifications, hazardous materials.*

THE MARKET

Market Definition

What markets are you competing in? If you make glove-compartment hinges, don't gush about the $80 billion automobile market. You make hinges—not cars—for that market, so tell us how many hinges were sold last year. Are there other markets where you sell your products?

We [expect to compete, are competing] in the [define niche] of the [define industry]. This market was approximately [$x] at [wholesale or retail] last [period available], according to [cite resource]. We believe, the major future trend in the industry will be toward [environmentally oriented, miniaturized, high-quality, value-oriented] product offerings.

Market research [cite source] suggests this market will [grow/shrink] to [$x] by [year]. We expect the niche in which we compete to [grow, shrink, remain stagnant] during this time. The major forces

affecting this change will be [falling cost of computers, explosion of home-based businesses, tendency for baby boomers to have fewer children]. The area of greatest growth within the industry will be [x]. *Identify where you got this information, and how up-to-date it is.*
Identify the market segment on which you intend to concentrate.

We define our market segment as [the writing and drawing instrument segment of the school/home/office products industry, the low-fat dairy products segment of the food industry]. This segment has been [volatile, steady] in the past few years. Industry experts [name them] forecast [x] for the industry in the next few years.

The major market segments [segment a, segment b, segment c]. [List, in general, the types of customers you are likely to reach (retailers, electrical contractors, catalog buyers, etc.)] The [a] segment of the market is based on [product type], which retail in the [x to y] price range. Most of the sales in the segment are delivered through the [catalogs, retailers, manufacturers' reps, other equipment manufacturers—those who use the product as a component of their final product].

Customer Profile

A typical customer for our product is a person who currently may use [alternative product or service] for [purpose]. They are motivated to buy our product because of [its value, its quality, its usefulness]. We know this from [customer responses, trade show input, ad inquiries] and feel our customers perceive our products as [good value, superior performance, great taste].

Our product, however, does have the following weaknesses: [higher price point than most other cheeses, weak brand identity in a commodity market]. We are working to position our product as [x] in order to reduce this vulnerability.

Marketing Plan

Our marketing plan is based on the following fundamentals:

We expect to penetrate the [x] segment of the market[s] and achieve this by using the [retail, mail order, multilevel marketing, Internet] as our primary distribution channel[s]. In time, we plan to capture [x%] share of the market.
Address the four P's.

Position
We will position our product as [good value for price, top quality, cheap and fun], which is a position not presently being addressed by the competition. One demographic group in particular, the [elderly, Hispanic, generation X, techies], has a particular need for this product, and we tailor our positioning accordingly.

Pricing
Our pricing strategy is [describe policy or, at least philosophy].
Is this pricing based on cost? Gross margin objectives? Market?

We arrive at our pricing based on [cost, gross margin objectives, market prices, perceived value]. We review this pricing [monthly, quarterly, annually] to ensure that potential profits are not squandered. Customers seem willing to pay as much as [$x] because of [explain reasoning].

Place (distribution channels)
The distribution channels we use for our product are [wholesalers, catalogers, mass merchant retailers, consolidators]. These make sense for delivering our product to the end user because [customer profile, geography, seasonal swings]. The competition uses the [wholesalers, catalogers, mass merchant retailers, consolidators] channel. Our channel will prove more advantageous because [x].

Our major current customers include: [list top five, with one- or two-sentence descriptions]. The attached chart demonstrates how our product reaches the customer [provide visual].

Promotion, Advertising, Trade Shows, etc.
Your purpose is to introduce, promote, and support your products in the marketplace. Although considered a cost, a properly designed and executed campaign is an investment.

[The company] has developed a comprehensive advertising and promotion strategy, which will be implemented by the best possible firm when funding is completed. We expect to have a presence in several national magazines as well as the trade press.

We will produce our own ads and be a part of ad campaigns of our joint venture partners or OEMs. Our publicity plan is to remain in constant contact with editors and writers of [trade journals that serve our industry] and seek stories and coverage that will [enhance our reputation, introduce us to buyers, etc.].

We plan to promote our product through a variety of [on-site product sampling, demonstrations at high-profile events, giveaways at fundraisers] and other high-leverage events. The objective of all our promotions is to [expand the audience, position our product as a premium brand, strengthen our ties to the community].

[The company] participates in the following trade shows: [list trade shows, briefly describe organization that sponsors it and who attends, and describe presence there]. We have [display booth of knock-down construction that allows us to display our existing products and introduce new ones]. *or* We prefer to attend trade shows as visitors and walk the show while displaying our wares only to prequalified buyers who will come to our nearby hospitality suite].

The following factors are taken into account when considering a trade show: Will this event help deliver our message to our target audience? Does the location of the show have significance? Is the time frame convenient? Is it a "must-go show"?

COMPETITION

Describe key competitors in regard to product, price, location, promotion, management, and financial position. False or incomplete information here translates as dishonesty and negligence to investors, bankers, etc. Do not delude yourself (or your investors) about your competition.

Look in your telephone book's yellow pages. Look in the industrial directories at your local library. Search on-line databases that provide competitive profiles of other companies. Read industry magazines and look for advertisers.

We have no direct competition, but there are alternatives to our [product or service] in the marketplace. *or* We compete directly with [competitor a, b, and c].
Provide a sample of each.

[For example, Acme, Inc., is a $3 million sales manufacturer and marketer of pencils in the Northeast region. Acme, Inc., is a division of Acme Corp, a public company with $800 million in sales. The division sells pencils, pens, and other writing and drawing instruments. The recent trend for the division has been static, as the parent has not provided working capital to modernize machinery. Acme, Inc., is managed by one vice president who has been there for six months. The previous manager worked there for 11 months.]

The competition [does, doesn't] [use the same means of distribution as (the company), advertise in the same trade journals]. *(If the advertising is regular, it probably works!)*

Our [product or service] is unique because of [x], [and/or] we have a competitive advantage because of our [speed to market, established brand name, low-cost producer status].

RISK/OPPORTUNITY

Business Risks

Knowing your risks and having a strategy is a must for attracting an investor. There are several kinds of risk, especially among entrepreneurial, growing businesses. Be sure to address the following, and provide your strategy for dealing with them.

Some of the major risks facing our development include [limited operating history, limited resources, market uncertainties, production uncertainties, limited management experience, dependence on key management].

Opportunities

Use this section to provide excitement and promise.

Although our business today has its share of risks, we feel we can overcome these risks because of [x]. We will address [market risk] by [doing a comprehensive study, partnering with a larger company who knows the market]. We feel we can address [pricing risk, product risk, management risk] by focusing on [x].

If we are able to overcome these risks, our company has the opportunity to [dominate a niche in the marketplace, become a major force in the industry]. We feel our brand could become known as the [place entrepreneurs look for financing help; the place people look for good tasting, low-fat cheese]. We think we can achieve this goal in the next [x] years.

Specifically, our lead product [x], has the chance to [change the industry, affect many lives, improve performance in the (x) field]. This would also enable us to tap markets we have not yet begun to approach, such as [international sales, ethnic market, generation X].

MANAGEMENT TEAM

Describe your managers, and how they work together as a team.

Our team has the following members to achieve our plan. [v] men and women who have a combined [w] years of experience—[x] years in marketing, [y] years in product development, and [z] years in [other disciplines].

Officers and Key Employees	Title
[A],	President
[B],	Vice President of Marketing
[C],	Vice President of Sales
[D],	Vice President of Finance

Ownership

[The company] has authorized [x] shares of common stock, of which [x] are issued and outstanding. The following persons or organizations are significant owners of the company:

Name	# Shares Held	% Ownership
[A. B. Founder]	52	[52%]
[C. R. Inventor]	22	[22%]
Management Team	10	[10%]
[Seed Ventures]	10	[10%]

Professional Support

We have assembled a team of professionals, including: [corporate attorney]; [accounting firm]; [other consultants].

Board of Advisors [or Directors]

We have also secured the assistance and support of the following business and industry experts to help in the decision-making, strategizing, and opportunity-seizing process: [highlight your board members, detailing where and why they add strategic importance, what experience they have, and what contacts they can contribute.]

CAPITAL REQUIREMENTS

We seek [$x] of additional [equity, subdebt, or senior financing] to fund our growth for the next [two years, year, month]. At that time, we will need an additional [$x] to reach a positive cash-flow position.

The initial stage of funding will be used to [complete development, purchase equipment, introduce and market our new/next product line, fund working capital, acquire a competitor]. Here is a breakdown of how the funds will be spent:

complete development	[$x]
purchase equipment	[$x]
market our new/next product line	[$x]
fund working capital	[$x]

Exit/Payback Strategy

We can provide an exit for this [loan, investment] within [x] years by [a dividend of excess profits, recapitalizations, sale of company, or public offering]. [Define how much time you will require to pay back the loan or provide a return to investors. Describe how the repayment will be accomplished, and what strategy will be used to acheive that exit.]

FINANCIAL PLAN

Assumptions

The attached projections assume the following: [state significant assumptions].

Financial Statements

Income Statements
Financial statements are generally monthly for the first year or two, then quarterly thereafter. Incorporate year-to-date figures if they exist.

Sales will increase with the introduction of the [new line, improved line]. We plan to introduce these products roughly on the following schedule: [detail here]. We expect to be able to sell at the rate of [x] units per month within [x] months of introduction.

Cost of goods sold will decrease [x%] as we are able to buy more efficiently in the marketplace and use our new equipment to produce more units at lower cost. Gross profit will remain static as [e.g., new introductions will be at higher margins, while we expect margins of older lines to erode].

Selling and administration expenses will increase in absolute dollars, but decrease as a percentage because while expense is increasing, [name largest items here, or items that will change most significantly] sales will be growing faster. Research and development, which will appear as a high percentage of sales early, will be reduced as a percentage over time.

Our head count will increase after funding to [x], which will include a [VP Sales, paid on commission; VP R&D, ($x); VP Finance, ($x); VP Operations, ($x)].

Keep in mind that projections do not stand on their own. The rationale of how you prepared the numbers is important to investors. Tie in the discussions you made about market size, time to market, market acceptance, and competitive pressures into these numbers. Discuss any large numbers or numbers that change significantly from period to period. Include discussion of sales growth rationale, expense growth, and so forth.

Balance Sheet Summary
Comment on any large or unusual items, such as other current assets, other accounts payable, or accrued liabilities.

Cash Flow and Break-Even Analysis
These are critical statements, even more so than the balance sheets and income statements. Cash, and how much you have at the end of the day, is everything to investors.

We have assumed that our suppliers will be willing to grant us terms of [x] until we reach monthly purchases of [x]. At that time, we have assumed that our terms will be stretched to [x] days.

We have also assumed that we can collect our billings within [x] days because of [special programs with large customers, factoring arrangement, credit card and COD sales].

We have assumed that the first part of our [loan, investment] will be made in [month], and the balance in [month].

We can reach break-even by the [x] month. Sales are expected to be at the [$x] level by that date.

Conclusion

Be bold. This is the finale of the entire document.

Based on our projections, we feel an [investment in, loan to] [the company] is a sound business investment. In order to proceed, we are requesting an [investment, loan] of [$x] by [date].

EXHIBITS

A common beginner error is to bog down the body of a plan with too much detail. That's what the exhibits are for. Exhibits give an investor a better feel for the company behind the numbers. Be sure to include illustrative material such as product literature and brochures, media coverage, relevant patents, market research data, past advertising campaigns, useful photographs of facilities, warehouses, and so forth.

Notes

1. Deloitte & Touche LLP (www.dttus.com).
2. "Step-by-Step Business Planning," *Home Office Computing* (November 1996): (www.brs-inc.com/homeoff.html).
3. www.nfibonline.com
4. Stephanie Gruner. "When Mom & Pop Go Public," *Inc.* (December 1996): vol. 18, no. 18, p. 66(6).
5. "Microbrew Raises $1.6 Million in Unprecedented Internet Offering," Wit Capital (www.witcapital.com) (2/26/96).
6. David Stegall. "A Seven Point Checklist for Your Business Plan," Financing News (www.datamerge.com/financingnews/SB7point.html) (© 1996).
7. Lynne L. Jacobus and Alvin D. Gottlieb. "Presenting Your Company to Investors," *Entrepreneurial Edge* (www.edgeonline.com) (© 1997).

CHAPTER

The Complete Entrepreneur: Post-Start-up Challenges

8

Chapter Objectives

After completing this chapter, you should be able to

■ Discuss and understand some of the difficulties of taking a business from start-up to profitability.

■ Apply the principles of activity-based costing to add focus to our product mix.

■ Manage the balance sheet to maintain adequate working capital.

■ Use financial ratio analysis to measure our company's performance, and refine our strategies.

■ Consider growth strategies for successful businesses.

■ Evaluate international opportunities, and our readiness to take them on.

START-UP "TRAUMA"

The amount of time required for a new venture to reach profitability is a critical factor in whether a business survives the start-up trauma. *Start-up financing does not mean the struggle is over.* A promising new business, well on its way to viability, can still experience severe cash-flow problems; sometimes these can be fatal. Even beyond the start-up period, strains on cash can severely limit company growth.

The best way to illustrate some of the bumps in the road to profitability is through real-life case studies. A critical reading of these cases, followed by the expert opinions of those who are knowledgeable about the industry and familiar with the venture, can help prepare us for dealing with difficulties that were not foreseen in our plan.

The first case concerns an entrepreneur who successfully executed a private stock offering at start-up, but then had to borrow to keep the company going. Form your opinions of the viability of the business and its strategy as you read the case, and then see "What the Experts Say" at the end.

CASE STUDY 8.1
Icon Acoustics, Inc.

The following was adapted from "Sound Strategy," by Edward O. Welles.[1]

THE INDUSTRY

Most stereo equipment is sold through dealers. But to small and craftsmanlike speaker builders like Dave Fokos, audio dealers sell a relative handful of popular, mass-produced models, effectively denying more customized offerings access to the mainstream market. What Fokos wanted to do with Icon Acoustics, Inc., was to bypass what he saw as a dealer cartel.

Icon seeks to sell direct from the factory. Customers can call Icon on an 800 number and order speakers. Icon pays for shipping and any return freight, and customers can try out the speakers at home without obligation for 30 days. If questions or problems arise, Fokos is available, via his 800 number, to give advice.

Fokos sees several advantages for his customers. Not only is the dealer markup—100% or so—avoided, but with the home trial, buyers can listen to the product in their actual environment before making a decision. Most important, direct selling makes available to the listener a niche product that would not be profitable for most dealers.

There are about 335 stereo-speaker makers in the United States selling to a $3-billion-a-year market (for all audio components). About 100 of them sell to the low end and midrange of the market—say up to $500 per pair of speakers—which accounts for about 90% of that $3 billion. That leaves roughly 235 specialty companies fighting over a market that amounts to no more than $300 million.

Most of those 250 companies are undercapitalized and therefore unknown. Plowing most of their resources into building speakers, they have little left over to market them with. That, too, was Icon's problem. How would Fokos get the word out?

THE BUSINESS

Icon's product line consists of two models. Its Lumen speaker stands 18 inches high and weighs 26 pounds. A pair currently sells for $795. The Parsec, 47 inches high and 86 pounds, currently sells for $1,795 a pair. Both models have components of very high quality that in many cases cost 10 times what the equivalent part in a mass-produced speaker does. In that way, they embody the Icon ethos: cram the speakers with quality components and craftsmanship—and then sell them for half the price a dealer would charge.

Fokos defines his target market as people who love to listen to music, equipment junkies, the audio-addicted. They tend to be educated, affluent, and obsessed. As Fokos puts it, "These people would rather buy a new set of speakers than eat."

START-UP FINANCING

The generally positive reviews Fokos received as a speaker designer for an employer enabled him to raise some money to start Icon. He had acquired a following among some hard-core customers, and several of them became Icon investors.

Fokos wanted Icon to be debt-free. He decided upon a private stock offering, and by early 1989 he had sold 42% of the company for $189,000, or $4,500 per 1% share. That would be his working capital. (He kept 58% of company ownership.)

Icon Acoustics began life on April 1, 1989, and quickly ran into trouble when Fokos couldn't immediately get his hands on that money. He needed regulatory approval for his private stock offering in the states in which his investors lived. Fokos's lawyer told him that would take three weeks. It took three months. It wasn't until August that Fokos had access to his working capital.

Without that, he had to use his $10,000 stake in Icon to pay the rent starting on May 1. Fokos had figured he would build his prototypes in the spring and early summer and have production speakers for sale by October. Now he knew he'd be lucky if he had the prototypes done by the first of the year. By early 1990, with most of his money plowed into inventory and equipment, Fokos had to abandon his debt-free strategy and seek a $50,000 loan—a loan from which he would not receive the proceeds until midyear. "That money was spent before I had it," he recalls.

OPERATIONS

By June, Icon was beginning to look like a real company. Its hit-or-miss marketing strategy, relying on magazine reviews and word of mouth, was starting to hit.

In a report on the High End Hi-Fi Show in its August 1990 issue, *Stereophile* magazine said this about Icon's speakers: "The overall sound was robust and dynamic, with a particularly potent low end. Parts and construction quality appeared to be first-rate. Definitely a company to watch." In a vote dubbed "The Best Sound at the Show," with ballots cast by attendees, rating 200

brands, Icon's Parsec speakers, selling at the show for $1,495, placed 15th. In the top 10 the least expensive were $2,400 a pair, and six of the systems sold at prices ranging from $8,000 to $18,000.

Fokos sold 20 pairs of speakers in October and another 20 in November. He also invested in one slickly produced four-color display ad, featuring the Parsecs, in the buyer's guide issued in October by *Stereo Review,* the consumer magazine with the largest circulation (506,000). That dovetailed with a generally favorable review in December in *Stereophile* magazine. For the last six months of 1990, the company's sales registered $70,000.

But just when Icon started to roll, it hit more snags. It was running low on a key component, woofers for the Parsecs, because of a mixup with the German manufacturer. Then Fokos's bank failed, denying Icon's customers the ability to charge their orders on credit cards. In mid-

---

Icon Acoustics, Inc. Projected Operating Statement ($000)

Icon Acoustics, Inc., Billerica, MA.

Concept: Sell high-end stereo loudspeakers direct from the factory, with a 30-day free trial period.

Hurdles: Financing a marketing effort to achieve name recognition in a crowded and highly fragmented market.

	1991	1992	1993	1994	1995
Speakers Sold (Pairs)	224	435	802	1,256	1,830
Total Sales	$303	$654	$1,299	$2,153	$3,338
Cost of Goods Sold					
Material/Packaging	$130	$281	$561	$931	$1,445
Shipping	$43	$83	$157	$226	$322
Total CGS	$173	$364	$718	$1,157	$1,767
Gross Profit	$130	$290	$581	$997	$1,571
Gross Margin	43%	44%	45%	46%	47%
Expenses					
New property/eqpt	$3	$6	$12	$15	$18
Marketing	$13	$66	$70	$109	$135
General/admin	$51	$110	$197	$308	$378
Loan repayment	$31	$31		—	
Outstanding payables	$30		—		—
Total Expenses	$128	$213	$279	$432	$531
Pretax Profit	$2	$77	$302	$565	$1,040
Pretax Net Margin	1%	12%	23%	26%	31%

January, the Persian Gulf war broke out, and Icon's phone fell silent.

In February the phone started to ring steadily. Fokos was getting about five queries a day. One out of seven callers bought speakers. People had seen his handful of ads. They had heard of the speakers by word of mouth. Icon had more magazine reviews to look forward to in late spring, including one in *Stereo Review. Stereophile* was going to put the Parsec on its Buyer's Guide list of recommended components.

Maybe now there was hope. Maybe Icon's best days lay ahead.

But for now Icon's is still a tale written in red ink. Fokos recites his litany of financial woes: "Last year I paid myself $9,500 in salary; the year before that it was $8,300 for nine months. The company has $50,000 in bank debt and $30,000 in bills that need to be paid. My interest on the bank debt alone is $500 a month." He draws an audible breath, considering the weight of it all. "This is certainly the toughest thing I've ever done," he says. "It has influenced my health a little. I can feel the stress inside. At times I ask myself, Is it worth it?" He pauses, then smiles. "But that doesn't last very long."

WHAT THE EXPERTS SAY

OBSERVER: *John Atkinson, Editor of* Stereophile, *a consumer magazine for audiophiles.*

One function of dealers is that they become your first customers. They'll tell you right away if the product isn't selling and why. They become your final test site, and by selling direct Fokos doesn't have that.

More important, if you look at all successful mail-order companies, they devote a large portion of their budget to promotion—and have something like a major advertising program or a direct-mail catalog. You have to advertise continually before people will take you seriously. Fokos's promotional efforts, in contrast, are largely one-time events. The general wisdom in this industry is that product reviews are good as part of your overall promotion, but if they are your sole means of promotion, the risks are too high.

OBSERVER: *Robert Blattberg, President of Blattberg Consultants marketing firm.*

Fokos is making a classic mistake that a lot of entrepreneurs make: He's underestimating what the distribution channel can do for him. There's a reason for the 100% markup dealers charge: They advertise. They provide an easy way for the customers to find the product. They deal with product returns. They service the product after the sale. They hold inventory. Those are all problems that Fokos himself now has to deal with.

And dealers offer a forum for customers to compare products. There's no way Fokos's potential customers can do that. I'm sympathetic to some of his points, namely that dealers sometimes set up unrealistic listening environments, push products that are better sellers or have higher margins, and so on. But he also has to realize that there's value there.

Can he continue to generate enough leads simply through reviews and word of mouth? He should think about more advertising and possibly direct mail. His advertising should create an image of him as a guru. That's what people are really buying: a special product designed by a special man in a special market.

OBSERVER: *Katie Muldoon, President of Muldoon & Baer.*

There are two types of successful direct marketing: a onetime product that has high margins and is marketed with lots of advertising space, or a continuing business built on an entire product line, often sold through catalogs. Fokos's business is neither.

He might be better off attempting to strike some sort of cooperative venture with an established catalog, like Sharper Image, a venture that would allow him to tell his story without bearing the whole cost. Credibility is essential if he's going to sell direct. And he doesn't have a famous name. A company like American Express might be able to make a direct-mail campaign work for him because it would be endorsing him.

COMPETITOR: *Frank Reed, CEO of Boston Acoustics, Inc., a loudspeaker manufacturer.*

Fokos suggests that the quality of his product is demonstrated in the expensive components he uses. But the cost of his components doesn't really relate to the quality. It relates to his inefficient economies of scale.

He says the retail audio market is stifling, but it isn't as cutthroat as he contends. I don't believe any single manufacturer has 10% of the market. He says it saves a lot of money to sell direct. But I suspect his costs of sales—advertising, freight costs—will be as high as those the guy selling through dealers has. He says he didn't want to sell through dealers because it offers limited distribution. Why can't he have a small network of esoteric dealers and supplement that by selling direct wherever he doesn't have a retailer?

FINANCIER: *Henry Morgan, Partner, Innovative Capital Partners.*

I agree with Fokos's assessment of dealers. I'm an investor in Cambridge Soundworks (another direct seller), and I've seen that audio retailers always want to push something new. So your product doesn't have a long life cycle. I agree that for Icon, selling direct is probably the right way to go.

But I think Fokos is overestimating the size of his market. His projections of about $3 million are high—$1 million is more like it. He doesn't have the name recognition right now that would give his products clear superiority over some of the stuff people currently like to buy.

Also, I don't think this is a price-sensitive business, and I think he has to get at least 50% margins, or else he can't support himself or afford to advertise effectively. He has to raise his price, and he must get his costs down. He's very fussy about how he buys components, but a lot of that quality he's striving for isn't going to be perceived by the customer.

Also, in direct marketing, customers want quick, reliable delivery time. Fokos has to have enough inventory to fill orders quickly. He has to eliminate some of the glitches he's already experienced with his suppliers.

The next case concerns another entrepreneur who succeeded at start-up financing, with a combination of family money and investment by a friend. He was trying to make his way in an industry that had not quite taken shape yet. Again, form your opinions of the viability of the business and its strategy as you read the case, and then see "What the Experts Say" at the end.

CASE STUDY 8.2
The Plastic Lumber Co.

The following was adapted from "Plastics!" an article by Paul B. Brown.[2]

THE INDUSTRY

Alan Robbins, president of The Plastic Lumber Co. of Akron, Ohio, is betting everything he owns that the world will pay more for picnic tables, mailbox posts, and speed bumps if they're made from recycled plastics. And no doubt there's a desperate need for someone to do something with what the industry calls post-consumer (used) plastics.

With Americans producing 160 million tons of solid waste a year—that's better than three pounds per person per day—landfills are beginning to overflow. And while plastics account for only 7% of those garbage heaps by weight, they make up 13% of their volume.

Besides, as Robbins points out, the potential market is huge. In 1989, only 250 million pounds of plastics were recycled, yet the demand for materials that plastics could replace was thousands of times greater, according to Robert A. Bennett, associate dean of the college of engineering at the University of Toledo. For example, last year Americans used some 3 *billion* pounds of treated lumber, and roughly 7.4 billion board feet of wood just to build pallets.

Robbins is not looking to replace all that wood—just a splinter of it. In 1989, convinced he was on to something, Robbins formed The Plastic Lumber Co.

THE BUSINESS

Plastic Lumber Co. is woefully undercapitalized. There's no money for a marketing staff. In fact, there's not much of a staff at all. The entire company consists of Robbins, his administrative assistant, and the four plant workers who actually turn out his product.

The company lost $55,000 during its first three months. When sales failed to come close to forecasts in January and February of 1990, Robbins reduced salaries and eliminated his public-relations program and most of his advertising. The Plastic Lumber Co. is still losing money.

Robbins assumed he would average 20% pretax profits. He budgeted raw materials cost at 44% of sales, labor was expected to be just 9%. But he also expected he'd fetch a premium price for his products. "Purchasing agents are trained killers" is the way Robbins puts it. So far, pretax margins on the speed bumps and car stops he has sold to commercial accounts have been lower.

Robbins sublets from his brother-in-law. Says Robbins: "By sharing space with him, I didn't have to worry about going out and buying fax machines and copiers." He pays $2 per square foot—about half the going rate—for his production facility in an old tire plant that the state of Ohio is trying to turn over to small businesses.

CAPITALIZATION

By combining interest from a CD with a term loan in a linked-deposit program, Robbins has borrowed $154,000 at about prime. He sold stock and options in the company, totaling 24% ownership, to a friend for $50,000.

Plastic Lumber Co. Operating Statement

The Plastic Lumber Co., Akron, Ohio
Started in 1989 by current president, Alan Robbins.
Concept: Recycle plastics into products such as picnic tables, mailbox posts, and speed bumps.
Projections: Profits of about $6,000 in 1990, almost $500,000 in 1991; pretax profits of 40% and 44%.
Hurdles: Defining market; convincing customers that paying more now for products made with recycled materials will save them money in the long run; overcoming lack of technical expertise.

	1990	*1991*
Sales	$495,000	$2,075,000
Cost of Sales		
Raw Materials	222,000	913,000
Direct labor	44,500	186,750
Rent	21,132	23,000
Electricity	11,535	48,349
Total Cost of Sales	299,167	1,171,099
Gross Profit	195,833	903,901
Gross Profit %	40%	44%
Expenses		
Production	53,120	150,568
Marketing	42,000	72,000
General & Administrative	55,000	114,684
Finance costs	15,000	14,737
Depreciation	10,529	41,736
Other	13,400	24,000
Total Expenses	189,049	417,725
Net Income	$6,784	$486,176

But the money is going quickly, thanks to a combination of lower-than-budgeted sales and cost increases primarily caused by operating problems. Expenses are as low as is practically possible.

Having contributed almost his entire savings to this arrangement, banks are reluctant to loan any more. What is needed—and soon—are additional equity investors. "We've been putting off looking for outside funding," says Robbins. "The better shape we can get the company in before offering stock, the higher the valuation will be. But we are now starting to hold serious meetings with venture capitalists."

The question is, of course, whether the money will come in time—and in sufficient amounts. There's little doubt that someday there will be a huge market for products made from recycled plastics, but which products? And even if Robbins does figure out which products the market wants, can he muster the technical expertise to make them? Good questions all, says Robbins, who remains sanguine nonetheless. "We'll be OK."

With plastic lumber . . . well, let's quote the business plan: "The plastic lumber market can only be considered in its infancy."

WHAT THE EXPERTS SAY

FINANCIER: *Nancy Pfund, General Partner, Hambrecht & Quist, a venture capital firm.*

I think Robbins was correct in perceiving there's a tremendous market opportunity here. The concept of the business, broadly defined, is sound; there will be exponential growth in the waste minimization segment of the market. But Robbins has made things difficult for himself by focusing on the lower end of the business, with its very competitive pricing. Better margins are available to the manufacturer that adds real value, for example, by creating recycled products with the characteristics of virgin materials—that's where money will be made.

If I were Robbins I would upgrade the technology and therefore the end product. How do you do that? Perhaps through strategic partnerships. He's got marketing contacts and distribution experience; he should weave that into some kind of relationship with a plastics recycler with a little more know-how.

He also has a little business that could feed into the activities of another firm. There are all kinds of options: a co-marketing arrangement, or a subcontractor, or supplying components for larger products. He certainly has a lot of energy and enthusiasm, which could be put to better use.

One of the common mistakes is to think people are going to buy products just because they're environmentally correct. It certainly can help, but people are very dollars-and-cents oriented. Recycled plastics products do not have to be more expensive than what they're replacing, and in the long run they can't be. In the long run they have to be cheaper.

OBSERVER: *Thomas J. Penrice, Director, Plastic Consulting for Strategic Analysis, Inc.*

I'm bullish on Robbins's idea and his chances for success. His sales forecast is quite modest. His raw materials cost, relatively high now, could become negative before long. As communities collect all this plastic, they will need someone to take it off their hands.

The major problem that I see is in the underestimation of marketing costs. If he uses the $72,000 he has budgeted (on $2 million of projected sales) to hire a marketing person, there won't be any budget for mailings and travel. You have to go to the trade shows and network.

Eventually there'll be many viable consumer and industrial applications for recycled plastic products. However, Robbins's company must first survive the next several months. I would begin by working directly with major producers of plastic resins, such as Dow and Du Pont, and take the plastics they can't use in their recycling programs, the co-mingled plastics, and see if they would be willing to buy picnic tables and the like from him. These companies all have active recycling programs and are eager to promote recycling. Once the applications are demonstrated to be practical and cost effective, however, Robbins must reach a broader market.

The next case describes a start-up that met its sales goals, but did not watch expenses closely enough. Here, the experts work with her on repositioning the company rather than commenting after the fact. Use the study questions at the end to make sure you are sensitive to the lessons learned.

CASE STUDY 8.3
Diamond Courier Service

The following was adapted from "Are We Making Money Yet?" an article by Susan Greco.[3]

THE BUSINESS

As Claudia Post pursued the simple idea of running a downtown Philadelphia bicycle-courier business, other related opportunities arose and she added several to her product mix. Now, besides bike-messenger services, Diamond Courier Service found itself in driver deliveries, truck deliveries, airfreight services, a parts-distribution service—and even a legal service that served subpoenas and prepared court filings.

Although all the businesses shared some common resources, each had its own line workers, manager, and administrative-support person, as well as its own steady customers and unique pricing and billing practices. The question was never, What do we do best? It was always: What else can we sell?

She had started Diamond Courier in August 1990, determined to outperform the downtown courier company that had just fired her from a sales position. Post plotted Diamond's sales growth on a straight trajectory, and it took her only 17 months to achieve her first objective, $1 million in sales. She nearly doubled that volume during the next year. "What she did was incredible," says the admiring owner of a Florida-based courier company.

In 1993, its third full year, Post's company had $3.1 million in sales. By then Diamond employed some 40 bike messengers and 25 back-office staffers and provided steady work for 50 independent drivers. There was never any ambiguity about Post's role in the business: master networker and fearless cold caller—the sales whiz every struggling young company needs. Post put the "star" in start-up, and she was happy. "I was busy having a great time selling."

Cash flow? Profit before taxes? "I didn't know how to figure out any of that stuff," she says. She was a selling machine. And to be sure that she could keep on selling, Post recruited a former colleague, Tony Briscella, to step into the sales manager's role at Diamond.

It was early that year, however, that symptoms of underlying problems in the business first became apparent. The usual start-up cash crunches grew more serious and arrived more often until eventually they became chronic. By the latter part of the year, Post was helping her staff shuffle the accounts payable and decide whom to pay and when.

Briscella, her new sales manager, who'd previously worked for Federal Express, had begun to complain that he couldn't get accurate operating results. "I'd hear things like 'We either broke even or made $6,000.' That," he says, "drove me crazy."

Despite Diamond's continued growth, it wasn't much longer before Post had to resort to drastic measures, selling her jewelry and liquidating long-held stocks, to generate the cash she needed to pay her employees. Of course, the more her cash problems mounted, the more Post, the consummate salesperson, wanted to get out and sell.

By the spring of 1994 the company was undeniably sick, and Post remembers thinking, "Here I am with a company that's doing $3 million plus, and I have no money. I'm working a gazillion hours a week. There's something terribly wrong here." But what? Desperate and scared, Post asked a friend in the industry to examine her books. "Claudia," he said after a cursory look, "you're headed for the rocks."

A MIDCOURSE CORRECTION

It wasn't diversification *per se* that had brought Post's business to the brink of failure. Any of the businesses Diamond now found itself in could conceivably have been profitable. The problem was that Post simply didn't know which, if any, of them were.

She didn't know because she was operating on a set of reasonable but unexamined assumptions. She assumed, for instance, that if she kept selling and priced her services at market rates, she would build a profitable business. She assumed that growing volume would generate economies of scale. She assumed that if she took good care of customers, the business would take care of itself. She never took the time to question or test these assumptions. Post continued to believe that sales would be Diamond's salvation when, in fact, nearly every sale she made pushed the company a little further into the red and a little closer to failure.

"Most entrepreneurs have no idea what it really costs them to produce a product or service," asserts Al Sloman. He's the veteran industry consultant recommended to Post by the friend who had examined her books and sounded the alarm. His goal was to teach her the business side of the business—to get her to understand and acknowledge that in addition to dollars in (sales), she also had to deal with dollars out (costs).

Chief among the tools that Sloman showed Post how to use was profit-center analysis, which amounted to showing her how to build an income statement for every business line Diamond was in. A profit-center analysis can reveal which activities—or, for that matter, which sales territories or branch operations—are making money and which are not. For Post the analysis proved to be eye-opening.

The key to building a profit-center statement is knowing how to identify all the costs associated with a particular business activity. Sloman helped Post extract sales and cost data for each of the businesses Diamond was in by poring over work records and computer files. Line by line, they compiled the labor costs, the operating costs, and the administrative costs directly linked to each of the six business lines.

They could have stopped there, but the profit picture would have been incomplete. Because Post's back office had grown so rapidly and come to generate such a large portion of total costs (sales, general, and administrative costs made up about 30%), they also had to allocate those indirect costs among the various businesses. *How* the overhead costs were allocated was crucial, because the allocation rationale would, in part, determine which businesses showed a profit and which did not.

Sloman urged Post to use an allocation system known as activity-based costing. Essentially, activity-based costing assigns overhead costs to the various businesses not in proportion to their revenue shares (which is the conventional technique) but in proportion to their respective use of the company's resources. "If employees and man-

agers could say how they used their time, we used that," says Sloman. "If not, we looked at the level of activity, say, the number of jobs per profit center" as the basis for allocating overhead.

Nowhere had her earlier assumptions been more misleading than in Diamond's original business, downtown bicycle-courier services. For instance, Post had assumed that if competitors could make a living with prices lower than hers, then she had to be making money, too. She had assumed that the revenues generated by her bike-messenger business contributed handsomely to total company revenues and profit, since the bike customers were among her oldest and largest accounts.

How wrong she found that she was. The bicycle division, which she thought of as Diamond's core business, generated just 10% of total revenues and barely covered its own direct-labor and insurance costs. Worse, the division created more logistical and customer-service nightmares than any other single business, thereby generating a disproportionate share of overhead costs.

Diamond wasn't making money on bicycle deliveries. It was charging customers $4.69 per job, but with fully allocated costs of $9.24 per job, the company was losing $4.55 every time a cyclist picked up a package.

	Est.	Actual
Revenue	$4.69	
Messenger's pay	$2.35	$4.23
Overhead	$2.11	$5.01
Profit (loss)	$0.23	($4.55)

How could her estimates have been so far off? Messengers were averaging less than half of the three deliveries per hour Post had assumed. This meant that many never qualified for the 50-50 commission split on which Post had based her mental profit model; instead they collected a guaranteed hourly wage.

In distributing her overhead costs on a per-delivery basis, she could see the problem clearly. Bike jobs, Post discovered, ate a disproportionate amount of each dispatcher's time (dispatcher's pay: $0.54); messengers called in to the office frequently (telephone charges: $0.14); office expenses included bikers' T-shirts (miscellaneous: $0.07). Service reps handled customer relations and kept records, a lot of work for such low-ticket transactions (customer service: $0.57).

The single biggest overhead allocation was the per-delivery share of the company's general and administrative resources used by the bicycle service (allocated overhead: $3.69). This category covers Diamond's managerial and administrative salaries, rent, insurance, collection costs, etc.

Sloman showed Post how to perform the same kind of analysis on Diamond's other operations. She was shocked to see that four of the six—all except driver and truck deliveries—were generating losses.

On January 3, 1995, Post shut down the bicycle-messenger business, which was killing the rest of the company. She saw that it was pointless to compete with operators charging $3 per delivery when she had to charge $10 just to cover her costs. (After all, the $3 operators were smaller companies focused on bikes.)

And it made no sense to try to run the bike work simultaneously with the suburban and regional vehicle work, which was profitable, each job generating an average of $27.60 in revenues to cover $21.23 in costs. "We didn't need the bike service to have the vehicle service," says Post. "I knew I couldn't delay the decision, because every second was costing us money."

Was there a way to jettison the bicycle-courier business gently without losing the profitable driver jobs that came from the same customers? Post and Briscella nervously rehearsed what they'd say in face-to-face visits. A few customers wouldn't stand for it, and Post wasn't surprised when 4 of her top 30 accounts took *all* their business elsewhere.

"I wanted to be clear and direct with my client base, and I think I gained credibility that way," she says. In the end Post kept all the large accounts that used her drivers more than her bikers.

Within a few months, Post closed two more of Diamond's *un*profit centers—airfreight and parts distribution. Using the profit-center analysis, Sloman had prepared a pro forma income statement that showed Post she could actually increase profits by reducing sales.

He showed her that by cutting $521,000 in unprofitable sales, she could eliminate $640,000 in costs. Sloman wanted Diamond to eliminate all services and customers that didn't generate a profit, but Post couldn't do that and didn't think she should.

She decided, for instance, that some services she couldn't afford to operate herself, such as air-freight, were worth brokering on occasion in order to retain clients that generated profits for her elsewhere. And she replaced a few of the bikers with walkers, who now service select customers at a premium price. Still, in 1995 she forfeited sales of about $400,000—most of them willingly.

Post also raised prices for some of the work Diamond did. Now that she knew how to wield a calculator and could compute her average cost per job, she realized that she'd priced too many jobs at or below breakeven.

Diamond managed to finish 1995 in the black with revenues from more profitable operations. Overall, revenue per job has more than doubled, from an average of $13 in 1993 to about $28 in 1995. Post and her managers think about sales differently, too. They're as likely to argue about which customers to drop as which prospects to pursue.

Now Post counts her blessings. "I mean, I could have just spun out," she says. She knows so much more now. "I know what I need to break even every day," she says. "I monitor my payables. I know what my cash flow is and what's going into the bank every day. We created a budget, and I understand what it means to manage according to budget targets."

A computer program provides her with a daily report of revenue per job. "Look, I'm never going to be a serious financial person," she concedes, "but you own a business, it's your responsibility. I can't slough it off on somebody else. I have to know."

STUDY QUESTIONS

1. Could the bicycle service have been retained with some change in operations? How can Diamond's competitors make a profit?

   _____

   _____

   _____

2. Is this type of analysis appropriate to your venture? What are your profit centers? How would you allocate general and administrative costs to the various profit centers?

   _____

   _____

   _____

3. How would you describe Diamond's marketing strategy before the corrections? What is the current strategy? Could there have been some intermediate approach?

_____

_____

_____

_____

Resources

The information contained in the resources that follow can help entrepreneurs think smarter about costing, pricing, and business-unit profitability

Articles

A free three-page executive brief on activity-based costing, a useful tool for companies whose overhead is growing as fast as their direct costs, is available from ABC Technologies, in Beaverton, OR (800-882-3141). A 16-page manufacturing case study, "Why You Should Consider Activity-Based Costing," can be obtained free from *Small Business Forum* (800-419-5018). To see how the practice works in service companies, order a reprint of "Tracking Costs in a Service Organization," published by *Management Accounting* (800-638-4427, extension 280) in February 1993, which explains how Fireman's Fund uses activity-based accounting.

Books

Accounting and Financial Fundamentals for Nonfinancial Executives, by Valarie Neiman and Eileen J. Glick (AMACOM, 800-262-9699, 1996, $18.95), covers the basics of cost accounting, the contribution concept, and other management tools. Two recent works demystify pricing and are well suited to service companies: *Priced to Sell,* by Herman Holtz (Upstart Publishing, 800-829-7934, 1996, $27.95), and *No Apologies Pricing* (Home Based Business Association of Arizona, 602-464-0778, 1995, $9.95), a 52-page booklet worth its price because of its wonderful simplicity.

On-Line

A primer on how to do a business-unit "contribution-margin analysis" is available at Inc. Online (www.inc.com) in the Interactive Worksheet area. The worksheet is titled "Is a Product or Customer Costing More Than It's Worth?" Tracking costs is made easier with the "job costing" modules available with major accounting-software packages. See "Ledger-demain" in the June issue of *Inc. Technology,* also available at Inc. Online.

CASH-FLOW AND PERFORMANCE MEASUREMENT

Managers, particularly in survival-stage businesses, must track their financial data closely. Many are very conscious of what the income statement tells them, but not enough manage the balance sheet as well. Cash is the foundation for a strong balance sheet.

Proper cash management permits the owner to meet the cash needs of the business, take advantage of special buys and discounts, minimize interest expense, and ride out slow periods. A good cash position allows the owner to maintain an adequate level of inventory, to replace equipment as needs arise, and to seize expansion opportunities.

Cash demands are often cyclical. On an annual cycle, inventory can be worked down (in essence, partially liquidated) as a slow period approaches, and restocked as the prime selling season returns. On a monthly cycle, the daily balance on the bank statement can show the ebb and flow of cash; a manager can track cash requirements and create inducements for customers to pay in time to fill in "troughs" in the cash balance.

Cash Management

Cash, in a business management context, refers to funds that can be drawn on immediately, generally the balance in the active checking account of the business plus incidental amounts of legal tender kept on hand for minor expenses.

Many observers confuse cash with profits. Profits, while necessary to survival, do not ensure survival. Profitable businesses have been known to fail because they could not meet cash demands placed on them.

You may have heard the saying that "anyone who hasn't met payroll doesn't know what it is to run a business." For salaries and bills to be paid on time, and for money to be spent on equipment and inventory, cash must be managed efficiently. The only way to do that is through an effective and well-monitored system.

An effective system begins with meaningful financial statements. Financial or cash-flow statements are like a map. They chart the trail of cash in and out of your business. If the map is difficult to read or does not provide you with sufficient and accurate information, it is time to redesign it.

The expense section of the income statement is particularly important. Are the categories sufficiently detailed to assist in tracking expenses?

For example, is a "Vehicle Expense" category likely to be as useful as separate categories for "Gasoline and Oil" and "Repairs"? With the latter breakdown, we may be more able to track month-to-month changes that indicate that we may be making unnecessary trips, or that one of our delivery trucks is becoming too costly to maintain and should be replaced.

Another valuable component of a cash management system is the budget. The main purpose of a budget is to establish reasonable targets for sales, profits, and the various expense categories, and to measure performance against these targets. Several months of operating experience is generally required before a budget can be developed. It then must be evaluated and refined on a regular basis.

Harvey Goldstein, a certified public accountant and author of the book *Up Your Cash Flow,* recommends two budgets: a realistic budget and a survival one. A realistic budget is one containing figures for achievable sales, honest operating expenses, and reasonable profits.

Goldstein recommends the survival budget "because most people operating a small business generally don't react to change and economic conditions quickly enough. The key triggering mechanism for going from a realistic budget to the survival budget is a steady decline in sales."

Collections

The type of business you are in often determines whether sales are mainly for cash or credit. A small bakery might sell completely on a cash basis; their daily sales and daily cash receipts are the same. Sales charged to bank credit cards are basically cash sales where the funds, less a service charge of 2 or 3 percent, are electronically deposited to the merchant's account as the sale is made.

Larger retailers, wholesalers, and manufacturers must generally extend in-house credit to their customers, in addition to accepting bank credit cards. Credit helps to attract new customers and increases the volume and regularity of purchases by steady customers. Money due the company on such charge accounts is termed "accounts receivable," and is a line item on the balance sheet.

These sales also have a service charge in the form of the increased expense of recording sales, and billing expenses, such as mailing invoices and monthly statements. A greater potential downside of in-house accounts is the risk of non-payment by the customer, or the need to turn accounts over to a collection agency with their fees, starting at 10 percent of the amount collected and going as high as 90 percent for older balances.

Be sure to establish a firm credit-granting policy. Overly liberal policies, designed to promote goodwill, can result in a large number of slow-paying customers, viewing their balances as interest-free loans.

Carefully screen credit applicants and require a signed application that spells out credit terms. You can investigate a customer's credit rating through such sources as local credit bureaus, merchant associations, and national credit agencies.

Take immediate action on past-due accounts, and earn a reputation for pursuing defaulters and bad-check artists. Do not be reluctant to cut off credit for those who are beginning to owe you more than they are worth. An accounts receivable aging schedule can help track your credit payments by listing the names of customers, their credit limits, their balances, and any amounts 30, 60, 90, or more days overdue.

Bill Hall, the retired owner of an industrial distributorship, advises, "Don't wait too long or until you you're in the mood." One of the biggest mistakes is to delay collection efforts so you don't antagonize a customer. No one likes to ask for money owed, but you need to have a method for collecting it. "And it's not difficult. If you have a computer, buy software that has accounts receivable aging schedules on it; you can punch out a schedule every week if you want."

Hall suggests a system that begins with a 30-day billing statement. "After 60 days have passed and still no payment, send a letter. After 90 days, turn the delinquent account over to a credit service such as the one run by Dun and Bradstreet. They send a letter out on their stationery, follow it up with phone calls and if still no payment, turn the matter over to the attorney."

"You have to show you're serious," Hall continues. "The person who speaks the loudest gets paid first." Don't wait to send out the first invoice. Customers seldom pay before receiving a bill, so the longer you delay in invoicing, the longer you wait for payment.

Arrange your billing cycle to meet your cash needs. Some owners offer discounts to customers who pay within a specified period, such as 2 percent off this month's purchases if paid by the tenth of next month. These are often the terms of your suppliers, and payments from your customers arrive just when needed. You can also charge interest, generally $1^1/_2$ percent per month, on balances due after 30 days.

Other Cash Considerations

Another source of cash-flow control is accounts payable management. Delay purchases as long as possible. Take advantage of all available discounts. Pay bills just before you have to. Negotiate extended credit terms where possible, but do not abuse your vendors. Pay promptly when cash is there, and ask their help when it is not.

Other balance sheet items can offer opportunities to improve your cash position. Has your physical plant exceeded what is business-necessary? Can excess space be leased to other tenants? Can an extra truck be sold, generating some cash and cutting insurance costs?

Show an expense consciousness, and the attitude will spread to your employees. Periodically review insurance and benefits costs. Keep tight reins on the purchasing function. Clear out dead and excess inventory; there is a cost to carrying it.

Is there a point at which a company's cash position can become too strong? Maintaining a cash balance that far exceeds a comfortable operating cushion in a non-interest-bearing account will certainly drag down the rate of return on your business investment.

Short- and intermediate-term excess could be invested temporarily in interest-bearing instruments that can quickly be converted to cash. Longer-term excess can require a strategic reevaluation, to consider expansion, diversification, paying down debt, or a huge bonus to the owner.

Performance Measurement

How can we measure a company's performance relative to these guidelines? While the financial statements give us values for many of the parameters we use as management controls, some relative measures can be even more meaningful. These measures are often expressed as ratios of standard financial statement items. There are several widely used ratios that allow us to compare our performance to norms for our industry, as illustrated by the following example.

MINICASE 8.1   How Are We Doing So Far?

The tax return for Tammany Supply, Inc., for 1994 is complete, and TSI president John Vinturella has decided that it is time to look at some company performance measures. He has routinely calculated some basic percentages, but would like to delve a little deeper this time.

The columns of the table show summaries of TSI's Income Statement and Balance Sheet, with key management control variables underlined. John would prefer to have a slightly higher gross margin, but the observed 18.7 percent is satisfactory given their aggressive sales effort; for the past three years TSI has posted sales increases over the previous year of more than 20 percent.

The net margin of 1.69 percent is acceptable, near industry norms published by the American Supply Association (1.75%), while returns on investment and equity comfortably exceed norms. Collection days, or average days from invoicing to collection, are 20 percent better (i.e., less) than is typical for similar businesses.

John then calculated financial ratios that TSI's accountant suggested that they track. These provide indicators of TSI's performance over a wide range of criteria. Financial consulting firm Dun and Bradstreet publishes norms for building supply businesses for these ratios, and we will use these values to add some perspective to our evaluation. (See the table on page 244.)

1. Liquidity and Indebtedness (indicators of financial stability and leverage).

   The liquidity of a firm indicates its ability to meet cash requirements, ride out difficult times, and expand in good times. Ratio 1, current assets to current liabilities, is a widely used measure of liquidity, referred to as the current ratio. TSI is a little more current than the norm, with 2.62 times as much in ready assets as in current debt. Ratio 2, the "acid

	1994		12/31/1994
Income:		**Assets:**	
Sales	$4,362,904	Cash	$101,407
Cost of Goods Sold	$3,545,747	Accounts Receivable	$430,486
Gross Margin	18.7%	Collection Days	36.01
Other Income	$10,813	Inventory	$326,554
Total Income	$827,970	OthCur Assets	$148,312
		Total Current Assets	$1,006,759
Expenses:		Total Fixed Assets	$105,713
Personnel	$379,544	**Total Assets**	$1,112,472
Operations	$174,857		
Sales	$51,561	**Liabilities:**	
Administration	$98,738	Accounts Payable	$356,320
Depreciation	$29,296	OthCur Liabilities	$27,777
Total Expenses	$733,996	Net Working Capital	$728,375
		Long-Term Debt	$0
Profit/Loss BIT	$93,974	**Total Liabilities**	$384,097
Taxes	$20,201		
Profit/Loss, after tax	$73,773	Equity	$738,375
Net Margin	1.69%	Return on Equity	9.99%
Return on Investment	6.63%	**Total Liab/Eq**	$1,122,472

test," or "quick ratio," is thought to be a better measure because it uses current assets less inventory (generally our least liquid current asset). A value over 1 is considered good. Is TSI too liquid? What would illiquidity convey? What are ways of improving liquidity?

Ratio 3, often called the "debt ratio" shows total liabilities to be less than 35 percent of total assets. A value of less than 50 percent is considered favorable. Ratios 4 and 5 are further indication that, compared to norms, TSI is not very dependent on debt. This excess debt capacity could be used to borrow for expansion, a process called "leveraging."

Is the fact that TSI is not very leveraged a positive or a negative? Should TSI borrow $250,000 to be more in line with norms? What might it do with the money?

Ratio 6, current debt to inventory, is high relative to norms. Is this inconsistent with the previous ratios? Do we need more information? Is this more of an indicator of TSI's rapid inventory turnover?

2. Sales and Profitability (indicators of performance).

Ratios 7 and 8 show that TSI is getting 30 to 50 percent more sales per dollar of equity and working capital than the norms. Ratio 9 is a tangible measure of its rapid inventory turnover, triple the industry norm!

Combined with earlier indicators, should TSI borrow to increase its inventory? Do we know if their level of inventory is holding the business back? Should they consider a greater depth of existing inventory, or additional product lines? What market factors would determine their actions?

The profitability measures in ratios 10, 11, and 12 also comfortably exceed norms. These represent, respectively, the percentage of each sales dollar that TSI brings to the "bottom line," its return on equity, and its working capital growth rate. What do these ratios say about TSI as an investment? What types of management actions produce

	1994	D&B
Ratios:	**TSI**	**Norms**
Liquidity/Indebtedness		
1. CurAssets/CurDebt	2.62	2.24
2. "Acid Test"	1.77	
3. TotLiab/TotAssets	34.53	
4. CurDebt/TangNetWor	52.0	75.0
5. TotDebt/TangNetWor	52.0	124.7
6. CurDebt/Inventory	117.6	81.2
Sales/Profitability		
7. NetSales/TangNetWor	5.91	3.84
8. NetSales/NetWkCap	7.01	5.39
9. NetSales/Inventory	13.4	4.5
10. NetProf/NetSales	1.69	1.58
11. NetProf/TangNetWor	9.99	7.29
12. NetProf/NetWkCap	11.85	8.66
Other Normed		
13. FxAssets/TangNetWor	14.3	32.8
14. Inventory/NetWkCap	44.8	93.3

these results?

3. Analysis and Conclusions.

Ratios 13 and 14 offer two more normed indicators of TSI performance. Fixed assets are a relatively low percentage of equity, indicating that additional investment in vehicles and equipment could reasonably be considered. Inventory is less than half the industry norm as a percentage of working capital, another indication that either TSI should increase inventory, or that it is managing what it has very well.

What does all of this tell us? Is TSI management too conservative about debt? What might happen to the positive indicators on sales and profits were TSI to get more leverage? Are we using the ratios properly by assuming deviation from the norm is indicative of a problem?

Has John developed a strategy that provides a comfortable living while making it easy to sleep nights? Is that all bad?

Study Questions

1. How applicable are norms for an entire industry to a specific small business? Are differences from norms more reflective of quality of management, operating strategies, or competitive conditions?

_____

_____

_____

2. Is rapid increase in sales volume a valid reason for a low gross margin? What is the mecha-

nism by which this occurs? Does an acceptable net margin validate this approach?

_____

_____

_____

3. Does a return on equity of 9.99 percent represent an effective use of Vinturella's personal resources? What are his options, and what is their likely return?

_____

_____

_____

By examining the business ratios of peers or successful industry leaders, business owners and managers can project and plan to make adjustments, matching industry averages or role models.

"Businesses shouldn't hesitate to compare themselves to their industry peers," says David Grand, an Entrepreneurial Advisory Services partner with Coopers & AMP Lybrand's Albany, New York, office. "We hear from many who say that their company is unique, and they don't do peer analysis because they don't fit into the mold. Sadly, this is a common trap in which business owners get caught, rationalizing why their business is not as efficient or as profitable as others."

"In order to get a true picture and make reasonable planning projections," says Grand, "you've got to compare your financial ratios to those pulled from a national poll of similar companies. "Firms like Dun and Bradstreet and Robert Morris Associates collect millions of financial statements across industries in the U.S., then they take those financial statements and compare them, to arrive at normative information on how the businesses of a certain type, size, and region of the country are performing. With this data, companies are able to compare themselves to the financial ratios of the best, average, and below-average performers in their industry."

"Small Business Traps"

According to the Small Business Administration, three out of five small businesses fold within the first five years. Sadly, few experienced lenders would find this statistic surprising, because they have seen how often mistakes can be fatal to a small busi-

8.1   *Expert Opinion*

James V. Schermerhorn, senior vice president of the Mellon PSFS Business Banking Division, hosts popular radio spots called "Tips on Growing Your Business." He gathered the following tips in an article entitled "Steering Clear of Small Business Traps."

Source: www.edgeonline.com/main/edgemag/archives/finan441.shtml (©1997).

ness. Small business owners can dramatically increase their chances for success if they are aware in advance, and have prepared for, the problems they will encounter.

UNDERCAPITALIZATION

Small business owners often want to run their companies on a shoestring, and thus avoid borrowing money. But adequate capital is needed, sometimes suddenly, to invest in the materials, equipment, staff and real estate that will lead to profits and, hopefully, success. Small business owners should always allow for a safety margin when estimating their capital needs. Overcapitalization can't kill a small business, a capital shortfall can.

IGNORING BUSINESS PROBLEMS

A small business doesn't fail overnight. There are always warning signs, and entrepreneurs must recognize and respond to them. Too many small business owners ignore cash flow problems, payroll shortages and other signals. When they finally approach a lender for financing help, it's often too late, the business is in a hole too deep to escape.

USING THE WRONG TYPE OF FINANCING

The relationship between the type of financing and its purpose should follow simple logic: long-term loans should be used for long-term investments, such as equipment, while short-term loans should be used for working capital. Repayment terms should always make good business sense. For instance, the owner of a construction company shouldn't finance a new truck over 10 years. In that industry, the truck may be replaced in as little as four years, and the owner would be paying for an asset that no longer exists.

MIXING BUSINESS AND PERSONAL FINANCES

When small business owners face personal financial pressures, such as college tuition, second homes, etc., they sometimes "borrow" money from the business to cover personal obligation. Despite good intentions, this money may not be paid back, and the end result could be the failure of the business. Entrepreneurs should exercise strict discipline in this area, and remember that any money in the business is there to cover future business—not personal—obligations.

OWNER'S DEATH OR HEALTH PROBLEMS

People start businesses because they want to be independent, but they shouldn't assume sole responsibility for every facet of the operation. We have seen many successful businesses fold because the owner dies or has long-term health problems, and no one else can sustain the momentum. Small business owners need to ensure that the company is not overly dependent on themselves and should put in place life and/or disability insurance adequate to sustain the business in the event it is turned over to heirs or sold. Someone else should know enough about the business and its finances to take over, if only temporarily.

SECOND- OR THIRD-GENERATION OWNERS LOSE INTEREST.

Most entrepreneurs would like to pass the "family" business on to their heirs. But they need to consider if this is the best choice. Are the children and grandchildren interested in and enthusiastic about the business? Do they have the necessary drive and skills? These are hard questions, but every entrepreneur needs to ask them and make realistic succession plans—in advance.

SIDE VENTURES

Success brings its own traps, including the lure of side ventures. The owner of a mature business may become bored and may start looking for new challenges. This could lead to a side venture, perhaps in an industry in which the owner has little experience, a significant handicap for any business. The new venture may take excessive time and resources away from the main business, effectively ending both businesses.

EXTERNAL ECONOMIC FACTORS

Even the most profitable small business will feel the effects of a regional or national downturn. And, for a business that's already struggling, a recession can mean the end. While entrepreneurs have no control over the economic climate, they should prepare a contingency plan that accounts for inevitable economic swings.

FAILURE TO PLAN AHEAD

The biggest pitfall for small business owners is short-sightedness. Owners need to prepare for periods of growth, new product development, physical expansion, etc., well in advance—and consider every possible outcome of their actions before proceeding. In addition, they need a sound financial plan that allows for variations in capital requirements, equipment and real estate needs, personnel, marketplace demand, etc.

An experienced small business lender can be an invaluable resource for information about financing options, capital need calculation, personal finances, financial and estate planning, and other issues that are critical to small business success. Entrepreneurs should sit down with their lender at annual or semi-annual intervals to discuss what's happened in the business recently, what the future holds, and what resources are available to manage the challenges of owning a small business.

SUCCESS: GOING FOR THE GROWTH

Many entrepreneurs' primary interest is in building a lifestyle business, that is, one which provides them a living (in varying degrees of comfort) while allowing them to do what they want to do. Other entrepreneurs want to take the business as far as it can go. Decision time comes when the business works its way through the start-up trauma to achieving some degree of stability.

Every business, committed to rapid growth or not, should always have a business plan in place that is updated annually. Even if our basic business does not change, our market does, the competitive environment does, and innovation and technology create more options for the consumer.

In the annual revision of the business plan, market and environmental data must be updated, and the strategic plan revisited and frequently revised. Actual financial data for the year recently completed must be compared with what was projected, and future projections adjusted accordingly. Reasons for deviations must be identified and addressed.

This ongoing review of the company's progress and the changing environment often indicates opportunities for growth. The challenge is in matching the requirements of the opportunity to the resources of the company.

How and Where Do We Grow?

Strategic options in a growth situation must be identified. Can we improve market share in the current market? Should we try to sell more to current customers by widening our product line? Can we cover a broader geographic area? Are there other channels of distribution that should be considered? Is our business concept franchisable? Should we develop a branch office network? How big can we get to be? How fast can we get there?

This process is very similar to start-up; we must do rigorous market research, clearly identify the specific market we will serve, formulate a strategy that effectively seizes the perceived opportunity, and develop financial projections to measure our progress. Case Study 8.5, at the end of this chapter, demonstrates this approach to growth.

Inc.'s Growth Strategy Consulting Group suggests the fundamental management and business practices that should be in place in order for a company to successfully manage and achieve long-term growth. They call these the "Critical Success Factors" for growth:[3]

- Market Intelligence—the company's ability to perceive and adapt to changes in the marketplace, including future industry trends, competitive environment, and customer feedback.
- Strategic Leadership—the CEO's ability to provide a clear source of direction, delegation, decision-making and long-term planning.
- Clarity of Purpose and Direction—a shared understanding of the company's identity and uniqueness, along with a detailed picture of the company in the future.
- Strategic Planning—the process by which the company determines specific action steps to achieve future goals.
- Internal Infrastructure—the company's ability to support the business strategies through its internal operations, systems and organizational structures.

A less formal and more operational perspective is offered by the following article from the Web.

ENTREPRENEURIAL RESOURCE   "Three Steps to Growing Your Business"[5]

One of the most common questions people ask me as a consultant is, "How do I grow my business?" It's a question that every business owner wants answered, preferably with ways that don't cost them a small fortune. My response to them is simple. There are really only three ways to grow any business:

1. You go out and find new customers.
2. You increase the unit of purchase.
3. You increase the frequency of purchase.

These are the only three ways I know of to grow any business. Let's take a closer look at what each one really means.

Most people believe that in order to grow a business, you have to prospect, cold call, advertise, do direct mail, or use the Internet to find new customers. While finding new customers may be one way of growing your business, it's also the most expensive and most risky way to go.

There is no guarantee that the thousands of dollars you just spent placing an ad in a national magazine is going to bring you new business, or that the 10,000 pieces of mail you just sent out will generate a profitable response. Yet many businesses spend the majority of their time and resources in this one area alone.

A better way is to focus more of your attention on the other two ways of growing your business. Although at first glance, these two might seem surprisingly similar, they are, in fact, very different.

The first one is to increase the unit of sale. What this means is that you want to make your current or even any new customers purchase more from you at each and every sale. In other words, if your typical customer buys an average of $100 worth of goods or services from you at each purchase, your goal is to try and move that number up as much as possible without losing that customer.

You might try adding complementary items to your product mix. An example that immediately comes to mind is a photo store I once worked with. To increase the unit of sale, instead of having the clients just come in for film or processing, I suggested he start offering photo albums, frames, and batteries. So when a customer came in to pick up their finished photos, they could also buy a nice frame or photo album, while they were thinking about it. This also saved them from having to go to another merchant for these items.

This increased the unit of purchase for the store owner, and inevitably increased his bottom line. Think about it, he had no additional advertising expenditures, he took very little risk, and he still managed to achieve his goal of growing his business.

The other way to grow your business is by increasing the frequency of sale. In other words, if your typical customer buys from you once a month, for example, you could offer them a reason to buy twice a month. An example that comes to mind is a client I worked with just last year. In this case we also had them offer an extended product line in order to increase the number of times a customer would purchase from them. This was a business services company that offered a wide range of services for the small office/home office professional. We looked at what people were buying and how often they were buying.

We decided to poll their customers directly and ask them what was missing. In just a few days, we had an answer. What they needed most were simple office supplies. For just a few hundred dollars, the owner of the business was able to bring in a full range of office supplies including paper, computer ribbons, cables, staples, ink, etc. These were the things these people frequently ran out of and by offering them in this location, they saved a long trip down to the office super-center.

It's always a good idea to talk to your customers on a regular basis. Find out what they really like about your business, but even more importantly, find out what they don't like and change it. You may find that if you were just to offer them the product(s) they needed either before or after purchasing your products, you could increase your sales exponentially.

These last two methods work for most any business because they have very little risk associated with them and can very easily have the same growth effect as finding new customers, but without the inherent risk associated with cold prospecting.

Another key advantage to using these two methods is that your customers already know you and trust you. They've done business with you in the past and they have some positive references about your company. In a cold prospecting situation, you are trying not only to sell a product or service, but you are trying to sell your prospect on your company's integrity for which they have no references.

A great question I often ask of my clients is how do they get most of their new business? Inevitably they'll tell me that most of their new customers come from referrals. So, my next logical question is, how much time and effort do you place into developing referrals? I'm always amazed to find out that although they realize that referrals are a major part of their business, they dedicate few, if any, resources to this powerful means of generating new business!

If referrals are a major part of your growth strategy, you've got to spend time developing programs that increase the number and frequency of referred clients to your business. An easy way to do this is to offer your existing clients a premium or discount of some sort for each new customer they bring you. What you are actually doing is turning your satisfied customers into a powerful, persuasive sales force and paying them only when they produce a result or in other words, bring you a new client.

Growing your business doesn't have to be expensive, risky, or even time-consuming. Unless you have a time-tested way to advertise that produces reliable results, try these other ways I've mentioned first. You might be surprised to find that they work as well as or better than cold prospecting at a fraction of the cost and with dramatically reduced risk!

Management consultant Aldonna R. Ambler suggests the following six points for growing your business.[6]

1. Introduce new products to existing customers.

Existing or local customers will consider purchasing new goods more readily than consumers who are unfamiliar with your company.

2. Increase control over the channels of distribution.

   Spur growth by entering into a joint venture with a distributor, retailer or exporter.

3. Acquire a competitor.

   This can be a complex and arduous process. You may not get what you thought you were buying if key people at that company resign because of the acquisition.

4. Franchise/license.

   If your business can easily be replicated, taught and controlled, this may be a good option.

5. Consolidate.

   Most businesses can't sustain continuous, uncontrolled growth. At some point, you must slow down and focus on your core efficiencies. During these periods of assessment, you can realize growth from improved profits, reduced waste, controlled inventories and decreased turnover.

5. Diversify/specialize.

   Success can breed success after your market knows you. However, there are problems associated with attempting to be a jack-of-all-trades; you could wind up being known as master of none. Therefore, it is better to consider combining diversification with specialization that will apply your area of expertise to a similar range of products or markets.

6. Expand geographically.

   Find other regions that share similar demographic features with your current market. The existence of business-service centers has helped service-oriented businesses expand geographically in recent years. Your company can also use flexible office space complexes, in which conference rooms, fax machines and photocopiers are leased on a per-unit basis, to test its capacity to attract and handle business in a new location. Be forewarned that you will have to learn new laws, familiarize yourself with regional differences, absorb more costs and spend a lot of time networking to make this option work.

As we consider our geographic span of operations, most small business owners think only in terms of domestic markets. International opportunities, they reason, are the province of the large corporations; "multinational company" has come to be synonymous with "huge company."

Typical reactions to suggestions of evaluating international markets include: "I don't have the time to deal with all the complications"; "there are too many ways to get burned"; "there are enough opportunities in the U.S. (Canada, etc.)."

Trade agreements are minimizing the complications and the dangers; Export Assistance Centers are opening around the U.S.; advances in telecommunications are shrinking distances and bringing us closer and closer to the truly global economy. Market information relative to global markets is improving in availability and timeliness.

Should We Look at International Opportunities?

In a sense, we are probably already competing in an international marketplace. We may only sell our goods locally, but some of the items competing with ours may be imported. Likewise, we may be reselling imported goods, or goods with a significant amount of imported components.

Active entry into the global market can take many forms. An expansion in point-of-presence could take the firm to a specific market in another country, to neighboring countries, or truly global; expanded representation could include assignment of salespersons to other home countries, or using company agents, native to the target market, in some fashion.

As tempting as international markets may be, however, the decision should be governed by the principle that internationalization should not be considered an end in itself, but as a means to enhance and/or exploit the firm's competitive advantage.

The following is a list of questions that will assist us making that determination.

1. Would it make us more efficient?

   Are there opportunities for performing each activity of our process of adding value at a lowest-cost site? Are there other markets with greater potential profits?

2. Would it give us access to new resources?

   Are there natural, human, or financial resources available in another market that would enhance our competitive advantage? Are there advantages over more localized competitors to the experience of operating in a larger "universe"? Can the observation of market trends over multiple countries give us an earlier sense of shifting market preferences?

3. Would it help us to diversify our risks as well as our opportunities?

   Market cycles are inevitable, but regional and national economies seldom rise or decline in unison.

4. Do current or prospective customers demand it?

   Are some of our customers operating internationally? Will our becoming international open new customer opportunities?

How Well Equipped Are We to Expand Internationally?

While internationalization creates marketing opportunities, it also creates significant organizational strains and challenges. What are the major components of a "fitness check"?

1. Financial strength.

   Internationalization of operations often drains a significant amount of capital before beginning to generate revenues. Once in operation, many of the costs of doing business increase dramatically, particularly transportation and communication costs.

   Banks are reluctant to lend to small- and medium-sized enterprises (SMEs) for expansion that they conservatively view as too rapid (remind them that tomorrow's best customers are today's dynamic businesses). Government programs to encourage entrepreneurship and exporting can sometimes be used for these purposes.

2. Organizational strength.

   Does your organization have sufficient management talent to take on the challenge without jeopardizing the existing business? Are current management systems sophisticated enough to serve an international company? Can communication systems and channels handle, or be easily upgraded to handle, the accelerating flow of information likely to occur?

3. Flexibility.

   Is the management team, or the family, committed to the challenge? Does it generate additional opportunity for up-and-comers to prove themselves? How serious are the language and custom differences, and the company's ability to bridge them? Does the company's distinctive competence transfer well? If not, what are the necessary adaptations?

4. Vision.

   Is company leadership aware of where they are headed? Where they would like the company to be in 10 years? Are they committed to incremental learning, and tolerant of the occasional misstep?

We Are Ready. Now What?

Next in the process come decisions related to the scope of our international operations, the optimal way to enter these new markets, and identification of the keys to success.

1. Where do we start?

   Each country has some natural trading partners, where cultural ties or past successes have lowered the barriers to economic cooperation. Beginning in an environment conducive to trade often leads to expansion to other regional neighbors, and on to a worldwide presence.

2. How do we make international contacts?

   You may already belong to international networks through your suppliers and professional organization memberships. Ask them for suggestions as to people who might help you orient yourself in what may seem at first to be a difficult environment.

   Most countries provide trade assistance through government agencies, business development centers, and trade associations. If you bank with a multinational, they can often be very helpful. These organizations also often sponsor trade missions and other events in the target country.

3. What information do we need on the target market?

   Feasibility studies in the international marketplace are similar to those for domestic markets, but with additional complications that could be troublesome. Certainly we need to be aware of the size of the market for our product, the competitive structure, and the costs of doing business.

   A common mistake at this stage is to base cost assumptions on experience in our home country. Among even neighboring countries, there can be wide variations in quality of market data, government restrictions and incentives, marketing systems, and distribution costs.

   Cultural factors, particularly relating to human resources, often lead to subtle but significant impacts on costs.

4. What form should the venture take?

   Are we confident enough to go it alone, or should we enter a joint venture with a company in the target market? Should we establish a network of distributors for our product, or sell directly to the users? Do tax laws, labor costs, and/or availability of raw materials favor one country over others? There are also issues related to our existing corporate culture, particularly, whether we partner well.

While each business is unique, there do seem to be some common characteristics of small- and medium-sized enterprises that have successfully met the internationalization challenge. Several rather generic "keys to success" have emerged along the experience curve:

- Concentrate in a limited number of product areas.
- Focus on specific customer requirements, emphasize product/service quality rather than commodity pricing.
- Balance marketing and technology—that is, sell them what they want, but lead the customer a little in advancement and improvements.
- Establish some local presence, but be wary of partnerships.

CASE STUDY 8.4
Conveyant Systems, Inc.

There's a long-cherished fantasy that you could easily make an enormous fortune if you could sell just one pair of shoes to every man, woman, and child in China. But that dream remains on hold. Protectionist measures make tapping into China's domestic consumer market an elusive goal for most foreigners. But there are opportunities to participate in a variety of government-driven economic-development plans designed to build up China's domestic infrastructure.

MARKET INTELLIGENCE ON THE PEOPLE'S REPUBLIC OF CHINA

Population: 1.2 billion. Ninety-five cities have more than 1 million people. Five cities (Beijing, Shanghai, Tianjin, Shenyang, and Wuhan) have more than 4 million people.

Official language: Mandarin is the common written language throughout China, but there are many mutually unintelligible spoken dialects.

Education: Compulsory through sixth grade. More than 4 million people are university graduates.

Economic:

- *Unemployment:* 2.3 percent in 1992, according to official Chinese government figures.

- *Inflation:* Nationwide, soared to 14.1 percent in the first quarter of 1993 (15.7 percent in major cities).

- *Gross domestic product:* The International Monetary Fund estimates China's GDP at $1.66 trillion, making it the world's third-largest economy.

- *Joint ventures:* U.S. companies have invested in more than 2,000 projects in China, with a combined contract value in excess of $6 billion.

- *Partners:* The United States is the third-largest foreign investor in China, behind Hong Kong and Taiwan, and just ahead of Japan. In 1992 a total of 48,764 new foreign direct-investment projects, worth $58 billion, were initiated in China.

- Total merchandise imports: $80.6 billion in 1992, up 26.4 percent from 1991.

This case is adapted from "In the China Shop" by Hal Plotkin, which appeared in the September 1993 issue of *Inc.* magazine.[7]

Michael Porter, author of *The Competitive Advantage of Nations* (Free Press, 1990), says that "companies, not nations, are on the front line of international competition."

It is generally believed that major international players are large. How large should a company be before it considers setting up operations abroad? According to tiny Conveyant Systems, Inc., not very.

Conveyant has achieved a 3% share of the enormous Chinese domestic market for digital private-branch-exchange (PBX) products, thanks to its 60% ownership of Tianchi Telecommunications Corp., in Tianjin, China.

With only 16 employees, Conveyant Systems, based in Irvine, California, seems an unlikely match for China's burgeoning market. Nonetheless, the small distributor of PC-based telecommunications gear is stealing some thunder from its larger, better-known competitors, such as Northern Telecom, Alcatel, Siemens, and AT&T.

Conveyant Systems' Joe Leonardi says his willingness to cut a generous deal over licensing rights, back in 1986, was the key to nosing out the big guys. The 53-year-old founder and president stitched together a complicated joint venture with Tianjin's local municipal government, the state-owned postal and telecommunications authority, and a local economic-development group.

For fiscal year 1993, the venture's 90 Chinese employees will produce about $10 million worth of PBX equipment in a 22,000-square-foot factory located in Tianjin. And China's businesses, starving for communications equipment, eagerly devour 90% of that output.

The news wasn't always so good, though. In its first year, Tianchi Telecommunications' sales fell far short of targets. But Leonardi fought back with a truly revolutionary idea. He proposed a commission structure for the Chinese sales force. Responding to his Communist partners' demands for recognition of every employee's contribution to a shared goal, he agreed to provide incentives to the factory workers as well, and sales of PBXs took off.

Now the company's 12 sales offices stretch from the Heilongjiang province in the northeast to the Guangdong province in the south.

Like Leonardi, most foreign entrepreneurs do business in China through joint ventures by providing capital, technology, or global-market-ing savvy. Leonardi credits his business's smooth operation to his well-placed Chinese partners. "The power never goes off, we always have running water, and we always have fuel to heat our building," he notes.

- Preserve those aspects of the corporate culture that made you a local success; build from within with highly motivated employees.
- Stick to basic strategies, and view the "latest" theories skeptically.

What Are the Risks of a Growth Strategy?

Many entrepreneurs see growing a business as highly desirable, or even necessary to survival. However, W. Michael Donovan, program director for Business and Technology Administration at Southern Maine Technical College, suggests that many overlook the effects that rapid growth might have on critical areas of the business that do not respond well to rapid growth. Donovan suggests that these areas are, typically, cash flow, price stability, quality control, distribution or delivery systems, and management decision making.[8]

CASH FLOW

Rapid sales growth requires an increased level of assets to maintain a desired standard of service and quality. At first, accounts receivable and inventories will rise. Later, additional storage space, office space or manufacturing facilities will be needed. As long as profits are sufficient, there may be enough cash to finance the increase in assets.

If sales growth exceeds the ability of the company to stay ahead of asset requirements, then profits will not be sufficient, and outside sources of capital may become necessary. The entrepreneur in a rapid growth mode must maintain access to outside funding through credit lines and communications with current and prospective investors. An alternative is to control growth to a manageable rate in the event that cash flow were to deteriorate to a dangerous level.

PRICE STABILITY

If rapid growth comes at the expense of a competitor's market share, a price war can result. Increased volume is often directly linked to reduced prices. In a small business, therefore, one must watch whether a sharp increase in volume prompts a large reduction in price by the competitor, which must, in turn, be matched. As a result, profits decline, and the firm's financial cushion may not be sufficient to adopt a wait-it-out strategy.

QUALITY CONTROL

Rapid growth in the number of units sold by a firm means additional inquiries, paperwork, installations, bookkeeping and client review. If the staff of the firm is not properly managed or expanded, then product or service quality may decline. Even though excess capacity may exist temporarily, small firm growth can quickly outstrip resources, thereby causing strain, mistakes, frustration and unhappy clients.

DISTRIBUTION AND DELIVERY

Quality deterioration is not the only reason why growth should not outstrip capacity. If a marketing program successfully attracts a bevy of new customers and the firm cannot satisfy sales demand rapidly, then its reputation in the marketplace suffers. Future strategies of growth may be ignored by clients. Further, moving from one volume level to a higher level might mean changes in technology or systems used to produce products or services. The new way of doing business, often adopted to gain a cost advantage, may take time to learn.

MANAGEMENT DECISION MAKING

The most critical issue is the ability of management to make decisions while growth is accelerating. The number of transactions increases to the point where control is difficult, employees are not certain of their duties, problems proliferate, and choices are voluminous. Delegation is critical, but there are not enough employees to handle the load. There is not enough time to think and plan.

Summary

Getting the doors open on a new venture is only the first in a series of challenges on the way to entrepreneurial success. In many cases, the survival stage of business development, that is, solidifying the viability of the business, can be even more difficult.

Another key to business success is to carefully monitor performance, and to act on the information this process yields. Newer businesses are particularly vulnerable to problems of cash flow, as the requirements of a growing business place continual demands on today's resources. Entrepreneurs must manage the balance sheet, particularly cash and receivables, as well as the income statement, that is, the instinctive focus on sales volume. Relationships between financial statement values, in the form of ratios and percentages, can be compared to industry norms as a way of grading ourselves.

Once a business reaches a level of stability and prosperity that may be considered success, the entrepreneur is at a crossroads. Many continue on a growth pattern, expanding the business in a variety of ways, sometimes even becoming international. Others become disengaged, often to the point of shutting down or selling the business.

Whatever path is chosen, the actions of the entrepreneur should always be guided by a current, well-researched, and considered business plan.

Review Questions

1. What are the stages in small business growth? How can we tell which we are currently in?

    _____

    _____

    _____

2. Why is cash flow so important to the growing business? What can we do to improve the cash flow of such a business? Can cash position ever be too strong?

_____

_____

3. How are the commonly used financial ratios helpful in managing a business?

_____

_____

_____

4. What are the common strategic options in growing a business? How do we choose between them? What are the primary limitations on growth?

_____

_____

_____

5. Why would a business owner not pursue a growth strategy?

CASE STUDY 8.5
Tammany Supply, Inc. (F)

INTRODUCTION

From its 1978 start-up through 1985, Tammany Supply, Inc. (TSI), of Covington, Louisiana, was the dominant plumbing supply wholesaler in western St. Tammany Parish. St. Tammany, an upscale suburb of New Orleans, was one of the country's fastest growing counties during this period, and TSI's growth rate reflected it.

The oil price collapse of the mid-1980s took a heavy toll on the Louisiana economy. In western St. Tammany Parish, an upscale suburb of New Orleans that had been experiencing explosive growth, new residential construction fell dramatically. For Tammany Supply, sales fell 40 percent from 1984 to 1987.

A modest recovery in TSI's fortunes occurred from 1988 to 1990, with a return to modest profitability in the next two years. Then, a building boom began in mid-1992. TSI sales for 1992 increased 20 percent over 1991. In 1993, sales in-

creased another 30 percent over 1992 sales, exceeding $3.5 million for the first time; profits were likewise the highest in company history. In 1994, sales rose another 24 percent, exceeding $4 million, and profits decreased only slightly (see "Sales and Profits, 1978–94" graph on page 257).

STAYING IN A GROWTH MODE

Company president John Vinturella had sensed some leveling off in growth of their core business in early 1995, and had begun evaluating alternative initiatives to maintaining the growth path the company had been enjoying. He reasoned then that new residential construction in west St. Tammany was reaching a saturation point, and began to investigate opening a branch in eastern St. Tammany, and broadening the TSI product line to include more items for commercial customers.

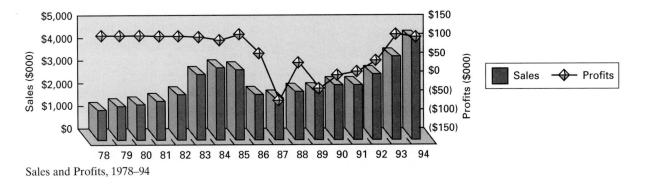

Sales and Profits, 1978–94

John had considered bringing in outside investors in 1995 (see Case Study 7.3), but decided that the company could finance the expansion itself, albeit at a slower pace. A gradual increase in their commercial offerings in 1995 did contribute to a modest sales gain by the standards of the three previous years (12%). The 1996 gain of 17 percent was largely attributable to increased commercial sales.

In 1997, he was glad that he had begun the diversification process, because sales for the past two years had barely exceeded his conservative projections (see "Sales, Projected and Actual, 1995–97" graph). The product-line broadening focused on utility products, consisting primarily of pipe and fittings for the water and sewer systems supporting municipalities and private developments. The new line had broadened TSI's geographic reach, as expected, but the inventory demands and low margins relative to residential products had caused some cash-flow strains.

In the fall of 1996, John began planning for a branch of the business in Slidell, the business center of eastern St. Tammany, about 25 miles from Covington via Interstate 12. As a courtesy,

John contacted the owners of the two supply houses located in Slidell; one of these businesses was rumored to be for sale, but the owner told John that the time was not right. John found a property just off the interstate where the owner was willing to build to TSI's specifications, and signed a five-year lease to begin operations in the spring of 1997.

A TIME FOR RENEWAL

There was something related to the decision to open the Slidell store that rekindled John's enthusiasm for the business. Over the previous several years, his outside activities, primarily teaching and consulting, had taken more of his time and attention. He was still clearly in charge of TSI, and it still formed a large part of his identity, but more and more of the details were being left to others.

John took an active role in the design of the Slidell store, modeling it after the Covington layout, but incorporating all the features that they wished for but did not have there. Once construction began, he hired a public relations firm to design a new logo and company brochure, revamp their advertising program, and create a publicity campaign for the Slidell opening. He built a company Web site, listing surplus items, and made a few sales.

The commitment to Slidell went well beyond the typical branch opening in the industry. This would not be a minimal location staffed by two or three people to test the market. It would be a state-of-the-art warehouse, first-class showroom, and a staff of seven people. To justify some of the added space, and give the branch a running start, the utility part of the business would be moved to Slidell.

In conjunction with the expansion, their already advanced computing operation would be upgraded, and the Slidell store would have a full-time data communications link to Covington.

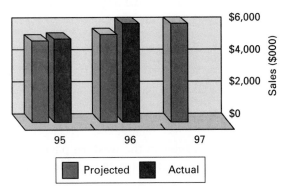

Sales, Projected and Actual, 1995–97

THE SUCCESSION PLAN BEGINS TO UNRAVEL

During this period, there were also several developments on the family business front. John's daughter, Vicki Olson, gave birth to her second child. Seeking a respite from the heavy work demands of her law career, she asked to work part-time at TSI.

Her timing was good, as the diversification campaign was making heavy demands on the administrative staff. Her legal training allowed her to effectively take over much of the collection work of the company, and the human resource function. Her proficiency in computing led to her assuming much of the systems and procedures work that previously only John could do.

Just as Vicki was getting deeply involved in TSI, her husband Scott announced that he would leave the company. John had chosen Scott to become the Slidell branch manager, on his way to assuming an increasingly important role in company leadership. Scott's reasons for leaving were not explicitly stated, but he had been unhappy in the role of "successor designate" for some time by then.

BACK ON TRACK

Dan White had been Scott's assistant in Covington, and was to move up when Scott went to Slidell. Dan had also begun to help in sales, and had shown tremendous initiative and talent in that role. When Scott left the company, John decided to give Dan a chance (at 23 years old) to manage the Slidell branch. With a lot of mentoring by John, Dan got the Slidell branch up and running by the target date.

Vicki was adapting well to her increasing responsibilities, and was indicating that she might be with the company for a while. Revisions to the succession program could wait a while, but John began to feel comfortable that the disruption of Scott's departure had been overcome.

From his mid-1997 perspective, John was pleased with the results of his concentrated efforts over the past year. The expected tapering off of Covington sales volume indeed took place, and the diversification program generated additional sales that showed signs of more than making up the difference. After only three months, the Slidell operation was running smoothly, and Dan confidently and effectively assumed the reins.

John returned to his disengagement program, having finished the entrepreneurship text he had been working on. He let his university contacts know that he was ready to return to part-time teaching in the fall of 1997. On July 1, 1997, the company began its twentieth year, and John began to think his goal of retiring at 20 years service (only a year away) might still be achievable.

Study Questions

1. Should John have taken in investors two years earlier, reaping the benefits of diversification beginning in 1995 rather than 1997? Do we have any information to indicate whether the "window of opportunity" was beginning to close on either of the two new initiatives?

   _____

   _____

   _____

2. Is there any chance that the perceived decrease in sales in the western part of St. Tammany Parish could be due to company leadership being spread too thin? What would be the best way to find out?

_____

_____

_____

3. Should John have waited before expanding into the Slidell area until the supply house owner there was ready to sell? Was the decision to open there with such a large operation a good one? What information might we gather to determine this?

_____

_____

_____

4. What was it about opening a branch store that generated John's enthusiasm in a way that it had not been for years? How is this similar to, and how is it different from, starting a business from scratch? Are many of the same entrepreneurial skills required?

_____

_____

_____

5. How do the peripheral activities, that is, the PR firm and Web site, relate to the diversification effort? Should a company review its image and marketing program periodically? What are the potential benefits? Is there any downside other than cost?

_____

_____

_____

6. What form might a new succession plan take at this stage? Is Vicki likely to assume next-generation leadership of the company? What other options are there?

_____

_____

_____

7. Is John being realistic about disengaging when the Slidell branch has only been in operation for three months? Can he leave the company completely in just a year? Where are problems most likely to arise?

_____

_____

_____

Notes

1. Edward O. Welles. "Sound Strategy," *Inc.* (May 1991): vol. 13, no. 5, p. 46(5).

2. Paul B. Brown. "Plastics!" *Inc.* (June 1990): vol. 12, no. 6, p. 70(6).

3. Susan Greco. "Are We Making Money Yet?" *Inc.* (July 1996): vol. 18, no. 10, p. 52(6).

4. *Inc.*'s Growth Strategy Consulting Group. "Critical Success Factors for Growth in Entrepreneurial Companies," Inc. Online: www.inc.com/consulting/consult_critical.html (9/1/97).

5. Robert Imbriale. "Three Steps to Growing Your Business," (www.global-homebiz.com/biztips-imbriale13.html).

6. Aldonna R. Ambler. "Growing by Design: Seven Channels for Growing Your Business," *Entrepreneurial Edge* (www.edgeonline.com) (© 1997).

7. Hal Plotkin. "In the China Shop," *Inc.* (September 1993): vol. 15, no. 9, p. 108(2).

8. W. Michael Donovan. "Beware of the Pitfalls of Growth," *Entrepreneurial Edge* (www.edgeonline.com) (© 1997).

Index